# CONTEST ORATORY:

## A Handbook for High School and College Contestants and Coaches

by

William Schrier

The Scarecrow Press, Inc.
Metuchen, N.J.          1971

The Library of Congress Cataloged the Original Printing of
This Title as:


Schrier, William.
    Contest oratory: a handbook for high school and college
contestants and coaches. Metuchen, N. J., Scarecrow Press,
1971.

    viii, 271 p.   22 cm.

    Includes bibliographical references.




    1. Oratory—Competitions.     I. Title.

PN4076.S3                        808.5'1                    71-171595
ISBN 0-8108-0416-6                                          MARC

Library of Congress            71 ₍60-2₎

# CONTENTS

## SPECIAL INTRODUCTION

To describe what oratory means to me has the overtones of a lesson in verb usage. I <u>was</u> a college speaker, I <u>am</u> a speaker, I <u>married</u> a speaker, and we <u>raised</u> two speakers.

It's obvious my interest in speech and oratory has had an immeasurable influence on my life. Now, as Governor of Minnesota, my background in public speaking has been an invaluable tool in effectively carrying out my responsibility. I give approximately 200 to 300 speeches each year in which I am expected to either inform, explain or inspire.

In order to communicate easily and accurately, each speech must be thoroughly researched, carefully constructed and effectively delivered. I firmly believe that a good speech doesn't just happen. A good speech is more than random remarks or casual conversation. A good speech is the result of thought, sensitivity, conviction and effective delivery. There is no substitute for competitive oratory work to train a person to write and give a sound speech.

However, the value of oratory in college is not limited to those who will be doing a great deal of public speaking in their careers. For every time a man speaks he opens himself to public inspection. "Speech is the mirror of the soul. As a man speaks so he is." Daily communication would be vastly improved if every man had the benefit of training in analysis, logic, verbal accuracy, and bodily action, eye contact and voice variation.

Harold LeVander
Governor of Minnesota
December 1970

v

# PREFACE

This handbook of contest oratory is intended for high school and college contestants and coaches. It could also serve as a text for advanced high school courses in persuasive speaking, as a supplementary text for college courses in fundamentals of speech, and in courses in the direction of forensics.

Quentin Reynolds wrote of his book on war experiences Only the Stars are Neutral: "This book is as personal as a toothbrush." This book is like that. I have tried to avoid the "editorial we" style. For me to refer to myself as "the writer" seems terribly stilted, and, in the words of the popular song, "I gotta be me!" I have written as if I were simply talking with my students or with coaches at a convention "gab-fest."

The book is a distillation of my views and methods used in coaching oratory for 40 years of my 45-year span of teaching. Contest oratory has held a life-long fascination for me, and has become a sort of specialty. It may not be inappropriate to mention my qualifications for writing the volume.

As a student, I took part in oratory contests for two years in high school, two years at Kalamazoo College, and two years at the University of Michigan. In 1924, my coach at Michigan was Thomas C. Trueblood, a great pioneer teacher. As a coach of oratory, I served two years at St. Louis University, one year at the University of Colorado, 12 years at the University of North Dakota, and 25 years at Hope College. I have sought to avoid being a "speechless speech professor," and bring to the book considerable experience in addressing a wide variety of audiences.

James Russell Lowell once wrote: "The art of writing consists in knowing what to leave in the ink-pot." This book is distinctive both for what it leaves out and what it includes. I resisted the temptation to write still another text on persuasive speaking of which there are already many

vi

excellent ones on the market.  Choice of material was rigid-
ly subjected to one criterion--is it pertinent to the oration?
On the other hand, it covers comprehensively the whole field
of oratory.  On matters of controversy, it takes a position
on each of them.

I believe contest oratory merits a book of its own.
In his Foreword to my publication, Winning Hope College
Orations, 1941-1966, President Calvin Vander Werf of Hope
College wrote that we are living

> . . . during one of the most revolutionary periods
> in the history of education.  Not the least of these
> factors in this revolution has been the sudden
> emergence of the notion that what the serious and
> enlightened college student thinks and says should
> be listened to and considered--that the conviction
> of today's college student may often become the
> basis for the public opinion, public policy, and
> legislation of tomorrow.

One distinctive feature of the present book is my firm conviction that educational oratory, revitalized, shorn of its excessive stress upon winning, and with more frequent appearances before off-campus audiences, can contribute toward
solving the ills of our troubled world in the here and now.
The current student rebellion provides an excellent opportunity for the expansion of this activity.  For reasoned discourse, and not violence, is the educated man's way of
bringing about needed changes in our society.

Tennyson says in his "Ulysses": "I am a part of all
that I have met."  I am in debt to so many that I cannot
remember them all.  I would be remiss if I did not express
my gratitude to all student orators, my own and others, as
well as colleague coaches with whom it has been my privilege
to work.  Pioneers in the speech profession such as Charles
Henry Woolbert, James Albert Winans, and William Norwood
Brigance have shaped and influenced my thinking.  I must
make special mention of my life-long friend whom I first
knew at the University of Michigan, Dr. Lionel Crocker of
Denison University.  His life and writings have been an inspiration to me throughout my teaching career.  He has read
the entire manuscript, and provided valuable counsel and
assistance which I appreciate more than mere words can
say.

# SYMBOLS FOR PERIODICALS,
## PUBLICATIONS AND ORGANIZATIONS

The following list contains the periodical, publication and organization symbols used in the text and footnotes in this book.

| | |
|---|---|
| AFA | American Forensic Association |
| CSSJ | Central States Speech Journal |
| IOA | Interstate Oratorical Association ("old-line") |
| IPSA | Intercollegiate Peace Speech Association |
| JAFA | Journal of American Forensic Association |
| MHSFA | Michigan High School Forensic Association |
| MISL | Michigan Intercollegiate Speech League |
| PKD | Pi Kappa Delta honorary forensic society |
| QJS | Quarterly Journal of Speech |
| SAA | Speech Association of America (now: Speech Communication Association) |
| ST | Speech Teacher |
| WHCO | Winning Hope College Orations, 1941-1966 |
| WO | Winning Orations (annual volume of IOA) |

Chapter I

ORATORY PAST AND PRESENT

## I. PREVALENCE OF ORATORY

This book concerns contest oratory, interscholastic
and intercollegiate. Oratory, a specialized form of persuasive speaking, has been with us since the days of antiquity. In all ages, it has played an important role in the history of our world. While there were historical periods
where the influence of the orator alternately waxed and
waned, in varying degrees that influence was never absent.

In our own country, oratory was prominent in its formation, was noticeably present during all of its turbulent
history, and exerts its influence to the present day. It
simply is not true, as some critics of high school and college competitive oratory say, "In real life situations no one
delivers orations any more." Certainly the Inaugural Address
of the late president John F. Kennedy is a superb example
of an oration. So, too, is the "I Have a Dream" speech of
Martin Luther King, Jr., at the Lincoln Memorial during the
March on Washington, August 28, 1963.

It is true that, outside of contest situations, such persuasive speeches are rarely called "orations." Sometimes
they are. For example, at annual ceremonies in my home
town on Memorial Day, the speaker is always referred to as
"the orator of the day." But why be concerned about the
word as long as the essence of oratory, getting over a persuasive message to a specific audience, is present? Thus
oratory, in its basic meaning, is being practiced all around
us every day in the year, before luncheon clubs, literary
clubs, study groups, conventions. Its practice will remain
with us as long as there are problems to be solved, and
Utopia shows no signs of being just around the corner.[1]
In short, the power of the spoken word has been with us
since time immemorial, is with us still today, and will be
with us until time shall be no more.

## II. EDUCATIONAL ORATORY

### A. Its Beginnings

Educational oratory, the study and practice of oratory in schools and colleges, all with the obvious intent of making possible more meaningful participation through speaking ability in the life of the world when school days are over, developed concurrently with the so-called oratory in real-life situations. Educational oratory is a training ground for the practice of oratory in later life. The purpose of oratory, in school or out, is, or certainly ought to be, essentially the same: getting over a message to a specific audience. The educational type of oratory has been with us since the ancient past, in the schools of rhetoric of Greece and Rome, in the Middle Ages, and right down to the present.

In our own country, educational oratory, both curricular and extracurricular, was present in our colonial colleges.[2] It was but natural that intra-mural competitive oratory, first among literary societies in colonial colleges, eventually led to the introduction of speech and persuasion courses into the curriculum of colleges, and later still, high schools.[3] Natural, too, was the development that intramural competition became intercollegiate and interscholastic in scope. Leagues and associations were formed for the purpose of competing for prizes in oratory. The oldest such organization, formed in 1874, was known as the Interstate Oratorical Association. It has been in continuous existence since then, and in 1974 will be celebrating its centennial.[4] Some famous people have represented their schools in IOA contests. For example, first-place winners were Senator Robert M. La Follette, representing the University of Wisconsin in 1879; Senator Albert J. Beveridge, representing De Pauw University in 1885; and John H. Finley, long-time editor of the New York Times, representing Knox College in 1887. The Northern Oratorical League, another pioneer organization, was formed in 1890 at Ann Arbor at the invitation of Thomas C. Trueblood, with the University of Michigan, Northwestern University, Oberlin College, and the University of Wisconsin as charter members.

Since real life oratory is not ever likely to pass from the mortal scene, since educational oratory developed concurrently and is the source from which most real-life orators emerge, it is a safe prediction to say that the competitive era of educational oratory will not pass from the educational scene. It may and should change its nature with changing conditions. Indeed, intercollegiate oratory--and the interscholastic has always tended to follow the lead of the colleges--has already done so during the century of its existence. It has successfully weathered "the winds of change" in the past and most likely will continue to do so in the future.

## B. Changes through the Years

Types and styles of oratory have changed through the years. In matters, for example, such as the nature of topics for oratory, the style of delivery and the composition of an oration, college competitive oratory has kept pace with changing trends and tastes in public speaking. It has survived through all these years because it has shown a resiliency, a remarkable ability to adjust and adapt itself to changing concepts of good speech techniques. In the area of subjects, for example, eulogies of persons, quite common in the early years, are not nearly so common today. In delivery, we have moved from a flamboyant, exhibitionistic elocution style to a much more direct, casual, and spontaneous mode of utterance. In the early years, grandiloquent phraseology--"purple patches" we used to call it--was common usage. Today there is evidence of more informality, more spontaneity and directness. For example, personal references and apt bits of humor, both of which would be considered anathema 40 years ago, are now quite commonplace.[5]

Just as educational oratory has kept abreast of and adjusted to change in regard to subjects of orations and to manner of delivery and style in composition, so, too, it has adjusted throughout the past century to the rules and regulations governing the conduct of contests. After the Interstate Oratorical Association was formed, other regional and state associations were developed. Most were governed by a Constitution which prescribed the conditions under which contests were held. Sets of rules were also instituted by the national honorary forensic fraternities for use at oratorical contests at their conventions. In addition, many articles were written in various speech journals suggesting changes in the conduct of contests, and many replies resisting change.

Some omissions were made permanent, as for example,

the provision in the old Michigan Oratorical League for two
sets of judges, one group, usually three, judging thought and
composition prior to the contest, judging a written copy, and
another set judging delivery, serving on the day of the contest.  The grades would then be averaged to arrive at the
winner.  This practice has now been discarded because most
coaches believe that an oration is an entity which should be
judged at one sitting during its delivery, all the while of
course keeping thought and composition in mind as criteria.


## C.   Under Constant Scrutiny

But other matters relating to contest procedures continue to be under constant scrutiny.  That is a wholesome
sign in that it indicates an unwillingness to stand pat if im-
provements are desirable and needed.  A random list of
some such items of procedure would include questions such
as these:

1)  Should there be a word or time limit for an
oration, and in either case, what limit?

2)  Ought a problem type of oration always be required to provide a specific solution?

3)  In judging which is the preferred method: a single
critic who is a speech expert, three such judges,
the coach-judge system, or civic judges such as the
local lawyer, minister and businessman?

4)  What critiques shall there be--none at all?   Oral?
Written?

5)  Should a uniform judges' ballot be provided, with
a listing of criteria?

Two issues very much alive today are being widely
thought about and discussed, and wisely so because they are
important.  They are:  shall we dispense with separate contests for men and women?  and, shall we continue to expect
memorization of an oration?  The January, 1968 issue of
Forensic, the official organ of the national forensic honor
society of Pi Kappa Delta, contained a provocative and stimulating article touching upon both these current issues.[6]  At
its May 3, 1968 business meeting, the Interstate Oratorical
Association voted not to include the words "from memory" in

its definition of an oration in its constitution, and voted instead to define an oration as "an original persuasive speech
delivered without the aid of notes or manuscript." It is
conceivable that in the future even the words "without the
aid of notes or manuscript" may be deleted. Thus oratory
contests are under constant surveillance and rules are
properly subject to change.

## III. ORATORY WILL SURVIVE

Upon most contemplated changes, I have some preferences and in a few cases rather strong convictions which
will be expressed in the relevant places throughout this
book. I make no pretense of saying the last and final word,
however, since these are controversial questions upon which
men of good will may well differ.[7] In the meantime, during
this period of change, let us as contestants and coaches of
oratory rest assured there is nothing inherently wrong with
high school and college oratory today which cannot be cured.
Let us have faith that we can solve our oratorical problems
in the future as we have always done in the past. Let us
continue to believe that oratory contests constitute an excellent educational device to train young people in public speaking.[8] So let's get on with our job knowing it is a most
worthy one. To this I next direct your attention.

### Notes

1. "Until human nature shall change, there need be no
   fear that oratory will lose its power . . . . The
   preacher, the lawyer, the legislator who must advocate measures before parliamentary bodies, the
   agitator, the reformer, and others whose business
   is to set the world to rights, need not be anxious
   lest increased diffusion of knowledge shall deprive
   them of their kingdom, or tremble lest they shall
   be dethroned and left to mourn because, like Othello,
   'their occupation's gone.' So long as men need to
   change their actions, or, at least, so long as men
   are not of one opinion as to what action should be
   in every case, so long will there be opportunity for
   the exercise of persuasive speech." Clark Mills
   Brink, The Making of an Oration, A.C. McClurg &
   Co., Chicago, 1913, pp. 74-75.

2.  Richard L. Johannesen, "Educational Oratory in American Colleges and Universities: An American Survey," CSSJ, Autumn, 1962, pp. 276-81. See also Chapter 2, "Our Rich Heritage in Oratory," E.C. Buehler and Richard L. Johannesen, Building the Contest Oration, The H.W. Wilson Company, New York, 1965, pp. 19-32.

3.  Donald E. Williams, University of Florida, "College Literary Societies and the Founding of Departments of Speech," JAFA, January, 1966, pp. 29-33.

4.  The first place men's winner in the 1947 IOA contest, John W. Low of Nebraska Wesleyan University, in the opening two paragraphs of his oration, "My Paper Doll," presents an interesting account of the program of the first Interstate contest on February 27, 1874, at Galesburg, Illinois. WO-1947, pp. 29-31.

5.  This trend toward informality may sometimes have been overdone, so much so that present-day oratory has been criticized on that score, viz., that it is no longer "speech in the grand manner." Charles T. Battin, University of Puget Sound, "Why Teachers of Speech?", Forensic, October, 1942, pp. 15-16. Thus, current oratory is attacked from both sides, by some because it's "too oratorical" and by others because it's "not oratorical enough." I, too, know of isolated instances where the subject-matter and treatment have been too light and frivolous. But in general I count the trend toward informality an asset.

    Articles have appeared commenting upon the change in the nature of oratory. Note, for example: "Oration is looked upon as a rather formidable word, suggesting what is tiresome and boresome. A person might 'hear an address' with ready willingness who would pause a long time before deciding to 'listen to an oration.' " Arthur Reed Kimball, "The Passing of the Art of Oratory," Outlook, 58:278-81, January 29, 1898.

    See also Max Eastman, "The Lost Art of Oratory," Saturday Review of Literature, 37:36, March 6, 1954.

6.  John E. Gow, Director of Forensics, Elmhurst College, "Re-examining Contest Speaking," Forensic, January,

1968, pp. 3-5. Excerpts: ". . . a recent report
as well as poll taking at the Pi Kappa Delta national
convention indicated that segregation by sex in contest activities may finally be discarded - more than
forty years after woman suffrage became a reality!"
(P. 3.) ". . . oratory usually requires memorization,
but memorization is neither required nor often possible in public speaking as actually experienced."
(P. 4.)

7.    For recommended reading of my views on the attitudes
citizens should hold toward controversial questions,
see "Decalogue for an Ideal Citizen," Vital
Speeches, Vol. XXIX, No. 6, January 1, 1963, pp.
186-92.

8.    "Speech contests, like any other educational device,
are, of themselves neither good nor bad.  Their
chief value rests on whether they stimulate the student to efforts he would not otherwise have made,
in situations that are measurably like those he may
meet outside of school.  Speech contests have a
long, and, in the main, an enviable history as devices for training superior students who are not
stimulated to their best efforts by the work of the
classroom."  Henry L. Ewbank, "Speech Contests
as Educational Technics," QJS, April, 1936, p. 188.

Chapter II

THE BENEFITS OF ORATORY

Not until human nature is other than it
is will the function of the living voice--the
greatest force among men--cease.  I advocate therefore, in its fullest extent and for
every reason of humanity, of patriotism, of
religion, a more thorough culture of oratory.

Henry Ward Beecher

A student may well ask, "Why should I come out for
oratory?  What'll it 'get me' besides a lot of hard work and
head-aches?  What benefits and values are there?  Are they
transitory or permanent?"  These are fair questions and deserve a frank and complete answer.

I.  OBVIOUS SPEECH BENEFITS
    A.  Interest and Research Ability in Public Problems

First, from wrestling with grave public problems, an
oratory participant acquires an awareness of and an interest
in them.  From seeking their solution, he also acquires
habits of scholarly research and preparation.  The general
public may not be aware of it but the conscientious, diligent
oratory student knows that the finished product of a written
oration represents only a small portion of the raw material
that has gone into its preparation.

    B.  Speech Composition

Second, oratory participation provides what amounts to
an intensive personalized course in speech composition,
usually under close supervision of a competent coach.  This
involves minute study, attention to matters of organization,
style and all the other concomitant rhetorical elements to be

16

studied in detail later in this book. And withal, by reason
of the need to adhere to prescribed word or time limits,
the student orator learns the art of compression, of discrimination, of saying "multum in parvo."


### C. Speech Delivery

Third, oratory participation obviously provides the
opportunity to improve one's speech delivery. All drills,
rehearsals, and public appearances have this objective in
mind.


### D. Social Growth

Fourth, oratory participation provides a subsidiary
sort of bonus value in the opportunity for mixing and
mingling with superior speech students from other schools.
Forensic participants are almost invariably among "the
cream of the crop" scholastically. Hence through travel
to contests-- another ancillary benefit, by the way-- one
becomes acquainted with some of the best intellects of
other schools, gets to share and exchange views with one's
peers.

These four briefly enumerated benefits of oratory to
the individual participant are obvious. They are not likely
to be disputed and require no elaboration. How these immediate benefits can result in the more lasting benefits of
enabling the orator to contribute toward a better America
and a better world, may not be so immediately apparent
and may need amplification. While this belief on my part
that it does is by no means original with me, and is
shared by many others, I am of the opinion that the speech
profession has "missed the boat," has never adequately
stressed this value aspect to their trainees, that is, the
powerful potential influence in improving America and the
world. I add "the world" since with instant communications, we have obviously become "one world." Hence, this
chapter and the next represent a basic statement of my
credos.

A mastery of language has always been recognized as
a valid educational objective. Today, the atomic age with
all of its potentialities for good and evil has made us aware
of the desperate need for improved human relations. This

in turn is inextricably bound up with better communication.
In June, 1968, Spectra, a publication of the SAA, said
editorially,

> Recent events, including the assassination of
> Dr. Martin Luther King, Jr., have underscored
> the necessity for a thorough re-evaluation of the
> educational and research postures of the commu-
> nication arts and sciences field. It would be pre-
> sumptuous to suggest that our community of in-
> terests holds the answers to national and interna-
> tional problems of poverty, racism and violence.
> Failure to apply our best thinking to these prob-
> lems, however, will represent an abdication of
> rightful responsibility.

In this proposed re-evaluation, the field of oratory
can claim an honorable place. For, while oratory is in the
first instance an educational device conducted for the purpose of developing competence in speech, it cannot be divorced from many lasting benefits resulting from the competent practice of oratory. For example, the subjects
dealt with in oratory concern major trends and movements
relating to great social, political, economic, moral and
religious problems. And as a first step in solving them,
there is just no substitute for the effective spoken word.

II.  LESS OBVIOUS LASTING BENEFITS
     A.  Knowledge of the World Scene - Current Events

A sizable unit in my fundamentals of speech classes,
from which orators are frequently recruited, is devoted to a
study of current events, the subject area from which many,
perhaps most, orations come. It seems nothing short of
silly for students to be studying ancient and medieval history
in school if at the same time, they are not alive to the
events of history in the making. In oratory work especially,
we are training ourselves in speech for practical, utilitarian
use of it, not merely as an ornament. Therefore, if we are
to be speakers in order to be leaders, we must have an
awareness of the problems which face us, their existence
and nature, about which we are to speak. We have a marvel-
ous country. True, it does have many faults and failings,
and in oratory work, where one is espousing a cause, en-
gaging in a crusade, those are constantly being pointed out.
But, remembering that one of the most precious things in

our heritage is freedom of speech, prospective orators, as potential citizens, are preparing themselves to exercise that freedom through their speaking ability. Thus we can help to keep our country the good country that it is and, through the medium of oratory participation, seek to improve it.

### B.   Worthy Citizenship

These lasting benefits are not mutually exclusive. One merges into the other. The knowledge of current affairs and interest in them leads to worthy citizenship. This has long been recognized as one of the seven cardinal principles of education. Familiarity with timely public questions, learning how to organize ideas, and how to present them effectively before audiences--all these are values which can and should lead student orators toward becoming better citizens as they take their place in the world. In his delightful volume, Public Speaking Without Fear and Trembling, Mark Hanna, Fresno State College, Fresno, California, asks:

> What is the primary purpose of good public speaking?

> The primary purpose is, of course, to enable one to be an alert, participating American citizen. Any American should wish to cultivate his ability to address others so that he can take active part in the discussions which are vital to this kind of nation and government. [1]

John P. Ryan, 13th president of the SAA, echoes the same thought:

> It is ... by means of speaking that you can make some contributions toward the permanency and perpetuity of the government that you and I, and all of us enjoy. [2]

### C.   Growth of Leadership

Oratory participation leads to growth in leadership qualities. From a detailed study of one problem, one's appetite is whetted for the study of others to the point where this becomes a life-long interest. Oratory participation in

high school and college contests serves as a training-ground
for our future leaders. It would appear that this idea would
be so in theory; it has actually worked out that way in practice. In the past, winners of IOA contests have for the most
part entered life professions requiring the exercise of their
speaking talents directly.[3] The late Dean of the School of
Speech at the University of Southern California, Ray K.
Immel, said many years ago:

> I have watched contestants develop through contest
> activities and I have watched their progress after
> they left school. They almost universally testify
> to the value received from these contests and
> their achievements generally support their
> testimony.[4]

If the classic definition of an orator by Quintilian is
correct--"vir bonus peritus dicendi" ("a good man skilled in
speaking"), --it would be tragic for any orator, young or
old, not to utilize his speaking talents to the uttermost to
make this world a better place in which to live. This
troubled world is beset with political, economic, social,
moral, religious problems of all kinds and descriptions.
The budding orator is the man with a message. Early in
life he becomes possessed of an interest in these problems,
grappling with solutions, organizing and presenting these
ideas effectively to an audience in a conscious effort to
bring about changes in society. This implies of course not
merely an interest in one topic but in many. Hence an
orator can be taking part in oratorical activity as a student
for some six years, during the last two years of high
school and throughout college years. And the interest
gained will presumably increase throughout adult life so that
his talents are continuously engaged in speaking out for
right, as God gives him to see the light, subject always to
change when new light dawns.

This is or should be the conscious goal of all who
aspire to excellence in oratory. Such a person must have
in his soul the crusading spirit. He should be a reformer,
one who sees a wrong and seeks to right it, who sees an
evil and seeks to remove it, who is gripped by a worthy
cause and wants to espouse and advance it.

D.  Self- Fulfillment

One could even look at this idea from a religious
viewpoint.  Cardinal Gibbons said:  "Every man has a mis-
sion from God to help his fellow-beings."[5]  Leo Rosten put
the idea somewhat differently:

> The purpose of life is not to be happy.  The pur-
> pose of life is to matter, to be productive, to have
> it make some difference that you lived at all.
> Happiness, in the ancient noble sense, means self-
> fulfillment--and is given to those who use to the
> fullest whatever talents God or luck or fate has
> bestowed upon them.[6]

In short, this world is faced with multitudinous problems
today, all of them properly subjects worthy of oratorical
effort.  These problems will not solve themselves.  I doubt
that God will solve them for us.  In my book Annie Mae
Flint's old hymn is still good theology:  "Christ has no
hands but our hands to do His work today."  Or, as the
late President John F. Kennedy put it at the close of his
Inaugural address:

> With a good conscience our only sure reward,
> with history the final judge of our deeds, let us
> go forth to lead the land we love, asking His
> blessing and His help, but knowing that here on
> earth God's work must truly be our own.

E.  Development of Public Opinion

Some may question the influence of "immature" students upon public opinion.  I do not.  I believe the tendency
to degrade youth is regrettable.  I have an abiding faith in
them.  Like Professor Lionel Crocker, in his presidential
address to the SAA, I too always rather

> ... liked the story of the professor who always
> tipped his hat to his students, for, he said, he
> never knew when he was in the presence of
> genius.[7]

During all of my 45 teaching years, I have been
preaching the gospel through numerous articles and addresses that we as speech teachers minimize the impact

which our student contest speakers produce upon public
opinion.  In our haste to acknowledge that there is undeniably present a game, sport, contest element, we tend to
lose sight of the obvious fact that our speakers are also
influencing the people who hear them.  Every participant in
a local, regional, state, and interstate contest has some influence upon any audience, be it large or small, which hears
him.  (I hasten to assure the distaff side that I am using the
word "him" generically!)  There is also a modicum of influence upon all who read the state prize-winning orations in
Winning Orations, the annual publication of the IOA.  Through
their orations, spoken and written, orators are contributing
their mite to the aggregate from which public opinion upon
the questions discussed, is formed.

It wasn't too many years ago that the national debate
question concerned federal financial assistance enabling in-
digent but academically worthy students to go to college.
No doubt many orators wrestled with the same problem.
On September 10, 1965, Time Magazine reported that
Congress

> Passed, by a 79-3 vote in the Senate, a bill
> authorizing the first federal scholarships for
> under-graduates and other substantial aid to
> higher education.

It is fair to assume that in some small measure the many
audience debates and orations on this subject helped to
bring about this result.

Addressing the PKD national convention March 28,
1961, a former president of the organization, Dean Edward S.
Betz, University of the Pacific, Stockton, California,
enumerated a number of significant social, economic and
political problems attacked through the years by thousands
of student members of PKD, and concluded:

> It is entirely possible that the consideration given
> by the top strata of the nation's colleges and
> university students did have a real effect on the
> climate of public opinion which made possible the
> adoption of these proposals.

I not only think that's possible; I believe it's certain.  Some
of my skeptical friends may say: "Why, you can't be
serious--you must be kidding."  I'm well aware, having

myself been a debate coach for 25 years, that this statement is what my debate friends would call an "unsupported
assertion." Allow me, therefore, to present a few ideas
which lead me at least to this inevitable conclusion.

I reject the notion that forensic events are solely for
the mere sharpening of tools in preparation for later participation in so-called "real life" situations. The high school
and college communities are already in a sense a slice of
real life rather than a mere preliminary to it. Consider
the active participation of the student speakers at Oxford and
Cambridge Universities in the problems of the day.

### 1. Leaders Who Affect Public Opinion

In 1963, Pi Kappa Delta held its Fiftieth Golden
Anniversary Convention at Southern Illinois University at
Carbondale, Illinois. Fifty Distinguished Alumni Awards
were presented to a group of 50 living alumni who had
"made distinguished contributions in their professional
careers for a more worthwhile way of life."[8] Among those
so honored were United States senators and representatives,
governors, Supreme Court justices, stars of stage and
screen, college and university presidents, leading educators
in the speech field, editors, ministers, missionairies and
top-flight business executives, all former college and university speakers. I realize it is risky for anyone, and
particularly the individual himself who is involved, to sort
out all the many environmental influences which contributed
in youth toward making him the person he is today. But
when all present bore brief testimony at the presentation
banquet to the debt they owed to their college speaking experiences, their judgments cannot be entirely ignored.

Any who heard this testimony could scarcely fail to
be convinced that persons trained in speech contests become
tomorrow's leaders. These men and women in their undergraduate days, no doubt in debate, extemporaneous speaking,
as well as in oratory contests, wrestled with significant
problems. Now I wouldn't pretend to know the perfect
answer as to how or even when a person matures.
Dr. Harry Overstreet once wrote a best-seller The Mature
Mind contending that many adults are immature and indica-
ting that maturation is more a psychological than a chronological matter. But it makes little sense to me to assume
that the influence of the 50 recipients of this honor began

only in some mysterious magical way the day after graduation.

## 2. Public Opinion and Pressure Groups

Whenever a debate team or an orator discusses a question, let us say relating to capital-labor relations, the publicity departments of the AFL-CIO and the National Association of Manufacturers are only too eager to supply information to the inquirers. That is true of rival organizations upon any controversial question. If these organizations did not feel that their positions on public policy would be enhanced and contribute to the public opinion favorable to their side by supplying this information, why would they be so eager to do so?

In the era when McCarthyism was in its heyday, the years 1954-55, the national college debate question was on the recognition of Red China. The debaters at West Point, the site of the national Debate Tournament, did not debate that subject that year, presumably lest some time in the future the loyalty of those speaking in favor of recognition might be called into question by being summoned before a congressional investigating committee. A few other schools likewise chose not to use the national question that year. While this failure to debate the question showed the low estate to which civil liberties had fallen in that era, does it not also show that there was a recognition that debating the subject would affect public opinion? While this example is in the area of debate rather than oratory, the point made is equally valid for one who delivered an oration on the subject of China recognition.

It might be noted too that many organizations anxious to promote a cause frequently use the device of holding a speech contest on the subject. Apparently the managers are convinced that public opinion is favorably affected by these contests.

## 3. Opportunities for Affecting Public Opinion - Off-Campus Audiences

College orations, and perhaps to a lesser extent, high school orations, are in demand and frequently delivered before off-campus audiences in non-contest situations. Obviously, any worth-while oration is suitable for delivery

before public audiences before, during and after the contest
season. Such public appearances have always been made by
our orators at the University of North Dakota and at Hope
College. I know that this practice prevails also at many
other institutions. Orators worthy of the name have a message of value to deliver and thus they are anxious to get it
circulated as widely as their time, and the energy of the
coach in providing dates, permits.

We shall say more of this in the later chapter on
audience attendance. But at this point allow two examples
from my own experience. One of our young men had gone
to Bonn, Germany, the previous summer as a community
ambassador from the city of Holland, Michigan, under the
Experiment in International Living Program. To sponsoring
groups, he delivered altogether from 30 to 50 speeches
throughout and even beyond the state, reporting on his experience. At about the midway point during the period of
these speeches, he did some severe cutting and prepared a
compressed version of the speech, "Bonn Report," and used
it as the oration which won the state Peace oratorical contest. He then later delivered this speech, with extemporaneous additions, to many additional audiences.

Another "old-line" state winner, with an oration
"God and Joe College," dealing with the problem of religion
among college students, delivered his speech some 20 or
more times before various religious groups, climaxing his
appearance the Sunday before the interstate contest by
delivering it in conjunction with the Sunday evening service
at the local Methodist church.

These outside appearances are in no way thought of
by the coach or contestant or audience as "exhibitions."
They are genuine speech appearances seeking the central
intent of all good oratory, to persuade the people present.
We here at Hope consider these outside appearances as of
equal importance with the contests themselves. In fact,
it's a bit of an open question which is primary and which
secondary, whether we look upon the outside appearance as
preparation for the contest or the contest as preparation for
the outside appearances. I suspect if we analyzed it deeply
enough, there is a reciprocal relation and each partakes of
the other.

There are times I attach more significance to these
outside appearances than I do to a contest. For example,

in 1964 Jacob Ngwa had just won the state MISL contest with
an oration on the problem of "apartheid" in South Africa,
and the following week the provincial PKD tournament was
scheduled for Grove City College, Pennsylvania.  I thought
it far more important, as did he, for him to keep his prior
commitment to speak at the neighboring Grand Haven Rotary
Club at their annual International Affairs Day than to use
him in the upcoming provincial tournament.

### 4.  Public Opinion and High School Oratorical Declamations

     High school oratorical declamation is not exactly my
favorite event.  For one thing, the declaimer gets no training in composition, very little in research, unless he is
asked to prepare some extemporaneous remarks on the background of his selection.  The prime emphasis is often on
delivery which may tend to become exhibitionistic.  My last
acquaintance with this event was as a judge in an afternoon
district contest with eight entrants, three of whom (one a
young lady) spoke Patrick Henry's "Call to Arms," a subject about which the few auditors present could do exactly
nothing.

     But a wholesome development in this event is the
increasing use of college orations.  Jimmie Trent,
Executive Secretary of the IOA, at its May 3, 1968 business
meeting, reported that 3, 000 copies of its Winning Orations,
mostly for use as high school declamations, had been or-
dered the previous year and that they were all disposed of
prior to February 1.  The Ohio Council of Churches is now
in its 46th year ('70-'71) of sponsoring the high school
Prince of Peace Declamation Contests, using selections
taken in whole or in part from the winning speeches of IPSA.
In 1966, I published Winning Hope College Orations, 1941-
1966, and hoped and still do that other college and universities would publish similar volumes to make their best orations available for declamation.

     A high school declaimer is old enough to know
whether or not he agrees with the sentiments expressed by
college orators.  The subjects treated are usually timely
and challenging to the audience.  When a community and its
high schools have good town-gown relations to the point
where audiences come out to hear student speeches, the
widespread use of these orations as declamations also

constitutes, in some small measure, an influence upon public opinion.

This belief of mine that high school declaimers do affect public opinion came to me rather startlingly and forcefully after I had been out teaching some eight years. Charles Finch, an orator of mine at the University of North Dakota in 1930, had worked out an oration entitled "The War Prayer," based upon Mark Twain's writing by the same title. It had been awarded first place in the national IPSA Contest. Copyright privileges were bought up by the Wetmore Declamation Bureau and copies were circulated throughout the country for use as high school declamations. It is impossible to tell how often it had been used. Some two years later, I was a judge at Warren, Minnesota, when a young man from Thief River Falls delivered this same piece at a high school declamation contest. To my best recollection, the audience numbered some 500 people. Earlier I had observed from judging similar contests that it is possible for high school students to become so absorbed with their selections and to assimilate its thought so thoroughly, that they speak the piece with probably the same animation and zeal which motivated the author. This happened in this case. The young man was old beyond his years and had captivated the spirit of the piece as thoroughly as the original author. The audience was visibly moved.

Now we have no way of measuring the true effects of presentations such as these. But it has been said by Clarence Darrow that "A pebble dropped into the ocean will stir all the waters in all the seas."[9] Analogously, I feel that the speaker with a message, by his speaking in the local contests and often before civic groups, both before and after the competitive event, exerts an influence which is not inconsequential. The thought that all the oratory being spoken by high school and college orators throughout the country have no effect whatever upon public opinion is, well, unthinkable. I have used guarded expressions such as "mite," "modicum," "in some small measure," "contributed." I wouldn't want to be guilty of exaggerating the degree of that influence. That would be a clear case of faulty causal relationship as in the classic example of the fly on the axle-tree of the chariot-wheel who, looking back, said: "My, what a dust I do raise!" In other words, I wouldn't want to maximize the causal connection. But the greater danger is for us as contestants and coaches to minimize the influence of our orators upon public opinion.

In summation, I do believe the power of both the
written and the spoken word through the oration is literally
incalculable.  What bright young orators have to say as they
grope for solutions to problems plaguing our country and our
world, deserves and does receive some measure of effect
upon the minds and hearts of both readers and auditors.
These impacts could conceivably change minds and contribute, if only in some small measure, to curing the ills of
our troubled world.

## Notes

1.    The Macmillan Company, New York, 1956, p. 164.

2.    As quoted by H. Clay Harshbarger, "Remarks on the
      Dedication of the John P. Ryan Speech Center,"
      CSSJ, November, 1964, p. 243.

3.    "The successful contestants in the Interstate Contests
      form a distinguished roll of honor.  Of the sixty-
      eight winners of first and second place who have
      been out of college twenty- five years or more,  the
      names of twenty- three- - more than one- third- - have
      appeared in Who's Who in America. These include
      one governor, one foreign ambassador, one bishop,
      two United States Senators, three congressmen,
      three distinguished authors, and six college presi-
      dents." William Norwood Brigance, Wabash College
      Orations, 1879- 1932, Journal and Review Press,
      Crawfordsville, Indiana, 1932, pp. 5- 6.

4.    "Contests Issue, " Speech Bulletin Supplement to QJS,
      December, 1931, p. 36.

5.    The New Joy of Words, J. G. Ferguson Publishing Co.,
         Chicago, 1961, p. 21.

6.    Leo Rosten, "Your Right to be Unhappy," Redbook,
         May, 1961, p. 17, 29ff.

7.    "Truth Through Personality," Presidential address,
         SAA, QJS, February, 1953, p. 3.

8.    Golden Anniversary Issue, 1913- 1963, Forensic, March,
         1963, p. 27.

9.    "Who Knows Justice?" Scribner's, February, 1932, p. 74.

Chapter III

## THIS BUSINESS OF WINNING

Perhaps it has not escaped notice that, in listing the reasons for coming out for oratory, the matter of gaining personal prestige and recognition in the form of awards, money and medals, trophies--in short, of coming out to win a contest--was not mentioned. To take part in order to win honors for yourself and for your school on a basis of school spirit is not a wholly unworthy objective, if kept within proper bounds. Surely everyone entering any contest, whether as contestant or coach, would rather win than lose, that's only human and understandable. It inheres in the very nature of man and competition. The worthy educational objective of oratory contests

> ... capitalizes upon a very natural and a very desirable rivalry between schools and individuals. The desire to win supplies a strong incentive to application and achievement and is wholly commendable in the degree that winning is correlated with performance of merit. [1]

## I. THE ROLE OF WINNING
### A. Past Over-Emphasis

Note in passing that in all of the educational oratory from the time of the ancient Greeks and Romans, contests were held. These probably were not always strictly oratory contests in today's sense, but were combinations of oratory contests with drama. [2] But the point is, contests were held even then. And incidentally, some of the undesirable concomitant side effects of an excess of this otherwise commendable desire to excel were present even in those days. [3]

Certainly in the past, here in Michigan we did overstress winning considerably. In the contests of the Michigan Oratorical League, some schools chartered special interurbans

to carry large numbers of the student body to the scene of
the oratorical contests.  Apparently this practice was true
in other parts of the country.[4]  Some schools followed an
oratorical contest victory with a "glory day" celebration,
complete with speeches and parades, including dismissal of
classes for the day and free movies at the local theatre.
Happily, this era has been passed now.  I find it hard to
justify disrupting the entire educational pursuits of an entire
student body, most of whom are non-participants in forensics, to do homage to some of their fellow-students who had
won forensic honors.

In Michigan, during my student days as a competitor
(1921-1922), it struck me that coaches and contestants over-
did the matter of rivalry.  They were much too tense and
on edge.  I well remember how at contests, a coach and
his contestant would purposely isolate themselves from other
coach-contestant combinations, eat by themselves because,
like Garbo, they "vanted to be alone."  Many coaches would
deliver last-minute pep talks to "do or die for old Siwash"
which usually had the effect, judging by its effect upon myself as a student orator, of getting orators tense rather than
relaxed.

### B.  A Proper Incentive

The desire to win cannot be ignored.  Winning gives
one a sense of satisfaction and reward for one's efforts.
This is not to be despised because if the resulting feeling of
elation doesn't "go to your head" and is kept modestly within proper bounds, there is a resulting confidence which will
stand one in good stead in whatever else one undertakes in
life thereafter.

At a provincial PKD convention in Orono, Maine,
many years ago, I heard a delightful oration by John Ahart
of Marietta College, Ohio entitled "Burn The Ballots and
Spin the Wheel."[5]  It made the point that the values in oratory are present whether one wins or loses and suggested
that, following a contest, we do what its title says.  For
what it is worth, I venture my opinion that in oratory we're
not likely ever to come to having a non-competitive festival
as has been done with other events which used to be competitive.  I could be wrong.  If we should come to that, it
might be a wholesome sign in that by that time we would all
have come to realize that the benefits of oratory are there

regardless of the outcome of the contest feature. I do rather suspect, however, that it would make the already difficult task of getting people to come out for oratory even more difficult, since this desire-to-win incentive undoubtedly motivates many to "give it a whirl."

Many minor criticisms of contest oratory spring from the perennial charge made against contests of all kinds, that there is an excessive emphasis upon winning. I agree heartily; but just how much is too much? There seems to be agreement that contests, short of this excessive emphasis upon winning, serve as an incentive and is a good educational device. It then becomes a matter of degree, of seeking a diminution of emphasis upon winning. And the success of such efforts will depend largely upon, and vary with, the individual coach. That this undue stress upon winning in oratory exists, I'd be the first to admit; that it is inevitable and widespread, I seriously question.

### C. A Subsidiary Role

Having made my bow of obeisance to what is good in winning, I now make bold to assert that winning as a motive for entering and participating in competitive oratory, both from the standpoint of the contestant and coach, should be relegated to a subsidiary role and never be pursued as a conscious goal. We ought never to make primary what should be secondary and incidental. Winning by itself is not a sufficiently worthy motive to absorb the efforts of contestants nor mine as a coach. The primary motivation in high school and college oratory should be to get over a message rather than winning a contest.

The degree to which student orators put winning as the primary goal varies with the individual orator. In the case of those who make this primary, the coach in his position of counselor is in a strategic position to steer the orator in the direction of de-emphasizing it. Upon further reflection, it strikes me that the two motivations, winning the contest or getting over the message, run concurrently. My own 40-year experience in coaching orators leads me to believe that as you seek mightily to influence your audience, which includes the judges, by so doing you as an orator are at the same time increasing your chances of winning.

D.  The Primary Role

Perhaps I may be pardoned for interpolating a personal reference to my own present method of motivation in
contest work.  The matter of winning is always kept in the
background, subsidiary to the main idea of getting over a
message to the specific audience addressed, whatever or
wherever that audience may be.  When a local winner is declared, and we start preparation for a state contest, the
orator and I have a little chat.  In effect, I say:

> In some circles, there's considerable stress upon
> winning.  Let's you and I just forget about that;
> let's do the very best job we can to prepare some-
> thing worth-while, and my experience is that win-
> ning or losing will take care of itself.  One never
> knows about competition; it's unpredictable.  This
> year you may be up against some extremely good
> orations in this tough league.  That is neither here
> nor there; your job is to get over the message,
> not to win.  If you go at this job with that attitude,
> I'll be happy and satisfied and you should be.
> From this point on, don't expect me to say anoth-
> er word about the competition you'll meet, the
> winning aspect, and don't look for me to give you
> a last-minute pep talk.  I just don't do that; I
> think it does you more harm than good, and it
> would be evidence that my mind is on what yours
> shouldn't be--winning the contest.

It would be a gross exaggeration to imply that in
every case I succeed fully in communicating this attitude to
all my contestants.  The fact of the matter is that I never
seek to exact a promise from them that this will be their
attitude; I just presume it.  I believe most of them through
the years have had this attitude.  But in general the degree
to which they do or don't absorb this philosophy is often
the measure of their success or failure in winning contests.
If one has this motivation, if the major stress is to get
over the message, if we forget about the contest element,
the results will take care of themselves.  That is, given a
fair amount of material in your school, as a coach, your
orators will win their share of contests; ours have.  There
will be times your orators lose when you expect them to
win.  But it will be balanced by having them win when you
expect them to lose.

E.   Present Improvement

Happily, this excessive stress upon winning which
used to prevail in Michigan, has long ago changed for the
better.   The desire to win no longer is so intense that
coach-contestant combinations at contests isolate themselves
and refrain from courteous social relations.   On the contrary, instead of eating in groups by schools, in 1947, during my regime as League Director of Oratory, we celebrat-
ed our 50th anniversary at a formal banquet.   Such sociali-
zing prior to the evening contest was not a common occurrence.   This de-emphasis upon winning is, I believe, true
elsewhere throughout the country, with perhaps some minor
exceptions in some areas.

Evidences in this direction appear in the withholding
of immediate announcement of results at conventions, the
use of ratings (Superior, Excellent, Good) rather than rankings (1, 2, 3) in announcing final results.   Recall that in the
opening chapter reference was made to oratory adjusting and
changing through the years with respect to nature of subjects, composition and delivery.   Similarly, a change has
occurred regarding the attitude toward winning.   Of much
more significance today than winning is the stress placed
upon the importance, both in the present and in the future,
of the potential influence for good inherent in the orator's
message.   For the ultimate intent of an orator, be he a
high school or college speaker or one in adult life, should
be to influence the conduct of the audience before him.

Unfortunately, even at state and interstate contests or
at provincial or national PKD conventions, the audiences are
rather sparse.   The conspicuous presence of the judges who
sometimes constitute the sole audience, noticeably accentuates the contest element.   Nevertheless, the orator's primary intent even there should be, is, and remains--if he
listens to, absorbs and applies the advice of this coach!--to
persuade the audience present whether large or small.   A
student orator, Miss Peggy A. Davidson, Michigan's woman
entrant in the IOA contest in 1953, raised the question
whether or not the orators have a continuing interest in
their subjects a scant year later, and then concluded, "It
all depends on what was more important, speaking your living thoughts or exhibiting your speaking talents."[6]   Miss
Davidson and I are in obvious agreement that "speaking your
living thoughts" should take precedence over "exhibiting your
speaking talents."   But I submit there is a false dichotomy

here.  It need not at all be "either-or"; it can well be both.
Most orators do express their living thoughts by and through
the medium of effective delivery of a good piece of composition.  I believe this to be possible because I have found it so
in my long experience in working with orators.


II.   THE ROLE OF THE COACH
      A.   Contestant-Coach Disagreement on Motivation

            In relation to "This Business of Winning," perhaps a
distinction should have been drawn between the attitudes
toward it of the contestant and coach.  It is best if both can
put winning as a motive into a subsidiary role and never
pursue it as a conscious goal.  But if a coach has in his
charge a young person whose personality is such that he
possesses a fierce desire to excel, what to do then?  Perhaps the best a coach can do is to allow it free rein, even
with considerable qualms and misgivings, knowing the difficulty awaiting the orator for trying to obey two masters at
the same time.  But who can really fully explore the re-
cesses of another's mind and heart?  Aside from caution
and admonition, there isn't too much a coach can do in
these circumstances without invading another's personality.

            The problem of a contestant not sharing the views of
his coach on motivation occurs infrequently.  The greater
likelihood is that oratory coaches lose out on some promising material as many of our brightest students are already
so disenchanted with all the hoopla of the medals and money
for winning, that they never enter oratory contests.  For
lasting satisfaction, at least we as coaches ought to view
our work in the context of a larger educational process
rather than to achieve the fleeting transitory goal of winning
contests.


      B.   Coaches - A Better "Selling" Job

            We as coaches must do a better "selling" job, in
seeking out these most gifted and public-spirited students
who do not come out for oratory.  We ought to convince
them that participation in oratory goes beyond the transitory
goal of winning.  We should stress its permanent values in
their own lives and in the life of the country and the world.
Often, in announcing the winners of a local contest, as an
encouragement to those who did not win, I have said,

"Participation in the contest, like virtue, is its own reward."
And that I sincerely believe.

This view of mine I have no copyright on.  It is held
by many others in the speech profession who coach oratory.
Among such is the late William Norwood Brigance, of Wabash
College, who has had phenomenal success in coaching college
orators.  In the Foreword of his compilation of Wabash College orations, he says:

> To some perhaps the verdict of victory is the goal.
> "He won, and that's what really counts."  But the
> winning of contests never can be the real goal, at
> least not with us whose pleasure it is to direct
> college students in this effort.  That goal is one of
> self discipline, of severe labor, and of the growth
> which comes only when men have given the best
> that is in them.  The winning of contests affords
> the stimulant and the immediate reward but not
> the victory.  In writing these speeches every stu-
> dent has grown greatly in the effort, and in grow-
> ing each has gained some semblance of what we
> are pleased to call education. [7]

C.  The Ethical Problem - An Awesome Privilege

In the preceding chapter, I cited as a value and goal
of oratory the making of a better America and of a better
world.  I am not so naive as not to know that speech, and
more specifically oratory, can be a bane to mankind as well
as a boon, that some orations may hurt rather than help.
But who is to say which is which?  It does appear to me
that an oratory coach is entrusted with the awesome responsibility not only to teach his students the acquisition of oratorical skill but to assure himself that they use it toward
worthy ends and not demagoguery.  He can and should convince them that "Nothing must be said which is not thoroughly and honestly believed."[8]  Since many public questions are
those with no clear-cut black and white distinctions and upon
which equally good men may, can, and do differ, this is not
an easy task.  In the realm of controversy, truth is not
always clearly known but is constantly in process of discovery.  Nevertheless, recognizing this difficulty, the conscientious coach should encourage his proteges to speak only
the truth as at the moment they are given to see it.  Since
a primary function of all education is to produce finer social

beings and to improve the lot and character of man, oratory coaches have a part to play in the process. In his role, an oratory coach has an opportunity and an obligation to imbue his students with a concern for the public good, thus strengthening the democracy we all enjoy.

In view of his huge responsibilities, and his privilege to be directing young men and women during their formative years, how can an oratory coach be less than enthusiastic about his job? There are times when the best of us are tempted to yield to discouragement. Our world is beset with problems of all kinds and descriptions, so much so that at times they tend to overwhelm us if we let them. The haunting torturous question poignantly faces everyone, What can I do? Well, aside from not being "speechless speech professors," and doing some talking on our own, we who coach oratory have the opportunity to influence young lives who in turn influence others in the here-and-now as well as in the future. I once heard Russell Conwell deliver his famous "Acres of Diamonds" lecture. Its lesson has never left me. Right in our own bailiwick, we can glean personal satisfaction in our job by the "Acres of Diamonds" right in our own back yard.

In summation, I can only repeat the words used earlier in this chapter. Winning as a motive for entering and participating in competitive oratory, both from the viewpoint of the contestant and coach, should be relegated to a subsidiary role and never be pursued as a conscious goal. We ought not to make primary what should be secondary and incidental. Some may say such an attitude is contrary to human nature; on the contrary, it is in accord with human nature and the laws of life as I read them.

I close with an analogy to explain and support my position. President Woodrow Wilson once said, "There is no more priggish business in the world than the development of one's character,"[9] and upon another occasion, "Character is a by-product."[10] One does not set out early in life and say to oneself: Go now, I want to succeed in life, and therefore, I shall set out to acquire a good character. Rather, one does his duty conscientiously, fills his life with deeds of love and service, and a good character follows as a natural consequence. Analogously, an orator's primary concern is to get over his message; if he does that, he has won a victory, regardless of the outcome of a contest. Winning is a by-product.

## Notes

1.    *Forensic News*, brochure issued by the Michigan High
      School Forensic Association, Sept. 10, 1967, p. 5.

2.    "Any sketch preliminary to the study of oratory would
      be incomplete without the mention, at least, of its
      place in the Greek drama.   Indeed, dramatic poetry
      and oratory were so near one another from the be-
      ginning 'that they often joined hands over the gap
      which separates poetry and prose.'   Accustomed to
      listen to long speeches in their assemblies, the
      Athenians tolerated a large interpolation of them in
      their tragedies, and so kindly that the oratorical
      element outgrew the others, and the speeches at
      length became the chief business of the play."
      Lorenzo Sears, Professor at Brown University, *The
      History of Oratory*, S. C. Griggs and Company,
      Chicago, 1896, p. 26.

3.    "Aristotle complained because the subjects chosen for
      debate in the school exercises of his time were not
      sufficiently true to life.   He was familiar, too, with
      the problems arising from decisions.... The Greeks
      had trouble with their judges.   So important did the
      winning of their dramatic contests become that the
      losers sometimes were lacking in good sportsman-
      ship.   Instead of smiling and running across the
      stage to congratulate the winners, they complained
      bitterly that the judges had been tampered with."
      Henry L. Ewbank, "Speech Contests as Educational
      Technics," *QJS*, April, 1936, p. 188.

4.    "So popular were the oratorical contests that it was
      not uncommon for railroads to run special trains to
      the site of the event, and school victories were
      celebrated with bonfires, blaring bands, and student
      parades."   E. C. Buehler and Richard L. Johannesen,
      *Building the Contest Oration*, H. W. Wilson Co.,
      New York, 1965, p. 29.

5.    *Forensic*, March, 1955, pp. 67-69.

6.    Peggy A. Davidson, "The Big Noise," *WO-1953*, p. 25.

7.    *Wabash College Orations-1879-1932*, pp. 7-8.

8.  Angelo M. Pelligrini, University of Washington, "Public
    Speaking and Social Obligations," QJS, June, 1934,
    p. 349.

9.  As quoted by Everett Dean Martin, "Education and the
    Basis of Morality," in Alexander M. Drummond and
    Russell H. Wagner, Problems and Opinions, Century
    Company, New York, 1931, p. 335.

10. William G. Hoffman, The Public Speaker's Scrapbook,
    McGraw-Hill Book Company, Inc., New York, 1935,
    p. 156.  Used with permission of McGraw-Hill Book
    Company.

Chapter IV

# WHAT IS AN ORATION?

## I.  AN ORATION - A PERSUASIVE SPEECH

What is an oration?  To some the very word is ob-
jectionable.  A most unusual suggestion to my mind is that
we should substitute a contest in persuasive speaking for the
oratorical contest.  This proposal strikes me as odd because
oratory is persuasive speaking.  Personally, I'm not overly
fond of the word "oratory," and I would have no objection if
throughout the country overnight all our oratorical contests
were to change their names to "persuasive speaking" contests.  Still, I see no urgent need to change our terminol-
ogy so long as the substance of what we would have would
still remain the same.  In this semantic age, we as adults
ought not to suffer from "word-fright."

An oration is simply a persuasive speech.  It's as
simple as that.  That's all the definition contestants and
coaches really need to know.  The aim of all orations is to
persuade--that's the common denominator.

## II.  THREE KINDS OF ORATIONS
### A.  Problem-Solution

Roughly, orations can be classified into three categories, and in all of them, persuasion, broadly interpreted,
is' the aim.  Today, probably 90 per cent of college orations
are of the problem-solution variety.  The aim here may be
either to stimulate or re-enforce a belief already held by the
auditors.  Or, more often, the aim is to urge them to accept
your proposed course of action as the solution to a problem.
In this broad sense, many sermons, except strictly expository ones, could properly be called orations.

### B.   Philosophical Type

A second type, for lack of a better term, might be called the "philosophical." Here the speaker presents a philosophical concept such as "the heterodoxy of one generation is the orthodoxy of the next." In this instance the intent is to urge that we keep open minds to new truths at all times, that we be loath to condemn new ideas and their exponents. Both of these first two types, probably embracing 95 per cent of all college orations, seek to persuade.

### C.   Eulogies

That leaves only the third type, the eulogy, whose general end, while technically called "to impress" or "stimulate," could also be thought of as persuasion in a broad sense, that is, urging auditors to think well of the subject of the eulogy.[1] The last orator I coached had an oration which was a combination of an eulogy to Dr. Frank Laubach, the "Apostle of Literacy," of "Each one, teach one" fame, coupled with an appeal to youthful auditors to "Go thou and do likewise" in some area of public service to humanity.

To say that an oration is simply a persuasive speech and that this information is all a contestant or coach needs to know, may strike some as incredibly naive. It certainly doesn't meet the peremptory demand of the debater, "define your terms." It admittedly side-steps the usual genus-differentia characteristic of definitions.

### III.   DIFFICULTIES ON GETTING AGREEMENT ON DEFINITION

An oration can better be explained and described rather than defined. For one could never arrive at a definition satisfactory to all. Those wishing to play the devil's advocate could find fault with almost any definition one might propose. Let us, therefore, undertake a mental journey together to see how we arrive at that conclusion. In that journey, we shall examine critically a number of representative definitions and descriptions by a number of recognized authorities in the oratory field, and ultimately arrive back at our starting-point that an oration is simply a persuasive speech.

A.   Three Representative Examples of Definitions

Here is a definition--one of the best--from an old but
rather good book.  "An oration is an oral address, on a
worthy and dignified theme, adapted to the average hearer
and whose aim is to influence the will of that hearer."[2]
This is quite acceptable although I would substitute the more
specific term "persuasive speech" for the general one "oral
address."

This definition makes no reference to the language
and delivery of an oration, so let's take one which does, also from an older book:  "There are three characteristics to
be found in an oration:  1) dignity of theme; 2) elegance of
diction; and 3) impressiveness of delivery."[3]

Personally, I agree with all three of these characteristics.  And yet, some might be inclined to be really hy-
percritical and object to all three.  As to dignity of theme,
while most certainly there would be agreement that the oration should deal with an important subject, if that is what is
meant, persons will differ on what's "dignified in theme,"
and what is not.  Certainly those subjects which deal with
the future destiny of our country and the world of mankind
are important and this type, particularly if winning is one's
chief goal, is most likely to win contests.  And yet, can
one not conceive of some orator feeling strongly about abol-
ishing tipping upon the grounds that it does violence to the
personality of both tipper and tippee, or about changing the
grading system at college?  Are these to be ruled out as
contest orations because they are not dignified in theme, as
long as they are important to the orator himself?  I cannot
see how we dare rule them out as subjects for treatment in
a high school or college oration.

Take elegance of diction.  What is one man's meat
may be another man's poison.  One person may receive an
almost ecstatic sense of aesthetic appreciation from an ele-
gant figure of speech whereas another might feel it just gets
in the way of the thought and that an orator should come
right to the point, and, to put it in modern slang, get to the
"nitty-gritty" and "tell it like it is, baby."  And beyond that,
is there not a likelihood that stress on "elegance of diction"
would soon lead to a return to the perfervid style in composition, the "purple patches" of a bygone era?

Take impressiveness of delivery. If by that is meant
earnestness, which is a sine qua non of good delivery of any
oration, there's no problem. But again, people differ in
their concepts of impressiveness. Take the matter of conclusion and climax. An effective "goose-pimple" conclusion
which would stir one auditor to the marrow of his bones
might leave some one else with a phlegmatic temperament
quite cold so that he would refer to it sarcastically as a
"maudlin tear-jerker."

A third example of a definition, to show the difficulty
at arriving at one satisfactory to all, is the latest definition
of an oration agreed upon at the May 3, 1968 meeting of the
IOA: "An oration is an original persuasive speech delivered
without the aid of notes or manuscript." Senator Edward M.
Kennedy's eulogy at his brother Robert's funeral would by
this definition have to be ruled out because he did follow a
script, even though he was by no means confined to it.

These three sample definitions of an oration, together
with my commentary upon them, illustrate the difficulty of
getting agreement upon a definition. Personally, I feel we
make a fetish of insisting upon the need for a definition. If
we can get common agreement on the genus--an oration is
simply a persuasive speech--then we can tolerate a wide
latitude in the differentia. [4]

Some may say this hasn't helped us at all. If we as
coaches and contestants can't agree on what an oration is,
then where are we? Well, we're right where we've always
been and always will be. For I assert that we are pursuing
a will o' the wisp when we insist upon agreement of what an
oration is; we don't need such agreement. We can conduct
oratorical contests with profit and value without it. Allow
me now to show how and why I arrive at that conclusion.

B.   Criticism of Lack of Standards in Definition,
      and in Judging

Oratory has been criticized for its lack of standards,
especially in this lack of agreement on the definition of an
oration, with its resulting lack of uniformity in judging. The
quite understandable desire for agreement on standards
prompted the IOA in 1950 to conduct a questionnaire which a
year later was published as the Diem Report. [5] The argument in favor of uniform standards sounds so very plausible.

There are standards in dog shows, horse shows, flower
shows, bathing beauty contests, therefore, why can't we get
more uniformity in judging oratorical contests? It all sounds
very good, but it just doesn't take into account human nature
as we find it. I recognize the need for getting such agreement as we can on standards, and have always cooperated
in endeavors to bring this about. At the same time I believe
the results of all such efforts will be minimal.

Tastes in oratory differ and they always will. Every
personality is unique. If we were all alike, there would not
be such a wide gap in our attitudes, for example, toward
our Vietnam involvement and the racial crisis in our country
today. Furthermore, if ever it were possible to agree upon
uniform standards, we would still be faced with the problem
of the interpretation of those standards. In any oration, the
human element in judging would still result in considerable
disparity in judgments. In the case of Supreme Court decisions, surely there each justice has received the same set
of facts, the same stimuli are presented to each. And yet
even this august body often comes up with opposing responses.
Witness 5-4 decisions!

Any experienced coach could cite scores of examples
substantiating the varying responses of different judges to
the same oration. Here's one concerning a state winner in
Michigan who had received widely divergent judgments under
the coach-judge system. She had the kind of oration which
you either liked very much or not at all. It was what I call
a "mood-piece," quite different from the conventional problem-solution approach. The young lady orator graphically
told of the excitement caused in her high school by the coming of World War II, of her own later enlistment and schooling

> in Mississippi, on the Gulf--in among the great
> airfields, under the roar of the planes. I lived
> for two years close to the men who fly; I danced
> with them and played with them.

She told of the glamour and glory of her experiences, the
adulation accorded her on furlough as she

> ... preened my navy blue feathers ... I hated the
> whole business. Yet I caught myself being afraid
> for the war to end.

Most of the oration consisted of superb narration and de-
scription. The wallop of the message itself was packed in a
few punch lines at the close:

> You know, it's almost easy to love war.   To hate
> it takes honest thinking.   To stop it?   We should
> try really wanting to![6]

This oration really stirred me when first I heard it; as a
judge, I took few notes (always a good sign when I am being
favorably impressed!), perhaps because it expressed so
beautifully what I have often thought.   A few other judges
were likewise favorably impressed, enough to make her the
winner of first place.   But the speech left some judges cold;
in particular, one of my friends whom I consider to be one
of the best oratory coaches in the business, said of it, "It
wasn't an oration!"

One other example.   In a state oratorical contest,
our man in the final contest won a unanimous decision of
five judges under the coach-judge system.   In the preliminaries also, he had received all first-place votes except one,
a third-place.   This judge volunteered to me that the only
reason he gave the orator third was that he had heard it
rumored that this speech had been delivered before to community audiences, and he felt that the speech should have
been prepared specifically for this contest.   What a difference in his philosophy and mine!   Verily, verily, one can't
please everybody, and my present point is that there is just
no use trying.   We ought not to be upset by these things but
learn to "cooperate with the inevitable."

The Diem Report previously referred to probably
says more succinctly what I have been trying to say here:

> May I say in conclusion that I do not think we
> need be confused because there has been so much
> difference of opinion among the men and women
> who contributed to this study.   Obviously it mere-
> ly proves that there is no one effective type of
> oratory.   As in all art forms, tastes with respect
> to oratory will differ with different people, and,
> may I suggest, with different moods in the same
> people.[7]

IV.   A PLEA FOR MATURITY

The desire to obtain uniformity in the definition of an
oration and consequent uniformity of standards in judging is
natural and legitimate.   Hence I intend no blanket disapproval of all those who seek these ends.   But let's face it--some,
but by no means all, of the clamor for standards and the
complaints of poor judging from lack of them, comes from
those who attach too much significance to winning.   But if
the preceding chapter has been at all convincing, what is so
earth-shakingly important about that?   The values inherent
in oratory participation still remain, regardless of the judging outcome.   If the contestant and coach have the proper
motivation for oratory, to pursue goals as outlined in the
chapter, "The Benefits of Oratory," if the major stress is to
register a message, as outlined in the preceding chapter,
you can well afford to forget about the contest element.

My plea is that we as judges in a kindly spirit "agree to
disagree," that we recognize that complete agreement on the
definition of an oration is impossible.   This much we can agree
on--an oration is simply a persuasive speech.   The best course
to follow is to refuse to take decisions too seriously, to take the
bitter along with the sweet, to join the human race and be reconciled to its failings and foibles, to take both defeats and victories
in stride, in short, to be mature.

## Notes

1.    A recognized expert in oratory excludes eulogy as a
       proper subject for orations, although he concedes
       that his mentor, Lew Sarett, includes it.   James L.
       Golden, "Achieving Excellence in the College Ora-
       tion," ST, September, 1965, p. 184.

2.    Clark Mills Brink, The Making of an Oration, A. C.
       McClurg & Co., Chicago, 1913, pp. 5-9.

3.    J. Thompson Baker, The Short Speech, Ch. XXVIII -
       "The Short Oration," Prentice-Hall, Inc., New York,
       1930, p. 293.

4.    Herewith are additional definitions and descriptions of
       an oration.   The reader can make his own decisions
       as to how satisfactory they are.
            a.   "The oration is a memorized, original, per-
                  suasive speech, dealing with worth-while subject

matter of timely interest, demonstrating qualities of logic, organization, language and delivery, and producing an effect of eloquence
which is far above the ordinary .... An oration is a creative effort by means of which
important ideas are illuminated, emotionalized,
ennobled, and dramatized. Its purpose is to
impress, convince or move the listener to action." E. C. Buehler and Richard L.
Johannessen, Building The Contest Oration,
H. W. Wilson Co., 1965, p. 15.

b. "Among the distinguishing characteristics of an
effective oration are high compulsion ideas,
clarity and vividness in style and versatility in
delivery .... Variety and contrast are indispensable elements. Thus the orator combines
logical and psychological appeals, general and
concrete details, social ideals and pragmatism,
yet conversational delivery." James L. Golden,
"Achieving Excellence in the College Oration,"
ST, September, 1965, p. 185.

c. "The writer of the treatise we know as
Longinus' On The Sublime, protesting against
the oratory of the schools of the first century
A.D., found excellence in oratory in five principles: (1) grandeur of thought--the power of
forming great conceptions, based on nobility of
character and on study of great models; (2) the
power of experiencing genuine feeling; (3) the
development of imagery through figurative language, appropriate to the idea and the emotion;
(4) noble diction, words appropriate to the
breadth of conception and feeling; (5) effective
sentence movement." Longinus' On The Sublime, Tr. by W. Rhys Roberts, University
Press, Cambridge, 1935, as quoted by Charles
W. Lomas, "The College Oration and the Classic Tradition," The Gavel, May, 1949, p. 78.

d. I rather like this explanation by my friend Dr.
Herbert L. Curry of Central Michigan University, Mount Pleasant, Michigan, an excellent
coach of orators, and recipient of the Province
of the Lakes PKD Distinguished Service Award
in 1962. "Oratory should be thought of as one
of man's most important means of affecting the

destiny of men's lives. It is simply the act of
communicating ideas and emotions to an audience
so that their ideas, beliefs, emotions and behavior will be affected by the speaker." Pamphlet, Herbert L. Curry and Emil R. Pfister,
Fundamentals of Forensics, The University
Press, Mt. Pleasant, Michigan, 1959, p. 24.

5. W. Roy Diem, Ohio Wesleyan University, "Factors of
Effectiveness in Oratory," WO 1951, pp. 2-6.

6. Jo Ann Westervelt, Hillsdale College, "The Years
Between," WO 1948, pp. 66-70.

7. W. Roy Diem, op. cit., p. 6.

Chapter V

A BROAD BACKGROUND FOR ORATORY

I.  IMPORTANCE AND RELEVANCE - FILING SYSTEM

A little boy, asked to write a book review of a book
about penguins, wrote this short one-sentence review: "This
book tells me more about penguins than I care to know about
penguins." Hopefully, the reaction to this chapter will not
be similar. The material may appear irrelevant to the young
orator intent primarily upon entering an oratorical contest.
On the contrary, it is quite basic to any student orator who
intends to engage in persuasive speaking during his entire
life-time.

For this larger goal, one needs a broad general education, the acquisition of a vast store-house of information
about men and affairs. Just as one needs specific preparation for a particular speech in the immediate present, one
who aspires to being a life-time orator must acquire the
ability to sense potential speech material in what he thinks,
observes and reads, just as a reporter must cultivate "a
nose for news." And, having acquired this, he must develop
a filing system making such information instantly available.

Any specially-prepared aids for the prospective public
speaker can be no more than a supplement, and not a substitute, for his own personal collection of ideas. One needs
ideas from within one's own experience, ideas that have gone
through the crucible of one's own mind and become a part of
oneself. In this chapter, we emphasize the need and value
of a personal filing system, divided into categories suited to
one's own temperament, needs and interests.

II.  TESTIMONY OF WRITERS AND SPEAKERS

A Chinese proverb says: "The palest ink is better
than the most retentive memory." Thoughts of possible

48

potential use in a speech are fleeting things; they should be
captured as they occur and recorded into a filing system.
Reliance upon memory is hazardous. Ernest Dimnet, in a
thought-provoking volume which was a best-seller in its day,
says:

> To keep no track of what one learns or thinks is
> as foolish as to till and seed one's land with great
> pains, and when the harvest is ripe, turn one's
> back upon it and think of it no more .... Most
> men who have made a name in literature, politics,
> or business have found it necessary to have a
> paper memory, and those who have thought it pos-
> sible to dispense with the drudgery of forming such
> a one have inevitably some day rued it. [1]

It is said of Jonathan Swift, the great satirist of Gulliver's
Travels fame, that he "used to jot down in the night as he
lay in bed any striking thought or lucky expression which
flitted through his brain lest it should be forgotten by morning."[2]

    The need for a broad background of general prepara-
tion for orators has been recognized since ancient times.
Aristotle in his Rhetoric recognized it and urged upon prospective orators a broad knowledge of men and affairs. Modern speech textbook writers urge a broad background of information for the cultivation of speech prowess. Many suggest specific categories of the kind of items worth preserv-
ing and filing.

    The testimony of able speakers themselves is over-
whelmingly in favor of this practice. They are not at all
hesitant to acknowledge that they have worked out in their
earlier years, and continue to the present day, a well-organ-
ized system of note-taking of their random thoughts, ideas,
and reading--all intended for systematic use later. Edgar
DeWitt Jones, in his American Preachers of Today, has 32
leading preachers describe their methods of speech preparation. Dr. William L. Stidger, head of the Department of
Preaching, Boston School of Theology and preacher of Copley
Methodist Church, the old Edward Everett Hale pulpit, was
asked how he could "find time to write scores of sermons, a
book or two a year, innumerable articles, to lecture, preach
and for the better part of the year meet [his] classes five
days a week."

A portion of his reply:

> ... as to my method of sermon preparation: I get
> an idea and file it away in a carefully kept filing
> system. That idea gathers material like a snow-
> ball. It grows in my mind. In a few months it is
> ready to be written. [3]

There is no need to belabor the obvious. Prominent
writers and speakers, ancient and modern, have disciplined
themselves to a system of record-keeping. That material is
then constantly at their disposal for use in either the written
or the spoken word.

III.  CATEGORIES
      A.  Original Ideas

We next address ourselves to the question, Just what
sort of thing does one file and preserve? We shall present
a few categories, recognizing that each prospective speaker
must work out his own to suit his needs and interests. The
first category is original ideas. Don't say you have none.
For if you believe it, you haven't a proper appreciation of
yourself as a human being. Having attained the status of a
high school or college student, you cannot fail to have encountered in your short life speech material galore. In support of the thought that you should not demean yourself as
unworthy to have original ideas, note this challenging excerpt
from Ralph Waldo Emerson's "Essay on Self-Reliance":

> A man should learn to detect and watch that gleam
> of light which flashes across his mind from within,
> more than the lustre of the firmament of bards and
> sages. Yet he dismisses without notice his own
> thought, because it is his. In every work of ge-
> nius we recognize our own rejected thoughts; they
> come back to us with a certain alienated majesty.
> Great works of art have no more affecting lesson
> for us than this. They teach us to abide by our
> spontaneous impression with good-humored inflexi-
> bility then most when the whole cry of voices is on
> the other side. Else tomorrow a stranger will say
> with masterly good sense precisely what we have
> thought and felt all the time, and we shall be
> forced to take with shame our own opinion from
> another. [4]

I cite two specific examples of original ideas from my own collection. Two items from my hometown newspaper in 1918, The Kalamazoo Gazette, contained contrasting words, one underneath the other, in the same size type:

> In loving memory of our dear husband and father, who passed away a year ago today ...
>
> I will not be responsible for any debts contracted by Mrs. _____ after this date!

Here side by side a picture of the harmony and love of life, contrasted immediately by its divisions and discord. You point the moral to adorn the tale.

Another example. I have heard it said that wars between nations are just as inevitable as the instinctive dislike of cats and dogs for each other. But out at my wife's Aunt Pherby's farm in Kansas, I noticed that the cats and dogs, six of one, three of the other, got along in perfect harmony, each respecting the prerogatives and rights of the other.

### B.   Personal Incidents

A second category of potential speech material is personal incidents. These are the things that happen in your life experiences directly or by observation. Incidents are happening daily in your life which constitute potential speech material. All you need to do is to cultivate an awareness of them. Record them in your filing system for later use in speeches.

Watching the Olympic games provided a minister friend of mine with an apt illustration. Referring to the relay races, in an opening address to beginning university students, he pointed out the responsibility of the older generation toward the younger, that is, that they should make a good transfer of the baton. Subsequently, from my acting as an official at track meets, I have made these remarks in the closing portion of a commencement address:

> I have never yet seen the anchor man of a losing relay team give up without trying and saying, in effect, "What's the use?" Always he goes pell-mell in pursuit, bent upon closing the gap.

C.  Humor

A third suggested category for a filing system is humor.  True, jokes are not extensively used in orations, at
least not the narrative Pat-says-to-Mike and Mike-says-to-
Pat variety.  But the clever quip or turn of a phrase which
epitomizes an idea have come into vogue in recent years, as
for example, the Linus remark in a Charlie Brown Peanuts
cartoon:  "I love mankind--it's people I can't stand."  I don't
share a feeling among some that to use humor is a sign of
weakness in a speaker, evidence he cannot hold his audience
without it.  We must take human nature as we find it and
people do respond to humor.  It is a common touch of humanity.  Its use in speech is psychologically sound.  Especially when used at the beginning of an oration, it is a device for unifying the audience.  Are we not better acquainted
when we have laughed together, responded jointly to the same
stimulus provided by the speaker?

The ancients did not overlook nor despise this element
in speech-making.  Indeed, judging from some observations
of Cicero, he had a high regard for humor:

> A jocose manner, too, and strokes of wit give
> pleasure to an audience and are often of great ad-
> vantage to the speaker ... [and] there is no sub-
> ject for jest from which serious and grave reflec-
> tions may not be drawn. [5]

Modern writers, too, speak highly of humor.  Marshall
McLuhan and Quentin Fiore say of it, "Our time presents a
unique opportunity for learning by means of humor--a per-
ceptive or incisive joke can be more meaningful than plati-
tudes lying between two covers."[6]

A few hints on humor.  A systematic classification of
jokes is worth keeping.  The subdivisions you use depends
upon you, your interests, your vocation, your likely uses for
them in the speech situations with which you are likely to be
confronted.  One should acquire a sense of their usability in
illustrating points.  For example, one speaker, addressing a
University Press Club at a state university, quipped that he
never fully realized the power of the press until he read an
announcement in a small town agricultural weekly, "Owing
to the crowded condition of our columns, a number of births
and deaths are unavoidably postponed this week." Naturally,
one should keep some kind of record of where one uses which

piece of humor so that the same jokes aren't inflicted upon
the same audience. It is good practice, too, to keep a rapid
turn-over in your joke collection, to throw out the old ones
and insert new ones.

### D.  Statistics

Statistics constitute a good fourth category for a filing system. It is true one can always go to the Statistical
Abstract of the United States to find valuable information.
But it is wise to have your own private record of statistical
data of a kind that interests you, which you pick up from
your general reading. Here are two representative samples
from my collection:

>  Americans spent approximately twice as much on
>  smoking in 1960 as they gave to their churches.
>
>  The United States has fewer clergymen than it has
>  bartenders. The nation has 193,467 bartenders
>  and only 167,471 clergymen, according to statistics
>  on occupations and professions in the annual edition
>  of the Statistical Abstract of the United States, pub-
>  lished by the Census Bureau. [7]

Statistics are often used in orations. Statistics often
are "b-l-a-a-h," hard to take, like pills; you need to do a
little sugar-coating. You must learn to "humanize" statistics in order to make them more palatable to the audience.
For example, in a foreign policy speech to the American
Society of Newspaper Editors, President Eisenhower said:

>  This world in arms is not spending money alone.
>  It is spending the sweat of its laborers, the genius
>  of its scientists, the hopes of its children. The
>  cost of one modern heavy bomber is this: a mod-
>  ern brick school in more than thirty cities. It is:
>  two electric power plants, each serving a town of
>  60,000 population. ... We pay for a single fighter
>  plane with a half-million bushels of wheat. [8]

### E.  Current Events

Current events constitute a fifth good category for a
filing system. More will be said about this caption in the

next chapter on subjects for oratory. This much should be
said now, in general terms. If you would aspire to be an
orator your whole life long, and this is presumed throughout
this handbook, you should read widely in keeping abreast of
the times. Being informed on major issues of the day is a
"must" for every truly educated person, and especially for
an orator. You ought to form at least tentative opinions a-
bout important issues, some of which may and even ought
later to ripen into convictions, after you have considered
and weighed the evidence. The able public speaker must be
well- read not only in books but also in magazines and newspapers. In your reading, you should learn of the editorial
slant of a variety of publications. You should try to balance
a liberal approach to public problems, such as is to be
found in New Republic and Progressive magazines, with the
more conservative approach to be found in U. S. News and
World Report and the Wall Street Journal.

       Even the lowly newspaper should not be forgotten.
Here too, as with magazines, it is well to expose yourself
to at least two, with opposing viewpoints and columnists.
The newspaper is a prolific source of material for your
speech file.

            Ralph Waldo Emerson once said that he hesitated
            before throwing away the smallest scrap of a news-
            paper before looking at both sides of it, "lest it
            should contain some thought or fact or verse wor-
            thy of preservation."[9]

Nor would I advocate skipping the funny page. The comic
strip is no joke. It is replete with the foibles of human nature. Most people read them, and therefore an apt and
timely reference to them gains the attention and interest of
an audience.


       F.  Quotations

       A sixth suggested category for your filing system is
quotations. It is true that whole volumes of them, such as
Bartlett's Famous Quotations, have been printed and are
readily accessible. But these will never be as valuable or
serviceable as those you pick up from your own reading and
experience. There are times when others have said things
upon which you just could not improve. They say things we
have often thought and wish we had said first. It is well to

capture and file such gems which mirror our own thoughts. Here, from my own collection, which numbers into the hundreds, are a few favorites.

Brooks, Phillips
     Do not pray for easy lives, pray to be stronger men; do not pray for tasks equal to your strength; pray for strength equal to your tasks.

Buchman, Frank
     There is enough in the world for the need of all, but not for the greed of all.

Buttrick, George A.
     God does not wish us to remember what He is willing to forget.

Carleton, Will
     Boys flying kites haul in their white-winged birds;
     You can't do that when you're flying words,
     Thoughts unexpressed may sometimes fall back dead,
     But God himself can't kill them when they're said.

Graham, Frank P.
     Let's remember this:  it takes both the white and black keys of the piano to play the Star-Spangled Banner.

Jones, E. Stanley
     You can be rich in two ways:  in the abundance of your possessions or in the fewness of your wants.

Kennedy, John F.
     Mankind must put an end to war, or war will put an end to mankind.

Mann, Horace
     I have never heard much of the resolutions of the apostles but a great deal about their ACTS.

Thoreau, Henry David
     There are thousands hacking at the branches  to one who is striking at the roots.


IV.  RECORDING MATERIAL

     As to how to record, so far as the physical details are concerned, and what kind of files to keep, what indices to have, there is not really much that one can say to be of help to another. This is an individual, personalized matter and our tastes differ just as they do in what we like for breakfast food or what girl we'll marry.

There are, however, some basic standard suggestions which may be of help.

1.  Use the card system, either 3x5 or 4x6 inch.

2.  Record only one idea or quotation per card, and give it some label which is meaningful to you.

3.  By all means be sure to record the exact source-- one just never knows when for a variety of reasons you may want to refer back to it.

4.  Some large bulky things you will want to put in large-size standard manila folders.

5.  Develop early some system of classification or categories into which your materials may be filed. Unless one does that, the material is as good as lost if you cannot find it on short notice.

6.  As your files grow, you may even want to insti- tute a card-file system, after the fashion of a library, to keep track of where your materials are filed.

7.  Develop a system of cross-references, i.e., drop- ping a memo in the proper slot when you have had to make a decision between filing something under subject-matter or by a person's name.

8.  In the case of items where you just don't know where best to file them, there is always the Miscellaneous file!

9.  Make a practice to leaf through your files peri- odically, maybe once a year. In that way, you can not only keep yourself thoroughly familiar with its contents, but dis- card some material that has become out-dated.


V.  SUMMARY

The values of a filing system are too numerous to record. It makes speech preparation easier and makes the problem become one of discrimination and cutting down rather than one of padding; it facilitates a systematic search for ideas. These advantages are both from the point of view of the speaker. From the point of view of the audience, such a system as has been described provides material with attention and interest value which, after all, is one of a speaker's major problems in speech.

There are objections to this method of speech preparation, but none that is not answerable. Obviously, any system can be overdone so that one becomes enslaved to it. You can, it is true, become a "pack-rat." But there is no reason why that should be allowed to occur. It can thwart originality, but only if one allows it to do so. Your filing system can be used to evaluate other articles and ideas you encounter. It becomes, in effect, a part of yourself.

The gist of everything I have tried to say in this chapter is probably summed up in the statement of Dr. S. S. Curry, of the Curry School of Expression in Boston: "Impression precedes expression."

## Notes

1. The Art of Thinking, Simon and Schuster, New York, 1928, p. 163.

2. William Matthews, The Great Conversers, S. C. Griggs & Co., Washington, D.C., 1874, p. 114.

3. The Gavel, May, 1934, p. 64.

4. W. C. Dubois, Essentials of Public Speaking, Prentice-Hall, Inc., New York, 1926, p. 131. By permission of Prentice-Hall, Inc. Note, too, this similar excerpt: "Our leaders do not always lead us somewhere else, or tell us something we did not know. They speak our own attitudes, and ideas more confidently and more persuasively." William G. Hoffman, The Public Speaker's Scrapbook, McGraw Hill Book Company, Inc., New York, 1935, p. 136. By permission of McGraw Hill Book Company, Inc.

5. Cicero on Oratory and Orators, tr. J. S. Watson, David McKay, Publishers, Philadelphia, 1897. Bk. II-LIV, p. 159, and bk. II-LXII, p. 171, respectively.

6.   The Medium Is The Massage, New York, Bantam Books,
     1967, p. 10, as it appeared in Robert L. Short, The
     Parables of Peanuts, Harper & Row, New York, 1968,
     p. 7.

7.   The two quotations are RNS (Religious News Service)
     releases from Washington, D.C., printed in the
     Church Herald, official organ of the Reformed Church
     in America, in its issues of 9/30/60 and 9/13/61,
     respectively.

8.   Eugene E. White and Clair R. Henderlider, Practical
     Public Speaking, The Macmillan Company, New York,
     1954, p. 289.

9.   Kleinknecht Gems of Thought Encyclopedia, C. F.
     Kleinknecht, Washington, D.C., 1953, Vol. II, p. 98.

Chapter VI

SUBJECTS FOR ORATIONS

Never confess that you cannot think of
anything to talk about; it is a concession either of fear or of poverty of life. That boys
and girls can arrive at upper-school and college age and not have countless good things to
discuss is inconceivable.[1]

Charles Henry Woolbert


I. GETTING STUDENTS INTERESTED - INTERVIEWS

In the kind of world in which we live, there is no
dearth of subjects from among which an orator may choose.
We live in a period of deep divisions and strong feelings upon both sides of many vital issues.

There is a question as to just how much a coach
should do in helping a prospective orator choose a subject.
I have undergone a considerable change of mind on that matter. In my early years of coaching, when some one would
approach me with the intent to "come out for oratory," I
would quiz him in an interview and put the inevitable first
questions, "What interests you? What 'bothers' you?" If the
answer was "Oh, nothing in particular," I remember saying
on more than one occasion, "Well, in that case, I don't
think you'd make an orator; if you don't now have something
in mind which just must be said, perhaps we'd better forget
about the whole thing."

But through ensuing years, I no longer assumed this
stand-offish attitude. As time passed, I would probe a little
deeper in the interview, and I considered my function to be
making the student aware of the many problems needing discussion. I came to realize that many a student wanted to
enter oratory from motives of personal glory or school spirit, or, in general, to improve his speaking ability. Many

59

appeared unaware, until I as a coach made them so, of the
many benefits of oratory. Furthermore, I came to see that
the coach, by finding out about the past life and background
of his students, can uncover for them many subjects, on the
basis of what he learns from the interview. Many prospective orators are secured from beginning speech classes, as
a result of a personal biographical letter from each student,
asking them to tell me about their background experience,
their fears, and their aspirations. C. Horton Talley, Dean
of the School of Communications at Southern Illinois University, an outstanding coach of orators, uses much the same
method in discovering oratory prospects. [2]

## II.   BASIC REQUIREMENT - VITALLY INTERESTED

By far the most important single requirement to be
an orator is that you should have a subject in which you are
vitally interested. This overshadows all other requirements.
It must be the thing about which you can get most "hot and
bothered," a cause about which you can speak with dead earnestness, in a desperate desire to have your auditors share
your concern. This basic requirement really encompasses
all the other criteria sometimes suggested for subjects, such
as: Is the subject important to the audience? Is material
available on the subject? Does it have emotional possibilities?

For if you as the speaker think your choice of subject is important, you will feel a challenge to convince an
audience it ought also to be important to them. There must
be material available on it, or you would not have become
interested, and it must have some emotional possibilities or
the subject would not have excited you!

### A.   Personalized Oration

The kind of oration which comes closest to meeting
this basic requirement, one which has come into popular use
in the last quarter century, is the Personalized Oration.
This is the kind of subject in which you have personalized
reasons for speaking with a high degree of authority. I mean
the type of oration where a Negro talks about what I choose
to call the black-white problem, a displaced person speaking
about the refugee problem, a handicapped person, literally
one without hands, talking about how we as civilians should
adjust our attitudes toward returning war veterans. [3]

Examples need not always be so obvious. The subject could be any kind which arises out of your experience
and on that account is close to your heart. Examples: a
speech on the problems of the ghetto by a white girl who had
spent two summers in the Hough district of Cleveland; a
speech by a sociology major who had spent her summers in
visiting old-age welfare clients; a speech by a young student
ambassador to Sweden, urging that we be more tolerant of
the customs of other countries and avoid the image of "the
ugly American"; a speech by an American aviator who visit-
ed Russia during World War II and spoke "On Getting Along
With the Russians."[4]

Such orations are "naturals"; oration subjects and orator are blended, merged into what becomes a moving effective speech. They are properly motivated; the opportunity of
getting over a message usually means much more to that
type of orator than winning a contest, as indeed it always
should in all contest oratory.

My first acquaintance with this type of oration was as
a student away back in 1922 at the Third National PKD Convention at Indianola, Iowa. The winner of that contest was
Habeeb J. Skeirik, a Syrian. The gist of his plea was:
"Treat the foreigner right; don't call him 'dago,' 'hunkie,'
'wop,' 'greaser.'" Many years have elapsed but I still vivid-
ly remember what a powerful speech it was. Another orator deservedly getting high honors upon that occasion was
Enrique C. Sobrepena of Macalester College, pleading for
Philippine independence. An interesting sidelight on this orator is that he returned to his native islands and became the
head of the United Christian Church. Following World War
II, he was accused and tried for collaboration with the Japanese, but was acquitted.

Since those early days, we have had innumerable
speeches of the personalized type. It is difficult to choose
among representative examples. There was the plea by a
hemophiliac for donations of fresh blood to those afflicted
with the dread disease of hemophilia.[5] There was the eulogy of John L. Lewis, "Something of a Man," by Doris
Schwinn of Southern Illinois University, a first-place IOA
winner in 1951, in which she lauded Lewis for the safety and
welfare measures he had secured for the miners, of whom
her father was one.[6] In that same year, there was the
speech of the war-bride, a resident of Casablanca, who returned with her soldier husband to a small Wisconsin college

and was appalled at the racial intolerance in that community. [7]

In my 1954 article in the <u>Forensic</u>, I said that I had never myself had a contestant who was an extreme example of such a highly personalized oration, but that I was nevertheless enthusiastically in favor of that kind. Since then, I have had two such, one by an Alaskan Indian who dealt with the problem of the religious confusion resulting from exposure to different types of Christian missionaries. The other was by an African from the Cameroun who spoke against "apartheid" in South Africa. [8]

And yet in some circles I hear criticism of the use of the personalized oration. One says such orations often represent exploitation of the individual for contest purposes. That may be true in isolated instances. I rather thought we were on the verge of that when, in a state contest which after all was a speech contest, I heard a stutterer plead in halting fashion for more public support for speech clinics. But the very nature and sincerity of the personalized speech makes exploitation highly unlikely. I know of one instance where there was certainly a studied effort on the part of the orator to avoid exploitation. Ron Gluski, Wayne State University orator, second-place winner in the MISL contest in 1957, had an excellent speech entitled: "So You Have Problems?" pointing out that we all do and should face life with courage. Only the following year did I learn that even as he spoke, he was suffering from an incurable disease from which he died before the summer was over. He made no mention of it whatever in his oration.

Personalized speeches have been criticized on the grounds that they cause unequal competition, that, as between a foreigner and a native-born American, the latter does not have an equal chance to win. Admittedly judges should not bend over backwards in favor of a foreign student. But since when do we give up in contest work because of admittedly tough competition? This type of oration should spur all on to greater efforts. Personalized orations are not unbeatable. Match them with a timely gripping subject, excellent composition, earnestness in delivery, and whatever advantage the personalized oration may have, can be overcome. [9]

Another criticism of the personalized speech is the charge that bad effects flow from efforts of other orators to compete against such "naturals." Partly as a result of the

alleged need to do this, and perhaps partly due also to the
need for compression in any oration, there has grown up a
tendency to use novel, startling, attention-catching devices at
the beginning and close of the speech. In the process of
doing that, according to one oration at the national PKD tournament and convention in Kalamazoo in 1953, "Simply for
dramatic effect, orators have been known to shift, disguise,
omit facts when it will aid the impression."[10] A case in
point was cited of someone speaking on the problem of the
hit-and-run driver:

> ... he made the problem intimate and dramatic by
> telling the story of a boy, whom he said was his
> brother, who had been killed by a hit-and-run dri-
> ver. In reality he had no such brother.

Such instances are not within the range of my experience. Nothing I could say in defense of novel approaches
and endings to a speech should be construed as condoning
such practices. The case cited cannot even be dignified by
calling it "a prevarication of the truth"; it is plain lying, and
unethical in the extreme. But if such practice, of manufac-
turing evidence for the sake of heightening an immediate impression, is becoming quite general throughout the country,
and I have my doubts, certainly it is not an inherent evil.
We had better combat such a trend in every way we can.
An obvious approach would be to get to work on the problem
of improper motivation, to seek constantly for a diminution
of the stress laid upon winning. I have aired these views of
the personalized oration because of its frequent use in recent years.


III.  SAMPLE SUBJECTS ON BASIS - THREE KINDS
      OF ORATIONS

We turn next to the three major kinds of orations:
1) the philosophical; 2) the eulogy; and 3) the problem-solution type. It is difficult to classify orations into types that
are mutually exclusive. For example, an oration by a resident of the Harlem ghetto, eulogizing Malcolm X, would be
an example of a personalized eulogy. I don't consider the
personalized oration as a separate kind. The three kinds
enumerated above will embrace most orations and serve our
convenience.

A.   Philosophical Type

The philosophical oration, a sort of "catch-all" category, deals usually with an abstract concept from which the
speaker seeks to draw some moral lessons.   An excellent
pioneering coach provides examples:

> Conservatism, progressivism, radicalism, liberal-
> ism, culture, efficiency, evolution, puritanism,
> loyalty, emotionalism, personality, public opinion,
> the common man, aristocracy, monarchy, demo-
> cracy, reform, compromise, materialism, lawless-
> ness, and character all have suggestions in them
> for philosophic discussion.[11]

Samples of this type cast into the mold of specific-purpose
sentences are:

> The heterodoxy of one generation is the orthodoxy of
> the next.

> One with God is a majority.

> Take time to live--do not rush about in a hurry con-
> stantly.

> The maligned men of today are often the revered men
> of tomorrow.

> There is joy in self-discovery, answering the ques-
> tion, "Who am I?"

> Equality is a delusion.

B.   Eulogies

This type of oration is most usually a laudation of an
individual, coupled with an exhortation to emulate his good
qualities.[12]   Mahatma Gandhi, Pope John XXIII, Albert
Schweitzer, Eleanor Roosevelt, Henry David Thoreau, Wilfred
Grenfell, George Washington Carver, Martin Luther King, Jr.
are examples of the kind of person one might eulogize.   In
amplifying and developing the eulogy, it is far better to use
the selective rather than the biographical method.   That is
to say, rather than using the chronological method of considering his life from birth to death, it would be preferable

to speak of the sources of his power, the outstanding lessons to be learned from his life, and/or the application of those lessons to today's problems.

### C.   Problem-Solution

The problem-solution oration is self-explanatory.   It is by far the most common type.   The following excerpt suggests a number of provocative issues which could be good subjects of orations:

> In a decade of discontent a handful of major issues has become focal points for intense and often virulent rhetoric.   One cluster of issues embraces civil rights, open housing, and equal educational and economic opportunity for Negroes and other minority group members.   Another cluster has been shaped by university students, and sometimes by professors and administrators, seeking greater participation in formulating educational policy, and rejecting the in loco parentis role of their institutions. A third cluster of issues has arisen from the incongruity of pockets of rural and urban poverty (Appalachia and the ghetto) in a nation with an expanding economy.   A fourth issue has been created by the conflict in Vietnam, which has shaped many related concerns about pacifism, the draft, and the role of the United States as world policeman.   While the prevalence of the "don't-trust-anyone-over-thirty" conviction might be doubted, much of the force behind the emergence of these issues has come from younger people, and many of them believe in a "generation gap."[13]

## IV.   A GENERAL LIST OF ORATION TOPICS (by key words)

1.   Abortion

2.   Academic Freedom

3.   Activism

4.   ACLU (American Civil
      Liberties Union)

5.   AFSC (American Friends
      Service Committee)

6.   Anti-Semitism

7.   Apartheid

8.   Arab Refugees

9. Auto Accidents

10. Automation

11. Bail

12. Bankrupt Cities

13. Bill of Rights

14. Birth Control

15. Braceros

16. Brain Drain

17. Capital Punishment

18. Censorship

19. Charity Racketeers

20. Christian Education

21. Church-related Colleges

22. Cigarette Smoking

23. Civil Defense

24. Civil Disobedience

25. Civil Liberties

26. Co-education

27. Comic Books

28. Communist Speakers at Colleges

29. Conformity

30. Congressional Code of Ethics

31. Congressional Reform

32. Crime

33. Demagoguery

34. Discharged Prisoners

35. Dissent

36. Divorce Reform

37. Drop-outs

38. Drug Addiction

39. Ecumenicity

40. Eighteen-Year Olds Voting

41. Electoral College

42. Ethics in Government

43. Euthanasia

44. Extremism

45. Farm Problems

46. Far Right

47. F.B.I.

48. Filibusters

49. Financial Disclosure

50. Firearms Control

51. Fiscal Reform

52. Food For Freedom

53. Foreign Aid

54. Formosa

55. Funerals

56. Gambling

57. "Good Samaritan" Laws

58. Greek Dictatorship

59. Guaranteed Annual Wage

60. Guilty Bystanders

61. Handicapped Employment

62. Head Start

63. Honor System

64. HUAC (House Un-American Activities Committee)

65. Hunger

66. Illiteracy

67. Immigration

68. Immorality

69. India

70. Indian (American) Problem

71. Inflation

72. Intercollegiate Athletics

73. Involvement

74. Israel

75. John Birch Society

76. Juvenile Delinquency

77. Medicare

78. Labor-Management Problems

79. Latin America

80. Law Enforcement

81. Law's Delay

82. Legalizing Marijuana

83. Leisure

84. Liquor

85. Listening, The Art of

86. Loyalty Oaths

87. Materialism

88. Mental Health

89. Migrants

90. Military Spending

91. Moon Race

92. Movies

93. My Country, Right or Wrong

94. Narcotics

95. NATO

96. New Left

97. Newspapers

98. Nuclear Warfare

| | | | |
|---|---|---|---|
| 99. | Orphans | 122. | Right-to-Work Laws |
| 100. | Parochial School Aid | 123. | Riots |
| 101. | Party Platforms | 124. | Sex Aberrations |
| 102. | Physical Fitness | 125. | Sex Education |
| 103. | Police Brutality | 126. | Slum Clearance |
| 104. | Pollution (Air, Land, Water) | 127. | Social Gospel |
| 105. | Pornography | 128. | Stoop Labor |
| 106. | Poverty | 129. | Student Rebellion |
| 107. | Prayer in Public Schools | 130. | Suicide |
| | | 131. | Supreme Court |
| 108. | Preventive Detention | 132. | Tax Reform |
| 109. | Pre-trial Publicity | 133. | Teacher Corps |
| 110. | Prison Reform | 134. | Television |
| 111. | Privacy | 135. | Temperance |
| 112. | Propaganda | 136. | Tipping |
| 113. | Public Apathy | 137. | Tolerance |
| 114. | Publish or Perish | 138. | Truth in Lending |
| 115. | Rackets | 139. | TV and Riots |
| 116. | Reapportionment | 140. | Unemployment |
| 117. | Recidivism | 141. | UNICEF |
| 118. | Relief | 142. | United Nations |
| 119. | Religious Confusion | 143. | Vandalism |
| 120. | Religion in Schools | 144. | Vietnam War |
| 121. | Responsible Journalism | 145. | Violence |

146. Voting Laws

147. Welfare Reform

148. What's Right With America

149. Wire-tapping

150. Women's Rights

151. World Government

152. World Law Day

153. World Neighbors

154. Yellow Journalism

155. Youth Rebellion

Two subject areas, the peace-war problem and the black-white problem, are likely to challenge high school and college orators for the next few decades. Therefore, in an effort to be helpful, I have prepared both a "key-word" and a "specific purpose sentence" list in these areas.

PEACE-WAR PROBLEM.

1. Africa

2. AFSC (American Friends Service Committee)

3. Atomic Warfare

4. Church Role in War

5. Children and War

6. China Recognition

7. Christians and War

8. Conscientious Objectors

9. Credibility Gap

10. Disarmament

11. Dissent

12. Draft Reform

13. International Police

14. Isolationism

15. Militarization of America

16. Morals in War-time

17. Pacem in Terris

18. Pacifism

19. Patriotism

20. Peace Corps

21. "Saving Face"

22. South Africa

23. Statute of Forces Agreements

24. Truth in War-time

25. TV and War

26.  United Nations                    28.  World Peace - A
                                            Realistic Possibility?
27.  Vietnam War

## BLACK-WHITE PROBLEM.

1.  "Apartheid" - South          11.  Neighborhood Schools
    Africa                            and Busing

2.  Black Panthers               12.  Police Brutality

3.  Church and Race              13.  Race Prejudice
    Relations
                                 14.  Review Boards
4.  Demonstrations
                                 15.  Slumlords
5.  FEPC
                                 16.  "Uncle Toms"
6.  Ghetto
                                 17.  Urban Renewal
7.  Gradualism vs. Now
                                 18.  What's Right With Race
8.  Integration                      Relations?

9.  Kerner Report                19.  White Backlash

10.  King, Martin Luther, Jr.


Before presenting the following two lists of specific
purpose sentences in the war and race subject areas, a few
preliminary words of explanation should be made.  Hope College takes part in the local and state contests sponsored by
the IPSA.  For the purpose of helping to recruit entrants in
the local Peace contests for men and women, it has been my
practice for some time to post a list of subject suggestions
on my class-room bulletin board.  This list is changed from
year to year.  These statements precede the listing:

1.  This list is suggestive only; you need not choose
from it; be original.

2.  The list endeavors to take the loaf of bread, the
peace-war problem, and to cut it in separate slices in the
form of specific-purpose sentences.  Don't try to cover too
much ground in one oration; be specific.

3.   Upon most of these subjects, there is some material in folders in my files, and I would be glad to have you avail yourself of its use.

4.   Feel free to take the opposing view from the statement as presented; simply insert a "not" in the proper place.

Item 4 attempts to avoid the impression that the sentences all bear my stamp of approval, although many do. In other words, students are quite free to express their sincerely held views whether or not they conform to mine. (This will be discussed later in the chapter, "Coaching The Oration.")

## PEACE-WAR PROBLEM.

1.   Christianity and war are totally irreconcilable.

2.   The Christian church should oppose war unequivocally.

3.   We can never expect a better world until we build upon Christian principles.

4.   Basic standards of right and wrong are destroyed by war.

5.   Peace is impossible without moral standards in international relationships.

6.   "My country, in her intercourse with foreign nations, may she ever be in the right, but right or wrong, my country," (Stephen Decatur) is an un-Christian slogan.

7.   Our nation should base its foreign policy upon principle, not expediency.

8.   America, in her international relations, is much too self-righteous.

9.   A spirit of repentance for our national sins would become us all.

10.  Prayer during war-time presents perplexing theological problems.

11.  The decline of public and private morals in war-time is inevitable.

12.  Propaganda in war-time is necessarily untruthful and unreliable.

13.  "Truth is the first casualty in every war."

14.  Obedience to conscience should prevail over obedience to country.

15.  The responsibility for peace is personal.

16.  Obliteration bombing is un-Christian.

17.  We should share our material abundance with under-developed nations.

18.  The American Friends Service Committee deserves support.

19.  The U. S. should rid itself of a "superiority complex" vis-à-vis other races in the world.

20.  South Africa's "apartheid" policy menaces world peace.

21.  Racial intolerance in Washington, D.C. menaces the cause of world peace.

22.  Improved treatment of foreign students in our colleges could measurably assist the promotion of peace.

23.  The Food for Peace Program deserves continuation and support.

24.  The academic community bears a special responsibility for the maintenance of world peace.

25.  "Operation Crossroads" of the Rev. James Harvey Robinson deserves support.

26.  The yearning for peace cannot be permanently defeated.

27.  You cannot kill an idea with bullets.

28.  We need to match and over-match for our cause the zeal and evangelistic fervor of the Communists for theirs.

29.  Dissent must be allowed, even in war-time.

30.  Peace is possible.

31.  There is hope for the world's future.

32.  The atomic age challenges the world to avoid World War III.

33.  The slogan "You cannot change human nature," is untrue.

34.  The slogan "War is inevitable; it always has existed; it always will exist" is not tenable.

35.  We should disarm unilaterally.

36.  We should encourage universal disarmament.

37.  Preparedness does not prevent wars, but makes them more likely.

38.  The slogan "In times of peace, prepare for war" is not valid.

39.  We should abolish the draft and replace it with a volunteer army.

40.  Deferring college students from the draft is unfair to other draftees.

41.  There is no logical basis for deferring seminary students from the draft.

42.  Our greatest enemy is not Russia or China but our atomic arsenal.

43.  No real defense is possible against nuclear warfare.

44.  "Co-existence is preferable to co-extinction."

45.  There is an imbalance between our expenditures for peace and for war.

46.  The predominant place of the military in our national life is deplorable.

47. Those who opposed our Vietnam involvement will one day be hailed as heroes.

48. Saving lives is more important than "saving face."

49. We must aid in solving the distress of displaced persons.

50. We must expand and improve the "Voice of America" broadcasts.

51. American movies in foreign countries cause ill-will against us.

52. Property, as well as persons, should be conscripted in war-time.

53. Bans should be placed on war toys.

54. Proper teaching of history in the grade schools would contribute to peace.

55. Cultural exchanges between countries contribute to peace.

56. The presence and conduct of our "occupation forces" hampers world peace.

57. We should recognize Red China.

58. We should free Formosa from the grip of so-called Free China.

59. The Arab view of the Middle East tensions is tenable.

60. The Israeli view of the Middle East tensions is tenable.

61. Communist "witch-hunts" must not be allowed to endanger civil liberties.

62. Chauvinism is a menace to world peace.

63. We should fight Communism indirectly by making democracy work.

64. The United Nations deserves our support.

65. The doctrine of national sovereignty is un-Christian.

66. The World Court deserves our support.

67. We need world government.

68. An international police force is necessary for the maintenance of peace.

69. Congress should ratify the International Bill of Rights.

70. Our newspapers are unduly alarmist in stirring up international friction.

71. Professional 101% patriots menace world peace.

72. We so much like the glamour and emotional excitement connected with war that we don't really want badly enough to stop it.

73. We must be prepared to pay "the price of peace" in time, money and effort.

## RACIAL PROBLEMS.

1. We are much too insensitive to racial injustice.

2. Our racial problems at home should take precedence over the Vietnam War.

3. White superiority is at the bottom of our racial difficulties.

4. Black power, properly interpreted and understood, is not reprehensible.

5. The Kerner Commission recommendations should be implemented forthwith.

6. Neighborhood schools bussing is not the answer to inferior Negro education.

7. Congressional reaction to rat control show its lack of concern for the Negro.

8. Civil disobedience is at times justified.

9.  You can't have law and order without first having justice.

10. The white backlash is real.

11. Open housing laws should be strictly enforced.

12. The cry "law and order" is often a euphemism for racial bias.

13. "A man's house is his castle."

14. White America should seek to atone for past neglect of the negro.

15. Gradualism is not an adequate response to the present needs of the negro.

16. Job opportunities and job training programs should be vastly expanded.

17. All miscegenation laws should be removed from the statute books.

18. "You can't legislate morality."

19. Police brutality does exist in many major cities.

20. Every major city should have a Civilian Review Board.

21. Negro history should be taught in the public schools and colleges.

22. Voting rights bills should be strictly enforced.

V.  MORE TOPICS - FUNDAMENTALS OF SPEECH
    CURRENT EVENTS UNIT

        The current events unit in my fundamentals of speech classes is one way of interesting students in "coming out for oratory." Class members are divided into groups, each with a chairman, and all in the groups give short talks, followed by contributions and discussions on their feet by other members of the class. A condensed version of a mimeographed sheet handed out to all members of the class provides some provocative ideas as subjects for orations. Here it is:

Groups as designated should meet at the call of the Chairman to discuss and compile questions such as these, which are <u>suggestive</u> only of the type of questions to be considered, all with the intent of <u>general</u> preparation on everyone's part and the emergence of a <u>topic</u> and SPS for everyone in the group.  (Avoid repetitive topics).

## BLACK-WHITE PROBLEM

1.  How do you react to the statement, we appear more concerned with the effects of riots than in doing something to remove their causes?

2.  Is the passage of additional civil rights legislation a case of "rewarding rioters"?

3.  Does TV coverage "add fuel to riot flames"?

4.  What in your judgment is the effect of Dr. Martin Luther King, Jr.'s assassination likely to be upon further progress or retardation of civil rights?

5.  What is the Kerner Report?  What was the heart and substance of its findings and recommendations? What were reactions of some prominent people to it?

6.  Will or should our society eventually arrive at the point where inter-racial marriages will not be a cause for comment--where such marriages will be considered ordinary?

7.  Are neighborhood schools the best answer to the problem of providing equally good schooling for all?

## VIETNAM AND THE DRAFT

1.  What were the ascribed reasons when we started bombing North Vietnam in February, 1965, and how well have these aims been accomplished?

2.  What is, or should be, the role of the churches in the Vietnam war?

3.  What is the nature of our commitment to "protect South Vietnam"?

4. Are we committed to South Vietnam to protect our own security?

5. What is meant by the "credibility gap" and what are often cited as examples of it?

6. Are we in violation of the Constitution because there has not been a declaration of war?

7. What were the "Geneva Accords"? Were its provisions ever carried out, and if not, why not?

8. What is the "domino" theory? Cite cases of persons favoring and opposing it.

9. Are we committed to the defense of Vietnam by the SEATO treaty?

10. Has television in its reporting of the war, played an appreciable part in making people feel more strongly about the war, one way or the other?

## VI. PROPAGANDA CONTESTS

This handbook aims to take a position on every conceivable controversial matter pertaining to oratory. In the past, some controversy has centered upon what has been referred to as propaganda contests. Groups wishing to promote a cause frequently sponsor oratorical contests for that purpose. I wish to make my position clear on three of the most common of these contests: (1) those on the peace-war problem, sponsored by the IPSA; (2) those on the liquor problem, sponsored by the national WCTU (Woman's Christian Temperance Union); and (3) those on the Constitution, for high school students, sponsored by the national headquarters of the American Legion.

Two preliminary observations should first be made. The first is that the prevalence of such contests is an open recognition that their sponsors believe they do promote their causes. If they are correct in this, it supports my belief that high school and college orators do exert an influence upon public opinion.

The second observation is that it is incorrect to assume that any and all propaganda is bad. The word "propaganda" for many carries a derogatory connotation which its dictionary definition does not support: "any organized, or concerted group effort, or movement to spread particular doctrines, information, etc." That doctrine can be either good or bad, depending largely upon one's point of view toward the subject-matter of the propaganda or, quite often, toward the methods of its promoters. It has been said in politics, for example, one party will think of its publicity releases as "educational material," while referring to material of the opposing party as that "ill-considered, puerile, demagogic stuff [they wish they'd thought of]."

The primary criticism of speech people against some propaganda contests in the past has been the manner in which they are manipulated by the agencies promoting them. Key questions are these: 1) Is the orator in any way hemmed in, limited, circumscribed in what he may say? 2) Is he allowed to say only what the sponsoring organization believes? 3) Are the sponsors willing to allow an orator some latitude and freedom of choice on how specifically to treat the general area of the subject-matter? 4) Are the judges competent from a speech point of view, or are they guardians and watchdogs to check upon the pre-determined position of the sponsors?

## A. IPSA - Peace Contests

The following is excerpted from the rules and regulations under which the IPSA currently operates:

> The Intercollegiate Peace Speech Association is a reorganization of the Intercollegiate Peace Association founded in 1906 at Earlham College by a group of representatives from Goshen, Bluffton, and Earlham Colleges, three of the historic peace church-related colleges. The new name for the Association stresses its relation to speech education. AIMS AND PURPOSES. The aim of the Association is that of hastening the era of international peace, and so the ultimate elimination of war in settling international differences of opinion and judgment. The work of the Association is confined to the undergraduate students in colleges and universities with the hope of arousing in them an interest in the importance and significance of international peace, a consciousness of the evils and barbarism of war, to

engender the highest ethical ideals of practical
statesmanship in all international dealings, and to
provide an outlet for student speakers who wish to
explore the frontiers of peace between man and man
and between nation and nation.

Who can quarrel with these aims? Who in his right
mind does not prefer peace to war? In my teaching career,
I have always taken part in these contests, and have found
no difficulty in recruiting interested students into taking part.
Executive Secretary-Treasurer Roy H. Umble, Goshen College, Goshen, Indiana wrote me in 1970 that each year some
40 to 50 colleges take part in these contests. The IPSA is
now in its 62nd year of operation, and its latest report (1968-
1969) shows organizations in 18 states.

The brochure of rules and regulations also states:

The sponsors of the contest believe that orations
and extempore speeches will have greater audience
interest and greater appeal if the theme of the oratorical contest is varied somewhat from year to
year. Suggestions from states or from member
colleges for a contest theme are solicited.

I can see some merit in this proposal. However, some ten
or fifteen years ago when it was first proposed that we do
this in Michigan, I opposed it upon the grounds primarily
that it was unwise to limit the orators in any way in speaking their minds freely, and confining them to a specific area.
A secondary reason was that the circumscribing of subject-
area would make more difficult securing entrants in the contest. No such limitation of a general theme has been followed in Michigan during my connection with these contests.

Since there is no stipulation as to specific topic, since
the IPSA endorses the "Code For Contests in Oratory" prepared by the AFA, since IPSA affairs are directed by state
chairmen all of whom are reputable leaders in the speech
profession, I can recommend participation most heartily.

B.   WCTU - Alcohol and Related Problems

In December, 1958, by pre-arrangement, directors of
MISL oratory met with Mrs. L. G. Rowley, President of the

Michigan WCTU and Vice-President of the national WCTU,
to hear her presentation and request that Michigan colleges
consider participation in the interstate collegiate oratorical
contest on alcohol and related problems.  Section 2d of the
printed contest rules reads as follows:

> Orations need not discuss Prohibition.  However,
> they should not be at variance with the principle
> to which the Woman's Christian Temperance Union
> is committed, - that Prohibition is the best method
> of "control" and that Total Abstinence, not Modera-
> tion, is the only safe rule of habit and conduct.

While deploring the undoubted evils caused by liquor, I explained to Mrs. Rowley orally that I regretted that stipulation in the rules.  Subsequently, upon my return home, I
wrote her and mentioned an additional very practical reason
for our not taking part:  the minimum requirement of five
contestants per school required by WCTU rules was far too
high.  We do well to get that many in the "old-line" and
Peace contests, for both men and women, in which we already take part.  In this letter, I called her attention to the
fine tongue-in-cheek sermon by Monk Bryan, "Six Reasons
for Drinking More Liquor,"[14] which I thought her organization might enjoy in promoting their cause.


C.   American Legion - Constitution

The contests among high school students emphasizing
the Constitution sponsored by the American Legion began in
1938.  E. C. Buehler and Richard L. Johannesen tell us
there are "some 350,000 participants annually,"[15] although
in a letter to me dated April 6, 1970, J. Edward Wieland of
the national headquarters, states that this number "in my
opinion, is [too] high."  A publicity release dated January 1,
1970, from the American Legion News Service, in connection with the finals of the 33rd annual contest at Houston,
Texas April 16, 1970 states that the contest "serves as one
of the Legion's vehicles for providing a new generation with
a better understanding of the U. S. Constitution as the basis
for this nation's freedoms."  Few would disagree with this
highly laudable purpose.  Most Americans, I believe, are
familiar with and would concur in the well-known statement
of William Ewart Gladstone: "The American Constitution is,
so far as I can see, the most wonderful work ever struck
off at a given time by the brain and purpose of man."  In

the light of the purpose of the contest, it is not surprising
to find many of the orations to be eulogies of our basic docu-
ment.

As a teacher of Speech, I am concerned that all sides
of controversial questions be allowed expression.  If one
says, "Oh, but the Constitution is not a controversial issue,"
I beg leave to differ.  The Constitution has been amended
25 times, and is not sacrosanct.  The first ten of those a-
mendments are referred to as the Bill of Rights.  Time
Magazine reports:

> Who could possibly quarrel with the basic freedoms
> guaranteed by the U. S. Constitution?  Most Amer-
> icans, according to a poll conducted by CBS News.
> A majority of the 1,136 people polled in a repre-
> sentative sampling of Americans in effect do not
> now support five of the ten protections of the Bill
> of Rights. [16]

If a student sincerely believed this sampling is a cause for
alarm, he ought to be permitted to say so.

The Constitution is constantly being interpreted by the
Supreme Court.  The sometimes virulent differences of opinion among people as between "liberal" and "strict construc-
tionist" judges are well known.  The "Impeach Earl Warren"
bumper stickers, and the Senate's rejection of President
Richard Nixon's nominees to the Supreme Court, Clement
Haynsworth and G. Harrold Carswell, attest to that.  Pro-
tagonists of both viewpoints ought to be allowed free rein to
air their views.

We live, as I write, in a violent time.  Crime is
rampant.  In an effort to curb it, Attorney General John
Mitchell initiated legislation in Congress for "preventive de-
tention" in a District of Columbia crime bill.  Senator Sam
J. Ervin of North Carolina, a former member of the Supreme
Court of that state (and incidentally, an outspoken opponent
of most civil rights legislation), denounced the bill as "an
affront to the Constitution .... a bill to repeal the Fourth,
Fifth, Sixth and Eighth amendments to the Constitution."[17]
If one shares Senator Ervin's concern, a student should be
permitted to voice it, and of all places in a contest on the
Constitution.

When Kingman Brewster, Jr., President of Yale University, addressed the ANPA Bureau of Advertising dinner, speaking of the "relatively silent student majority," he said:

> Most frustrating of all to the most highly motivated, concerned students is the glorification of silence; the disparagement of dissent and nonconformity; and the ease with which the presumption of innocence is overridden in the name of "law and order."[18]

Again, if one shared this view, a student orator should be permitted to say so, even in an American Legion Constitution contest.

Since my work has been exclusively in the college field, and since I have therefore not had any personal contact with the American Legion-sponsored high school contests, I was in no position to pass judgment upon them without first-hand information. Accordingly, I wrote for information directly from its source, the national headquarters of the American Legion.[19] I am happy to report that in none of their literature is there any indication that the expression of such views as I have indicated would be prohibited, either expressly or by implication.

Upon the contrary, there are a number of indications, some important and some less so but "straws in the wind," that lead me to look favorably upon this nation-wide contest. The fact that the American Legion has sponsored this contest for 33 years (1970) with increasing numbers of participants each year, would indicate they are satisfied it is accomplishing its worthy objectives.

Three features of the contest should be of special favorable interest to teachers of speech and to coaches of oratory. The first relates to the wide range permitted in choice of subject. Note this excerpt from the printed announcement of the 1970 contest:

> The subject to be used for the prepared oration in the 1970 Oratorical Contest must be on some phase of the Constitution of the United States which will give emphasis to the attendant duties and obligations of a citizen to our government .... The subjects listed below are recommended as desirable topics but not mandatory:

An American Citizen's Rights and Responsibilities
under the Constitution.
Fulfilling the Aims of the Constitution.
Checks and Balances - Our Basic Governmental
Principle.
Our Constitution - Worth Having, Worth Defending.
Our Constitution - Ordained by Free Men, Sus-
tained by Free Men.
The People's Constitution - Ours to Defend.
The Constitution in a Changing World.
The Constitution in Our Every-Day Life.
The Bill of Rights - Reciprocal Rights and Duties.
The Constitution - A Barrier Against Tyranny.
The Constitution - Guardian of the People's Rights.
In Defense of Our Constitution.
The Constitution - Temple of Liberty.
Our Living Constitution.
Communism's Threat to the Constitution.
The Constitution and the Federal Courts.
Powers of the States Under the Constitution.
Our Constitution and Free Capitalism.

A second feature of interest to speech teachers and
coaches of oratory is the requirement of an extemporaneous
feature of from three to five minutes from each orator. This
requirement is some insurance that there will be preparation
in depth, that an orator cannot "get by" with mere "words,
words, words" without some support in research. Again,
quoting from the 1970 announcement:

> The purpose of the Extemporaneous Discourse Fea-
> ture is to test the speaker's knowledge of the sub-
> ject, the extent of his research, and the ability to
> discuss extemporaneously the topic as related to
> the basic principles of government under the Con-
> stitution.

A third feature of the Legion-sponsored contest is
that no distinction is made as to sex, and that girls compete
on an equal basis with boys. From a "Fact Sheet," we
read:

> Nine girls and forty-two boys made up the fifty-one
> Department (State) winners certified into the Na-
> tional Contest in 1969.

Two girls have won first-place honors in the National High School Oratorical Finals Contest: Jeanne-
Mann Dickinson of Roanoke, Virginia, who won in
1951, and Patricia Ann Turner of Muskogee, Okla-
homa, who won in 1962.

In this, the Legion is ahead of the speech profession in that
in most state contests and in the IOA, separate contests are
still held for men and women.

Finally, as a "clincher" reason for endorsing this contest, it should be noted that the AFA "Code for Contests in
Oratory," which I endorse completely, was prepared by the
AFA Committee on Professional Relations in cooperation with
officials of the American Legion.

## Notes

1.  Charles Henry Woolbert, Fundamentals of Speech, Harper
     and Bros., New York, rev. ed., 1927, p. 305.

2.  "Manuscripts Win Oratory Contests," The AFA Regis-
     ter, Spring Issue, 1963, p. 14.

3.  John Steensma, Calvin College, Grand Rapids, Michigan,
     "Does It Matter?" First place, IOA, WO-1945, pp.
     46-49.

4.  Bob Underhill, Manchester College, North Manchester,
     Indiana, "On Getting Along With the Russians,"
     First place, IOA, WO-1946, pp. 45-49.

5.  Ralph Zimmerman, Wisconsin State University, Eau
     Claire, "Mingled Blood," First place, IOA, WO-1955,
     pp. 88-90. This oration is much spoken of in oratory
     circles in that Mr. Zimmerman fell victim to the
     disease before another year had passed.

6.  Doris Schwinn, Southern Illinois University, Carbondale,
     "Something of a Man," First place, IOA, WO-1951,
     pp. 9-13.

7.  Flavienne Hanson, Wisconsin State University, Eau
     Claire, "I Discover America," WO-1951, pp. 44-47.

8.  James W. Thomas, Hope College, Holland, Michigan,

"The Light of the World," WO-1962, pp. 98-100, and
Jacob Ngwa, "Our Common Tradition in Peril,"
First place, IOA, WO-1964, pp. 68-72. Thomas is
currently the Director of Public Relations of the National Congress of American Indians, headquartered
in Washington, D.C.

9.   In my judgment, this belief of mine was confirmed in the
     Women's IOA Contest in 1964. First place was a-
     warded to Miss Jean LeVander, Gustavus Adolphus
     College, St. Peter, Minnesota, with her oration
     "Change to Progress," WO-1964, pp. 22-26. It was
     the best oration I have ever heard delivered by a
     young lady. She incidentally comes from an "ora-
     torical" family. Theodore LeVander, her uncle, has
     for many years been a highly successful oratory
     coach at Augustana College, Rock Island, Illinois.
     Another uncle, Bernard, and her father Harold, now
     Governor of Minnesota, have participated in intercol-
     legiate oratory. In this contest, second and third
     places were awarded to two young black women,
     Miss Jean Heard, Sioux Falls College, Sioux Falls,
     South Dakota and Miss Irma Tyler, Ball State Tea-
     chers College, Muncie, Indiana, both of whom spoke
     excellently upon the black-white problem.

10.  Vera Gabbert, "The Search For Truth," Northwestern
     State College, Natchitoches, Louisiana.

11.  Egbert Ray Nichols, Writing The College Oration,
     Nichols Publishing House, Redlands, California,
     1950, p. 75.

12.  It could be the laudation of a city, as in Senator James
     Proctor Knott's well-known speech, "The Glories of
     Duluth"; or of a country, "The Magic of America,"
     Laurence Masse, Hope College; or of a group as "The
     Spirit of the Pioneers," Wilma Oleson, Mayville
     State Teachers College, Mayville, North Dakota; or a
     dog, as in the celebrated speech of Senator George
     West of Missouri in a legal case, as quoted in W. N.
     Brigance, Speech Composition, Second edition, F. S.
     Crofts and Co., Inc., 1953, pp. 171-72.

13.  J. Jeffery Auer, Introduction, The Rhetoric of Our
     Times, Appleton-Century-Crofts, New York, 1969,
     p. 4.

14.  "This sermon was delivered on Sunday, January 11,
     1959 in the Missouri Methodist Church, Columbia,
     Missouri.  Its unusual approach plus its concrete
     and specific evidence made a forceful impact upon
     the large congregation of students, faculty members
     and townspeople that heard it."  Loren Reid, Uni-
     versity of Missouri, First Principles of Public Speak-
     ing, second edition, Artcraft Press, Columbia, Mis-
     souri, 1962, pp. 386-89.

15.  E. C. Buehler and Richard L. Johannesen, Building the
     Contest Oration, The H. W. Wilson Company, New
     York, 1965, p. 31.

16.  Time, April 27, 1970, p. 19.  Reprinted by permis-
     sion.

17.  Tom Wicker, columnist, Detroit Free Press, March
     31, 1970.

18.  UPI News report, April 22, 1970, Holland Evening
     Sentinel.

19.  Address:  The American Legion,
               National Headquarters,
               700 N. Pennsylvania Street,
               Indianapolis, Indiana 46206

Chapter VII

DEVELOPING THE ORATION

If you want to get rabbit pie, your first
job is to get the rabbit.

Senator Karl E. Mundt

The preceding statement appeared in The Rostrum,
official organ of the National Forensic League, at a time
when this former speech teacher served as its editor. Assume the general area of your subject has been chosen. It
may have come from your filing system, from developments
in the day's news, a discussion in sociology class, a television documentary, or from a sudden flash of insight during a period of daily meditation. How do you go about the
further researching, refining and developing of the subject
into the finished product of an oration?

I. NO BEST WAY - VARIED APPROACHES

Three preliminary observations should be made in
answer to that question. First, there is no single set of
steps which everyone should follow in preparing an oration.
Speech preparation methods vary to some degree with every
individual. Second, just as individuals vary, so, too, do
orations so that preparation methods vary for different kinds
of orations. For example, some subjects may require your
doing extensive reading and library research. Others, particularly if the subject is very recent and novel, may lend
themselves more toward having extensive interviews with
acknowledged experts in the area of your subject-matter.
Some may bear the unmistakable stamp of your originality
and insight. Third, it is presumed that most students entering oratory contests have already benefited by many excellent texts on persuasive speaking. Hence, this handbook,
although covering some of the same ground, aims only to
present in considerably compressed form some high lights

relating specifically to the preparation of an oration.

## II.  MATERIALS
### A.  Sources

In the main, once the general area of your subject is chosen, there are four sources from which you get material for your oration.  They are:  1) yourself (think); 2) others (confer); 3) reading; and 4) listening to radio and television.

### 1.  Free Association

One of the best things to do is just to sit down and think of all the ramifications of your subject.  Allow your imagination free rein and do some hard thinking on your own. Don't be afraid of getting brain-fever; it's a rare disease. As you think, perhaps you can formulate at least some tentative opinions about the subject.  Hold these in your mind as a guide and touchstone as later on you read other, and often contrary, opinions.  Thinking through the subject yourself, before rushing off to the library, is a method of speech-making recommended by Senator Albert J. Beveridge of Indiana, a notable speaker in his day:

> The method commonly employed in speech preparation is incorrect.  That method is to read all books I can get on the subject, take all the opinions that can be secured, make exhaustive notes--then write the speech.  It is merely an arrangement of second-hand thoughts and observations and of other people's ideas.  It never has the power of living and original thinking.  The true way is to take the elements of the problem in hand and, without consulting a book or an opinion, reason out from these very elements of the problem itself your solution and then prepare your speech.  After this, read, read, read, read omniverously--in order to see whether your conclusion was not exploded 100 or 1000 years ago, and if not, to fortify and make accurate your own thought ....  Do not read other men's opinions on the subject before you have clearly thought out your own conclusions from the premise of the elemental facts. [1]

## 2.  Consultation

A second source of information is consultation with others, either in person or by correspondence.  If, for example, you are intrigued with the possibilities of the pass-fail system, or the evil of grades, or the value of an honor system, it would be well to solicit in-depth interviews with professors in the Department of Education.  They would no doubt be willing to be helpful not only in expressing their own views, but to direct you to some provocative articles in educational journals.  The same would be true of subjects and professors in other fields such as economics, political science, and sociology.

Others outside the faculty, expert and knowledgeable in the area of your subject, could and should be consulted. William Norwood Brigance, an outstanding coach of orators, in his Preface to a compilation of Wabash College orations, commends the diligence of some of his orators in this practice.  He writes of one "who wrote numerous letters to secure one fact set down in a single sentence of an oration"; of another who "bearded a great lawyer in a distant city and persuaded him to set four of his young attorneys at unearthing the entire history of contempt of court cases in that city"; and of still another "who, though paying his way through college, spent some of his hard earned money in going to Chicago to make first-hand inquiries from inside sources concerning the underworld of that city."[2]

## 3.  Reading

A third source of your research preparation is reading.  You should be posted on the history and background of your subject as well as in what contemporary authorities are saying about it.  Most subjects for oratory are controversial; they admit of two or more sides.  Especially in the problem-solution type of oration, be sure to read on all sides of the question.  In an oratory contest, unlike debate, there is no speaker present representing the other side, but be assured the arguments of the opposing views may well be present in the minds of the auditors.  Thus, in composing your oration, you should take cognizance of those views and answer them to their satisfaction in what we might call anticipatory rebuttal.

### 4.   Radio - TV

The reading you do by no means should be confined to books, magazines, and newspapers.  Public affairs pamphlets, the "Face The Nation," "Meet The Press," and "Issues and Answers" television programs, and often scripts of documentaries such as Edward R. Murrow's "The Harvest of Shame" on the problems of migrant workers, are readily obtainable from the broadcasting networks, sometimes gratis or for a nominal sum.[3]

### B.   Recording Materials

Some suggestions for recording materials on cards have already been made in Chapter V.  I have found helpful a method of assembling these cards which may be useful to others.  Knowing that every speech should at least have the elemental divisions of introduction, body, and conclusion, I prepare three standard size 8.5x11 inch heavier-than-average sheets, fold them in half, and label them "Introduction," "Body," and "Conclusion."  Insert cards from your reading, or even memos you write to yourself, into the proper slots. Ere long you will have many more cards in the "Body" slot than for the other two, whereupon you in turn prepare additional half-folded sheets within that body category, as some faint glimmerings of a semblance of organization begin to take shape in your mind.

Remember that you should gather far more information and material than you could possibly use in the compressed type of speech which an oration is.  My own formula-- it's admittedly a mere guess, not statistically verified--is that only 1/7 of the material collected actually later appears in an oration and that, like an iceberg, 6/7 of it remains beneath the surface.  And yet that unused material is by no means wasted effort.  It helps to instill confidence in you and in your subject, by reason of the knowledge of the thoroughness of your preparation.  It enables you to "hold your own" in a question-and-answer period following the delivery of your speech before non-academic audiences.  You are much more likely to err in doing too little research rather than too much.  Of course, there is a limit to what you can read.  There does come a time when you just have to call a halt.  However, all during the contest season, you should keep abreast of new developments, especially if your subject deals with a constantly changing current event.

III.  SPECIFIC PURPOSE SENTENCE (SPS)
      A.  What It Is

A specific purpose sentence is a terse, unadorned statement of the response you want from an audience, worded as if you were talking to them directly.[4]  Preparation of an oration involves many steps.  Efforts of textbook writers to set these apart into various stages are for learning purposes only.  It does not always mean that one's thought-processes need always to follow the same pattern.  In some cases, your SPS, as I usually refer to it in my classes, may conceivably have been formulated before you undertake your library or other research.  It may have occurred to you during the selection of your subject.  In such a case, your whole time in reading will be a search for material to support your pre-determined SPS.  But at other times, the SPS may come upon you all of a sudden during your reading.

One thing is for sure.  You are not just speaking to hear yourself talk.  You are speaking to achieve a result from your audience.  Therefore, sometime before composing your speech, you have to come to a decision and be able to state in one simple SPS the exact result you intend to achieve.  This is so elemental a matter that it is surprising that it is so frequently neglected.  Various authors of speech texts have said that the greatest single cause of speech failure is the failure to select and then to stick to a specific purpose.[5]  In short, when you are through talking, the audience should know quite specifically what, as a result of your speech, they are now expected to do, to feel, or to believe.  The story is told of President Calvin Coolidge, known as Silent Cal, that he attended church services one Sunday when his wife Grace was indisposed and stayed home.  Upon his return, she asked, "What did the minister preach about?"  He replied: "I dunno--he never said!"[6]  That should never be said of you!

B.  Where To Put It?

Where in the oration first to disclose the SPS will depend upon many factors, particularly upon the nature of the subject and the audience.  If, for example, you have a highly controversial subject highly charged with emotion, true of many "trail-blazing" type orations, one upon which members of the audience may hold views contrary to yours, also not uncommon, it certainly would not be wise for you to

mention the SPS boldly at the beginning.  The audience must
first be brought to a mood of giving your proposal a fair
hearing.   This can be done by many methods or by a combination of them,  such as stating first points of agreement,
making a plea for fairness,  urging the audience to take a
fair,  honest look at all sides of controversial questions.  For
you to state the SPS at once might immediately raise barriers
of antagonism needlessly which you would have difficulty overcoming later.   Hence a delay of the statement of your SPS is
a perfectly legitimate persuasive technique.  You must first
seek to create a favorable impression through your attitude
and words,  in the hope that the favorable attitude toward you
will later carry over to your proposition.  This was essentially the technique employed by Jo Ann Westervelt in the
oration, "The Years Between," previously referred to, where
the SPS was not fully disclosed until the end.

That instance,  however,  was an exception,  and there
are exceptions to all rules.   For example,  in spite of the
warning in the preceding paragraph against early disclosure
of the SPS on an explosive subject,  still,  for the sake of emphasis or shock value,  it might on rare occasions be the
opening sentence itself.   Note,  for example,  the oration on
Christian pacifism "Standards That Stand," delivered by
Calvin De Vries a month after the declaration of war in
World War II,  in which he began bluntly:  "Christian standards should be standards that stand."[7]

The SPS could come in the middle of the speech.  The
most usual spot for it is fairly near the beginning,  following
one or more introductory paragraphs.   A typical example of
such a one is that of Miss Joan Reidy,  first-place winner in
the Women's Division of the IOA contest in 1953.   After two
preliminary paragraphs,  she discloses her intent,  thus:

> I am aware that each of you having come from a
> different locality and having been educated in a dif-
> ferent manner,  is entitled to your particular view
> concerning politics,  religion,  and life in general;
> but I will warn you,  my purpose here today is to
> try to convince you that the Junior Senator from
> my home state,  one Joseph R. McCarthy,  is a
> man that should not be in power in the United States
> today,  because his influence for evil goes beyond
> the borders of Wisconsin.[8]

There are oration subjects where it is well to follow
a "scent-a-chase" technique, wherein you employ a sustained
curiosity-arousing beginning and in effect invite your audience
to go with you cooperatively in search of the answer to a
problem.  In such cases, the denouement in the form of the
SPS would more likely come in the late middle or toward the
end of the oration.  What we have said, then, in essence,
is that the SPS may appear just about anywhere in the speech.


## IV.  ORGANIZATION

Your subject chosen, your research done (although
that never really ends), your SPS selected, then, knowing
that time or word limits require you to cut your material to
a single slice of bread rather than trying to use the whole
loaf, you are now ready for the next step, which we shall
call organization.  Under no circumstances should you follow Rousseau's recipe for a love letter:  to start without
knowing what you are going to say, and to end without knowing exactly what you have said!

Every speaker develops his own individual method of
organizing his speech, and even he does not prepare every
speech in precisely the same way.  That being true, it is
futile to set down iron-clad rules for everyone.  However,
we shall present what might be called helpful hints on organization.

### A.  Preparatory Outline

Hint #1 - If not already convinced, sell yourself on
the idea that before proceeding to write you should prepare
some sort of outline.  Brigance writes:

> ... my study of great speakers leads me to the
> conclusion that, whatever may be the other details
> of a speaker's method of preparation, the one im-
> perative requirement is that, at some time or oth-
> er, he order his thoughts by an outline.[9]

An outline is an ordering of your main and supporting points.
The audience is in a sense being taken on a mental journey
with you, the speaker, as their guide.  At each step of this
journey, those auditors should know exactly where they are
in the speech.  This does not mean that there should not be

elements of suspense.  In other words, while they may not
always know where they are coming out, they at least should
always know where they are now.  To put it another way,
one test of a good oration is the discernibility of the framework, the organization.


B.   Relevant to SPS

Hint #2 - In the process of selection, of deciding
what ideas to include and which to reject, make sure that
each is relevant to the SPS, even though for surprise purposes the relevance may not be immediately apparent.  Hew
to your prepared SPS goal; avoid yielding to the temptation
to admire the landscape and scenery and pick up buttercups
along the way, but march straight toward your goal.


C.   Three Points

Hint #3 - As a general rule, have no more than three
main points in the body of your speech, and certainly not
more than five.  Remember, an oration is really a compressed version of what could easily be amplified into a much
longer speech.


D.   Outline Speech

Hint #4 - State the main ideas of your oration, subject to some exceptions for surprise reasons, at the end of
your introduction.  This makes for "instant intelligibility,"
a prime requisite for all oral discourse.  For example, Guy
Vander Jagt, in a state Peace contest oration, "Bonn Report,"
began with a humorous narrative of meeting his counterpart
in Germany in the Experiment in International Living who,
through a mistake in arrangements, turned out to be a girl,
Lizi.  Shortly thereafter, he indicated the divisions of his
oration in this fashion:

> It was while getting to know "Lizi" that I learned
> three lessons about war; its physical destruction,
> its corruption of the human personality, and its
> utter futility as a means of solving problems.[10]

### E.   Memorable Phrasing

Hint #5 - State the main divisions of your speech in
rememberable fashion.   Make them stick out like burrs.
While this is primarily for the benefit of the audience for
ready comprehension and retention, it is also an incidental
help to your own memory in keeping the speech in mind.   A
commencement speech entitled "The Three Looks" covered
the points:  1) a deep look within; 2) a long look ahead; and
3) a steady look on high.   An extremely effective chapel talk,
about the length of an oration, was delivered by the Rev.
Paul E. Hinkamp of Hope College when he said the Christian
religion gave us "pardon for the past, victory over the present, and assurance for the future."

There are many ways of stating your main points in
a rememberable way.   One is to present them alliteratively.
Dr. Joseph R. Sizoo, President of New Brunswick Seminary,
addressing an opening convocation, urged seminarians to possess the qualities of "conviction, character, and compassion."
One could compose a speech under the title of "Blind Spots,"
and in the development refer to intolerance, indifference, and
injustice.

### F.   String of Beads

Hint #6 - Consider the effectiveness of using what is
referred to as a "string of beads" type of development.   An
advantage of this type is that it allows you to cover more
than one subject, and yet retain a sense of unity.   For example, Don Moore of McKendree College in his oration, "De-
pose King Selfishness," deplored selfishness in various areas
of our common life.   "Not Sick, but Weak," an oration by
William Primm of Central Michigan University, deplored a
lack of control--in our personal life as to smoking, drinking,
over-eating, and loss of temper, and in our national life in
our suppression of civil rights, our uncontrolled violence in
labor disputes, and the climate of unrest and political emo-
tionalism resulting from the assassination of President John
F. Kennedy.

### G.   Problem-Solution

Hint #7 - In the problem-solution type oration, in
most common use today, do not begin emotional appeals

before having presented an adequate foundation of logical reasoning. Do not forget that you are prejudiced in favor of your SPS and from your research have abundant reason to believe in it. But the audience does not come to it with that favorable bias. They must be presented with some of the evidence that convinced you. A problem-solution type oration necessarily deals with causes, effects, and remedies. But in presentation the more effective and accepted order is to present first, early in the speech, the terrible status quo --the effects, then go on to ferret out the causes, before proceeding to the remedy--yours!

### H.  Clothe the Outline

Hint #8 - In presenting the various points of your oration, try to avoid word usage which calls conscious attention to the organization of it. At first mention, this may appear to conflict with earlier advice that an oration should have "instant intelligibility," but not really. True, the audience should sense and appreciate your transitions, but try to have them do that without their being made painfully conscious of your wording. Let me explain. In a debate, one doesn't hesitate to say: "first," "second," "my next point is ..." But in an oration, one uses transitions which in a sense are smoother, less abrupt, such as by the use of a "not only ... but also" approach. What I am trying to say here was better put by Lew Sarett and William Trufant Foster:

> ... when a speaker delivers his speech, he should not let the ribs of his outline stick out like those of a starved horse. Nearly two thousand years ago Tacitus said: "The beauty of an oration, like that of the human body, is perfect when the veins do not project and the bones cannot be counted, but a wholesome blood fills the limbs, rises through the flesh, and mantles over the thews and sinews with the comely hue of health." Nevertheless, the speaker himself cannot too clearly visualize the bones of his speech; and he may well do more than a writer need do toward revealing the structure to listeners. Listeners need more help than readers. [11]

## V.  TITLES

Somewhere in the development stage, you have probably selected a title. An excellent title will not save a poor

oration.   But it may help to entice an audience to want to
hear it.   Thus, even before a word is uttered, since you
yourself do not normally speak the title, a good title can
help to gain the attention of the audience.   And that's important, for you just cannot afford to leave a stone unturned to
achieve that end.   Hence, some advice on titles.

Three outstanding requirements of a good title are
that it should be short, attention-catching, and curiosity-
arousing.

Some 20 years ago in the "In The Good Old Days"
section of my home-town newspaper, there appeared an item
saying that a Senator from Iowa delivered a lecture and
spoke on "The Century In Which We Live and Its Present
Opportunities, with Some Suggestions as to the Career of the
Late President William McKinley."   The November 16, 1959,
issue of Time magazine reported that a Lutheran minister
addressed the Santa Barbara Kiwanis Club on the subject,
"Glimpses of the Political, Economic and Religious Aspects
in Hong Kong, India, Japan, Middle East, Kenya, and East
Germany."   Neither report mentioned the size of the audience.   It's a cinch they didn't come as a result of a short,
attractive title!

The two terms "attention-catching" and "curiosity-
arousing" are closely allied and in a sense synonymous.
But not entirely so for we tend to think of the former as a
broader and more inclusive term.   A title would not be fully curiosity-arousing if the intent of the oration were disclosed.   In other words, the curiosity should be aroused,
but not satisfied.   Here are some examples of curiosity-
arousing titles: "Apology for Worshipping With my Eyes
Open," "A Divine Command," "Shall John Have His Ears
Clipped?" "Pyramids, Sphinxes and Calla Lilies."

In addition to using questions, vivid, concrete and
pictorial language, two other means in quite common use
for getting attention-catching and curiosity-arousing titles
are by the use of alliteration and contrasts.   Examples of
alliteration:  Age of Accusation, America Ablaze, Backyard
Buchenwalds, The Challenge of Change, Constitutional Cow-
ardice, Courageous Crusader, The Grace of Gratitude, Inexcusable Ineptitude, Justice in Jeopardy, The Lariat Laugh-
maker, Men or Machines?, Passive Patriots, The Price of
Peace, Rattlesnake Religion, Standards That Stand, The Warrior and the Woman.

Here are examples of contrasts: Brains or Brooms?,
Black and White Keys, Charm vs. Harm, Tyranny or Tol-
erance?, Master or Victim?, Peace or Profits?, Bootstraps
and Moonshots, The Failure of Success, Taps and Reveille,
My Friend The Enemy, A Miss Is as Bad as a Mile, It's
Sometimes Dangerous to Play Safe.

## Notes

1.    The Young Man and the World, Appleton & Co., New
        York, 1905, p. 234.

2.    Wabash College Orations, 1879-1932, Journal and Re-
        view Press, Crawfordsville, Indiana, 1932, p. 7.

3.    Addresses of networks' audience-information depart-
        ments:

American Broadcasting Co.,          Columbia Broadcasting
7 West 66th Street,                        System, Inc.,
New York, N.Y.  10023                  485 Madison Avenue,
                                                    New York, N.Y.  10022

National Broadcasting Co., Inc.
30 Rockefeller Plaza,
New York, N.Y.  10020

Other addresses which may be helpful to know, in writ-
        ing for material:

AFL-CIO,                                      American Farm Bureau
815 16th St., N.W.,                          Federation,
Washington, D.C. 20406                  2300 Merchandise Mart,
                                                    Chicago, Illinois 60654

Chamber of Commerce                  Council on Foreign
of the United States,                      Relations,
1615 H Street, N.W.,                      58 East 68th St.,
Washington, D.C. 20006                  New York, N.Y.  10021

4.    While an oration usually has and should have rhetorical
        elements such as figures of speech, it is best to
        avoid them in the SPS; hence the inclusion of the
        word "unadorned." Many speech texts, in discus-
        sing outlining, encourage students to write at the
        top of a submitted outline, expressions such as
        "Specific Purpose: To show that we should do so

and so." It is no doubt a personal idiosyncrasy but I prefer to have students omit the infinitive expression "To show that..." and instead to add the word "Sentence" following "Purpose." To me the use of the infinitive puts the emphasis upon the student-teacher relationship in that you, the student, are telling me, the teacher, what you plan to do. I would rather, from your very first speaking experience, have you become audience-conscious and thus to word the sentence as if you were talking directly to the audience.

5.   Typical of many: "The question might be raised: does anybody ever speak in public without a purpose? In answer, it may be said that more people fail in speaking because they have no definite purpose in mind than for any other reason." Arleigh B. Williamson, Speaking in Public, Prentice-Hall, Inc., New York, 1937, p. 200. By permission of Prentice-Hall, Inc.

6.   The story is probably apocryphal. Another version: "What did the minister talk about?" "Sin." "What did he say about it?" "He was against it!"

7.   WHCO, p. 15.

8.   "Age of Accusation," Wisconsin State University, Eau Claire, WO-1953, p. 45.

9.   Speech Composition, 2nd ed., Appleton-Century-Crofts, 1953, p. 38.

10.  WHCO, p. 165. Hon. Guy Vander Jagt is now serving his fourth term in the U.S. Congress, Ninth District, Michigan.

11.  Basic Principles of Speech, rev. ed., Houghton Mifflin Co., 1946, p. 379.

Chapter VIII

INTRODUCTIONS

Speakers, like advertisers, are in business to get attention. This is not a mean, superficial thing. You may have an excellent plan to maintain world peace or quell industrial strife or lift the living standards of the sharecropper, but unless you get people to listen to you, your ideas are futile. [1]

Mark Hanna

## I. IMPORTANCE OF INTRODUCTIONS

The preceding excerpt from Mark Hanna expresses well a central problem in all forms of speaking, getting attention. An oration is a persuasive speech in compressed form. On account of word or time limits, it is essential to capture this attention at once in the introduction. For here is your initial encounter with the audience, wherein you lay the foundation for your oration and aim to elicit favorable responses to yourself and your subject. Just how do you go about doing that?

We shall mention a number of methods which have been successfully used in the past, cite a few examples of each, perhaps with a commentary, and always with the implied suggestion, "Go thou and do likewise!" Note that the various techniques cited are not at all mutually exclusive. Many overlap and may be a combination of two or more methods. Some examples cited do not contain the entire introduction but enough of it for you to "get the idea."

## II. KINDS OF INTRODUCTIONS
### A. Startling Opening Sentence or Sentences

This sentence, or sentences, may state either an obvious truth in a matter-of-fact way, or be a startling chal-

lenging statement, sometimes curiosity-arousing and at all
times attention-catching.

> More people have been killed in the name of Christ
> than for any other cause, person, or ideal.
> The early inspired followers of Christ had been ea-
> ger to suffer martyrdom; later, they were as eager
> to inflict it.  Jesus on the Cross became the sym-
> bol of an uncompromising, ruthless idealism that
> has inspired the most glorious and most terrible
> deeds in our history.  In the name of the One who
> preached peace and the brotherhood of man, Chris-
> tians have slaughtered millions of their brethren,
> chiefly their fellow Christians. [2]

Here Neil M. Weatherhogg of Texas Christian University, with his oration titled "Tyranny or Tolerance?" (1958-
59), uses a startling opening sentence.  The immediate reaction to it may be shocked disbelief, or, if it speaks your
mind as an auditor, almost gleeful agreement.  In either
case, it is challenging, and makes one want to hear more.
Shortly thereafter, he discloses that he speaks:

> ... not for the purpose of condemning religion ...
> but to show how many of our hypocritical actions
> today resemble the actions of the brutal and insin-
> cere propagators of Christianity in history.

Marian Korteling comes from missionary parents in
India, where only 1% of India's 400 millions are Christian.
Attending Hope College, she contrasts the vitality of the
Indian church with that in America, and its failure of "lead-
ership in correcting existing social evils," and pleads for
"Renascence," the title of her oration.  Note the unusual
opening paragraph:

> A prominent artist was asked to portray a dying
> church.  Every one expected a decrepit, ram-
> shackled, deserted old building.  Instead he paint-
> ed a magnificent city church with beautiful stained
> glass windows, exquisitely carved altar furniture
> and fashionably dressed parishioners scattered here
> and there among comfortable pews.  A strange in-
> terpretation.  But was he entirely wrong? [3]

Here is an introduction which probably, from its des-
cription of a couple in love, secures instant identification

from the average academic contest audience.  But the last
three words of the opening paragraph come as something of
a shock.

> On many a secluded street this evening,  under a
> dim shadow-casting street light or an equally ro-
> mantic moon,  a couple will stroll ... hand in hand,
> or arm in arm.  They may occasionally pause to
> embrace ... then continue their saunter.  Lost in
> thoughts of each other, with the rest of the world
> shut out, they are obviously in love.  Only one
> blur breaks the pretty picture ... both are men.
>
> The National Institute of Mental Health estimated
> in an October report that four million American
> men are exclusively homosexual, with millions
> more trapped in the borderline areas ... not know-
> ing which or is it 'what' sex to turn to. [4]

B.   The Use of a Quotation

Sometimes an oration can begin with and be built a-
round a familiar or even an obscure quotation by some well-
known person.  Even hypothetical quotations such as expressions in current usage can be effective at the beginning of
an oration.  Note how the first example capitalizes upon the
well-known wizardry with words of Winston Churchill,  and
in an area with which he is not usually instantly identified.

> 'The mood and temper of the public with regard
> to the treatment of crime and criminals is one of
> the most unfailing tests of the civilization of any
> country.'   These words of Sir Winston Churchill
> are as pertinent today as when they were spoken
> in 1910. [5]

The next example takes the well-known quotation from
Shelley, and with the immediate drawing of a parallel with
America,  draws a reaction from the audience.  That reaction relates to our sense of patriotism.  Some might react
by thinking "Oh no, not us; can things really be that bad?"
Others might be inclined to an "I'm from Missouri--show
me" attitude.  In either case, the audience is immediately
involved.

> I met a traveller from an antique land
> Who said:  'Two vast and trunkless legs of stone
> Stand in the desert.  Near them on the sand
> Half sunk, a shattered visage lies ...
> ...' and ... these words appear--
> 'My name is Ozymandias, king of kings:
> Look on my works, ye Mighty, and despair!'
> Nothing beside remains.  Round the decay
> Of that colossal wreck, boundless and bare
> The lone and level sands stretch far away.
>
> Thus the poet Shelley considered the ancient na-
> tions of the earth, their self-confidence, their
> boasting, and their power.  Today America in all
> her grandeur can learn from these colossal wrecks
> of old. [6]

Here is a beginning, not exactly a quotation except
that it is the title of a well-known sermon which immediately catches attention by the contrast Dr. Ralph W. Sockman
makes.

> Jonathan Edwards once stirred a religious revival
> in New England by preaching a powerful sermon
> 'Sinners in the Hands of an Angry God.'  Today
> we're in the situation, according to Dr. Ralph W.
> Sockman, famous radio pulpiteer, where 'the
> power of God is in the hands of angry sinners.'[7]

C.   Startling Opening Question or Series of Questions

The abrupt beginning of a speech by a Korean war
veteran might well shock some auditors.  It might even
make some bristle in disbelief, which can readily be dis-
pelled upon presentation of evidence.

> How many prostitutes have you bought lately?  Most
> of you moral, upright citizens may think you haven't
> bought any.  But I suggest you're wrong.  You have
> bought prostitutes and provided them to men like
> myself through your government.  War does things
> like that to people and governments.  Here at home
> our government frowns on prostitution.  But the
> moment a war breaks out, all of a sudden prosti-
> tution becomes a highly desired profession.  Oh,
> of course, not here.  Only where our American

> boys are outside of the country is such prostitution
> so desired.  Now, in most of the countries where
> we visit on our way to war, or on our way out,
> prostitutes are readily available.  But whenever
> they aren't, our government, with your tax money,
> makes sure they are provided. [8]

Many of the examples selected I have heard personally.  That is true of my second selection in this group, and
I can therefore testify to its effectiveness with the audience
hearing it.  Others, especially the judges, must have agreed
with me on the following opening since it was awarded first-
place in the 1950 IOA contest.

> How do you explain the fact that you have an album
> of Paul Robeson records in your home?  Have you
> ever studied Karl Marx?  Did you belong to the
> liberal club in your college?  Does your wife go
> to church often?
> These questions and scores like them or worse,
> have been asked by a mushrooming staff of loyalty
> snoopers of and about millions of American citi-
> zens.  And the people who give the answers to
> these questions, whether they be your neighbors
> with grudges, a subordinate who wants your job,
> or your personal enemy, are never made known
> by the government to you and can brand you perma-
> nently on the FBI files as a Communist.
> Understand me, friends, I'm not opposed to our
> government's seeking to protect itself against for-
> ces which threaten its very existence.  Court de-
> cisions have long ago established the right of Con-
> gress to ask questions and receive answers.  But
> I do object to the careless, vicious Nazi- like man-
> ner in which so many of these un- American activi-
> ties and loyalty investigations have been carried
> out and to the lack of safeguards surrounding them. [9]

D.   Humor in Various Forms

Humor, either in the form of a joke, a humorous narrative, a quip or clever turn of a phrase, is useful, and particularly so at the beginning of an oration.  Here is an example which struck my fancy when first I read it.  Even the
title captivates attention, "How To Tell Your Friends From
the Apes."

For several months I have viewed with alarm the
tendency for the mome raths to outgrabe the boro-
goves. This hyper-adenoidal globaloney has been
tergiversating long enough. There has been too
much whimmying under the miff tree, and the ther-
mothrockles--the thermothrockles have only obfus-
cated the matter. I stand four-square against all
such underattenuated blatherslaving and promise to
put all of the jam on the lower shelf so that the
little fellow can get some. I demand a return to
the principles of Jeffersonian democracy, and anyone who says the opposite is a dirty red communist!

I hope that I have confused you; I have just given
my impression of a typical campaign speech. Like
most speeches of this nature, it was quite nonsen-
sical. [10]

### E.  Painting a Word-Picture or Relating a
     Narrative Incident

This device is probably the most frequently used in
beginning an oration. Since contest rules forbid an actual
picture, you do the next best thing and provide a word-pic-
ture, one which sets the stage for, or even within itself em-
bodies, the gist of the oration.

The first example is from a depression-born oration
out of North Dakota, beset simultaneously with both depression and drought.

King Tantalus of Greek mythology was a great favorite of the gods. But Tantalus, humanly ungrate-
ful, abused the divine favor and revealed to men
the secrets of heaven. Famous in his punishment.
He was placed in a lake whose waters reached to
his chin, but at every attempt to quench his thirst
the water receded. Terrible hunger gnawed at his
vitals; directly over him hung branches laden with
delicious fruit, but always beyond his reach!
The new industrial era ushered in by the machine
has produced a modern counterpart to the Tantalus
of ancient Greece. We see a vast army of inade-
quately clothed citizens; yet the Farm Board advocates the plowing under of every fourth row of cot-
ton. We observe long breadline queues; but our

elevators and granaries overflow with wheat. Today
we count millions of jobless in the land of plenty.
Standing in the flood waters of economic chaos, they
grasp for the fruits of prosperity, always beyond
their reach. [11]

Mere words on a printed page cannot convey adequately the force of the next example. The unalloyed joy beaming
from the contestant's countenance was a delight to behold.
The opening paragraph got the orator off to a good beginning,
and no doubt played a part in having the judges award him
first-place in the IOA contest of 1964.

It was in Mbengwi, a small town in Cameroun, my
home country. The long-awaited morning had finally arrived. It was Independence Day, October 26,
1960. Our over-friendly tropical sun sparkled from
the eastern horizon with seeming approval for the
occasion. The newly-constructed Independence stad-
ium was already over-crowded with highly-excited
faces. The dramatic moment arrived--the drums
beat, the guns boomed. The orations were delivered, the flag was raised. A new African state
was born. It was happiness indeed. And all day
long with glamorous music and dancing, we cele-
brated the turning-point in the history of my country. [12]

The final example is from an oration delivered near
the close of World War II.

The scene: the interior of Hope College Memorial
Chapel. The occasion: Armistice Day, 1943. The
speaker: Major George Steininger, Chaplain in the
United States Army, a Hope alumnus. It was a
fine speech, the kind one would expect from a national oratory winner of 1916. The speaker impressed upon us a double dedication: to resolve to
win this war, and then, this time, to win the peace.
The speaker's eloquence reached its climax, and he
closed. Taps. Silence. Then, out of the din that
silence can sometimes be, as if from beyond the
veil, comes again the trumpet's lament, "Day is
done, gone the sun ..."
As I listened to that second cry, I could not refrain from thinking: What will become of our soldiers at the close of this war? Even the very

stones of the chapel seemed to shout:  Will youth
again be betrayed?[13]


E.   A Personal Reference or Experience

Dr. Paul Fried, Chairman of the Hope College History
Department and Director of International Education, is a refugee from Nazi Germany.  Both his parents perished at the
hands of the Nazis.  He served in our armed forces.  Here
is his introduction to an oration based upon his experience in
the service.

> On March 5, 1945, I knelt in the dimly-lit base-
> ment room of a German farmhouse.  It served as
> our battalion aid-station.  On a stretcher lay a dy-
> ing German officer.  While a medic gave him plas-
> ma, I questioned him--in German--about the direc-
> tion of his troops.  He tried to answer, but all I
> could hear was:  "Why did they shoot at me? ...
> why did you Americans come here? ... we wanted
> peace!"
> Could it be that the supermen who had attacked
> Poland, ravished Norway and plundered the Nether-
> lands and all of Western Europe, had become
> "peaceloving"?  I didn't think so!  But I am sure
> that in his last moments this young German sud-
> denly realized what an awful price he and his coun-
> try had to pay for the war.  And as I watched him
> die, he ceased to be the enemy to me, and I, too,
> saw for the first time the ghastly results of war.[14]

Today, the eviction of the Japanese citizens from
their homes during World War II and the herding of them into concentration camps is almost universally recognized as a
blunder.  Vivian Tardiff spoke up about it at the time, and
introduces the subject by reference to her own ancestry.

> In 1917 a young American doughboy sailed for
> France.  There for two years he served his coun-
> try.  Desolation and death lay upon that land, yet
> this soldier found happiness there.  He had fallen
> in love with a lovely French girl called Germaine.
> When the war was over, this soldier brought his
> young French bride to America.  That youthful
> couple were my father and mother.  That explains
> why my thoughts turn almost instinctively to the

> crushed, defeated land of once valiant France. Re-
> cently when I read about the forcible eviction of
> the residents of Marseilles and Lorient, it makes
> me want to talk about the plight of France. And
> yet, there is a problem that arouses my indigna-
> tion even more.
>
> For, speaking of forcible evictions, often within
> the past few months I think with terror what would
> have happened had my mother been not French but
> Japanese, had my skin been not white but yellow!
> Have you ever thought what might now be your
> plight had your parents come from Japan? Will
> you pretend for a few moments that I am not Vivian
> Tardiff but Mary Jane Yoshida, a Japanese girl,
> born in this country, attending a Los Angeles High
> School. [15]

In the personal reference type of introduction, one
needs to proceed cautiously. There is always the danger
that some auditors may get an impression that you are ego-
tistical. Much depends upon what the nature of your reference to yourself is, and even more upon the manner of
your delivery in expressing it. A good rule to follow is:
when in doubt, don't use it. Another example of what I consider to be an acceptable use of a personal reference comes
from a sermon by the Rev. Harry Emerson Fosdick:

> If we are successfully to maintain the thesis that
> the church must go beyond modernism, we must
> start by seeing that the church had to go as far
> as modernism. Fifty years ago, a boy, seven
> years of age, was crying himself to sleep at night
> in terror lest, dying, he should go to hell, and
> his solicitous mother, out of patience with the
> fearful teachings which brought such apparitions to
> the mind, was trying in vain to comfort him. That
> boy is preaching to you today and you may be sure
> that to him the achievements of Christian modern-
> ism in the last half century seem not only impor-
> tant but indispensable. [16]

## G.  Ordinary Colloquial Talk

Some may well be confused by mention of this category. It is true that oratory is a specialized form of persuasive speaking, that it makes liberal use of novel begin-

nings.  At the outset, a listener's attention and interest cannot be taken for granted, nor can it be commanded.  It must
be wooed and won.  The preceding six kinds are ways of doing just that.  And yet, not all introductions need to begin in
an unusual manner.  There are times, depending somewhat
upon the personality of the speaker, upon the subject, and upon the audience, when straight-forward, ordinary colloquial
talk will make the audience prick up their ears and want to
hear more.  Examples follow.

> I ran across Jack the other day.  I hadn't seen
> him for years, but he remembered me.  As a mat-
> ter of fact, he was a senior in high school when I
> was a freshman.  Jack's looking great, and say,
> he's doing fine, too.  He was dressed immaculate-
> ly, and was about to step into his car, a model
> I'm afraid I'll never be able to afford.  I asked
> him what he was doing and then he smiled and winked
> at me.  "Why, I'm in the biggest business in the
> country, maybe in the world, I don't know.  There's
> about four and a half million on our payrolls."  And
> then he told me about it.  I had never before rea-
> lized the immensity of that business.  Why, only
> last year its income was fully one quarter as much
> as all other American enterprises combined.  Its
> cash registers run up a total of 41 million dollars
> every day in the week, including Sunday.
> Jack is in the business of organized crime. [17]

Note that the following example was spoken in 1966.
The opening paragraph comment of the father represented the
view of all too many.  The continued resistance in the South,
and the white back-lash in the North were beginning to appear.  In retrospect, the second paragraph proved to be prophetic.

> When I told my father my oration concerned civil
> rights, he looked at me blankly and said, "Civil
> Rights--that's not really a current issue--it's now
> the law of the land."  Perhaps many of you, like
> Dad, may be tired of hearing another oration about
> the Negro and his problems, feeling that with the
> passage of the Civil Rights Act, that was the end
> of them.  But is it really?  The question that still
> faces America today is the application of the prin-
> ciples it proclaimed.
> True, the Civil Rights act was an important victory

for all of us interested in equal rights for all men.
But this victory, as Winston Churchill said of another triumph for freedom, "is not the end; it is
not even the end of the beginning." The problems
involving acceptance of equal rights can prove to be
even greater than those faced when enacting the law.
Indeed, the words of James Baldwin, prominent
Negro author, could very well be true: "The Negroes of this country may never be able to rise to
power, but they are very well placed indeed to pre-
cipitate chaos and ring down the curtain on the
American dream."[18]

## III. HELPFUL HINTS ON INTRODUCTIONS

Hint #1 - Once your subject, SPS, and the main ideas
of your speech are chosen, it is best to proceed to the writing of the body of your speech before proceeding to the writing of the introduction.

Hint #2 - Don't make the introduction too long. There
is no one preferred length for the introduction. It varies--
one test is whether or not the main functions of any introduction have been accomplished, which are to lay the foundation for what is to follow and to gain goodwill for yourself
and your subject. And that in turn depends upon attendant
circumstances. For example, if you know that your audience
may be inclined to be more than usually hostile to your viewpoint, it is well for you to take more time for you to lessen
that hostility. But the introduction is too long if a sizable
number or even a few of your auditors begin inwardly to
think, why doesn't he get to the point?

Hint #3 - It may be a personal idiosyncrasy, but I've
always rather liked a short opening sentence. Here, for
example, is one example.

The zero hour had come. The signal was given
and the fighting marines at Chateau-Thierry were
over the top. What meant this mad rush toward
those guns which exacted their terrible toll each
moment? The answer came from the lips of a
dying captain, "On, on to victory, and may war
come never again!" At Vimy Ridge and Chateau-
Thierry we won the victory, but the "never again"
is the task that confronts the world today.[19]

Hint #4 - Avoid a false lead.  In the effort to achieve
surprise, do not lead us to think you are going to talk on one
subject, and then talk of another.  See that the surprise element directs attention to your subject, and is not used for its
own sake.

## Notes

1.   Public Speaking Without Fear and Trembling, The Mac-
     millan Co., New York, 1956, p. 38.

2.   Neil M. Weatherhogg, Texas Christian University,
     "Tyranny or Tolerance?", 1958-59.

3.   Marian Korteling, "Renascence," SUPERIOR, National
     PKD Convention, 1947, WHCO, p. 39.

4.   Clifton P. Schroeder, Loras College, Dubuque, Iowa
     "Out of the Darkness," WO-1968, p. 58.

5.   Larry Izenbart, "The Real Criminal," WHCO, p. 101.

6.   Donald P. Buteyn, "Invisible Abutments," WHCO, p. 44.

7.   George Worden, "The Publican," First-place, IOA 1958
     contest, WO-1958, p. 66.

8.   Anti-war speech by Korean War veteran, in James
     McCroskey, An Introduction to Rhetorical Communi-
     cation, Prentice-Hall, Inc., Englewood Cliffs, New
     Jersey, 1968, p. 192.  By permission of Prentice-
     Hall, Inc.

9.   Howard Cole, St. Olaf College, Northfield, Minnesota,
     "Shades of Peekskill," First-place, IOA 1950 contest,
     WO-1950, p. 65.

10.  Raymond McCall, Allegheny College, Meadville, Penn-
     sylvania, "How To Tell Your Friends From the Apes,"
     WO-1948, p. 41.

11.  Harold Cram, "Men or Machines?" First-place, state
     contest, 1932, University of North Dakota, Grand
     Forks.

12.  Jacob Ngwa, "Our Common Tradition in Peril," First-place IOA contest, 1964, WO-1964, p. 68.

13.  Wilbur Brandli, "Taps and Reveille," WO-1944, p. 43.

14.  Paul Fried, "The Price of Peace," WHCO, p. 35.

15.  Vivian Tardiff, "Americans With Japanese Faces," WHCO, p. 20.

16.  "Beyond Modernism," Christian Century, December 4, 1935, p. 1549. Reprinted by permission. Copyright 1935 The Christian Century.

17.  Gordon B. Mills, Wayne State University, Detroit, "Public Business Number One," Robert T. Oliver, Rupert L. Cortright, Cyril F. Hager, The New Training For Effective Speech, rev. ed., The Dryden Press, 386 Fourth Avenue, New York, 1946, p. 354.

18.  Gretchen Steffens, "The Law of the Land," WHCO, p. 132.

19.  Estelle Cozine, "From Vienna to Versailles," First-place, MISL Women's Contest, 1919, Albion College, Albion, Michigan.

## Chapter IX

## CONCLUSIONS

## I. IMPORTANCE

An oration is an entity. Every part of it is important and none more so than the conclusion. It is your last chance to make a final impression, to influence your audience in the direction you want them to go. While appeals to the emotions may be scattered throughout your speech, it is here that they predominate by your deliberate intention. Here your appeal reaches its climax. Both by the words spoken and by your manner of delivery, the audience senses that you are nearing the end. They expect and are receptive to something different, to more exalted language.

## II. FUNCTIONS

To ask what it is the audience expects is the equivalent of asking: What are the primary purposes of a conclusion? In the main, they are three in number: first, a restatement and summary of your main points; second, an appeal to the emotional nature of your audience, sometimes accompanied by a plea for some specific action; and third, a showing of the significance and application of what has been said to the individual lives of the auditors.

A typical example of the summary type follows:

As I stand on the brink of my graduation, I have sought to appraise modern education. This I believe: we need to restore the hard core of the classics to our learning; we need to temper scientific advancement with genuine reverence for the Author of all knowledge; finally, we need to cloak our graduates with the idealism which alone can give meaning to education and to all of life.[1]

114

## III.  LENGTH

There are no hard and fast rules for length.   The conclusion should take only so long and no longer than to accom-
plish the ends sought, which are one or more of the objectives mentioned above.   To take longer would be analogous to
"talking yourself out of a sale," or to chatter interminably at
the door of your hosts following a social evening in saying
"Goodbye, thank you, we had a nice time."   Learn to make
a graceful and gracious exit.   It is better to err on the side
of abruptness than boredom.   Someone has aptly said:  "A
good speech always ends before the audience wants it to."
Better that than to have it said:  "He missed several good
stopping-places."

We make a distinction between the aims or functions
of a conclusion and the methods by which these are brought
about.   Our listing of categories is an arbitrarily selected
composite one.   Which kind is best suited for use in any particular oration is a decision which the orator himself must
make, being guided by his own nature and temperament, the
nature of his subject, and the actual audience he faces.   You
may detect in the listing of kinds some inevitable over-lap-
ping, although there are distinguishable differences.   Let it
also be clearly understood that the use of combinations of the
various methods is quite acceptable, provided always you are
mindful of avoiding excessive length.

We now direct attention to four major kinds of conclusions in quite common use in oratory.   They are:  1) prose
or poem quotation; 2) personal reference; 3) tie-up back reference to introduction; and 4) narrative illustration.   In each
case, we shall explain, give examples, and make some commentary upon their strengths and weaknesses.

## IV.  KINDS
### A.  Prose or Poem Quotation

The first example comes from the first-place winner
of the IOA contest in 1962, Douglas W. Anderson, of the
University of Denver.   It was a philosophical type oration entitled "Life or Living?"   It was my good fortune to have been
present at its delivery, and I well recall how tremendously
effectively it was spoken throughout, and especially so at its
poetic closing paragraph.

This is my manifesto--the experiences which those
who do aspire to a life, who do seek that certain
something for which to die slightly, might pursue.
It is unfortunate; unfortunate that no one else can
read and create or teach, for me or for you; unfortunate that the road to a life is the straight, the
rigorous and the lonely one; unfortunate that the decision is uniquely each man's, that the making of
it, and the doing something about it, belong each
to each alone; unfortunate--but there; unfortunate
that you and I, too, like the character in Robert
Frost's poem,

> ... shall be telling this with a sigh
> Somewhere ages and ages hence:
> Two roads diverged in a wood, and I--
> I took the one less traveled by,
> And that has made all the difference. [2]

A second example comes from the first-place winner
of the IOA contest in 1938, Delmar Neutzman, of Nebraska
Wesleyan University. Happily, the problem he was concerned with, exclusion of Negroes from membership in PKD,
has long since been resolved.

> And for you who have a cause that fires you like a
> living torch--a cause that means to you what anti-
> lynching means to black Walter White--pray the
> prayer of crowbars and steel spikes, of white stars
> and blue nights beaten from the great democratic
> heart of Carl Sandburg:

> > Lay me on an anvil, O God,
> > Beat me and hammer me into a crowbar.
> > Let me pry loose old walls.
> > Let me lift and loosen old foundations.
> > Beat me and hammer me into a steel spike.
> > Drive me into the girders that hold a skyscra-
> >    per together.
> > Take red-hot rivets and fasten me into the cen-
> >    tral girders.
> > Let me be the great nail holding a skyscraper
> >    through blue nights into white stars.

> I hold it high honor to be a crowbar prying at old,
> worn-out walls and foundations. I would hold it higher
> honor still to be a steel spike driven into the cen-

tral girders holding a real democracy together.[3]

In concluding with a poem, be sure it is germane to your problem, and particularly beware of using one which by reason of current popularity has lost some of its original impact. I recall, for example, being in a Michigan state contest following World War I wherein five of eight contestants quoted excerpts or the whole of the then popular poem, "In Flanders Fields" by Lieut. Col. John McCrae. You can well imagine that about the third time it was used, it had lost its effectiveness and provoked titters rather than solemn thought.

### B.   Personal Reference

The same caution against avoiding the impression of egotism in personal references in the introduction of an oration applies equally to conclusions. Here is an example which I was privileged to hear in person and which I thought was in perfectly good taste. The judges must have thought so too for the orator, Charles E. A. Moore, of Wabash College, with his oration "Profit in Loss," was the first-place winner of the IOA contest in 1935.

> Before sitting down, I would like to add a personal thought. I've called war a racket, but I'm not a pacifist. I would not oppose a war of self-defense, not one propagandized as such by munition-makers, but a real war of self-defense. If such were to come, I would shoulder a rifle, I hope I would, and march away to fight, and perhaps to die, with the same firm tread that marked all men who have marched before me; and my heart too would beat with patriotism, and I would feel, perhaps, that my uniform was more symbolic of a privilege than a duty. That is, as I said, if it were a real war of self-defense. But if I die in a war started by munition profiteers, I hope this inscription is written on my tombstone: Profit in Loss. This American died to make a profit for the manufacturer of the bullet that killed him. I would like Americans to understand its significance, for I think they ought to know.[4]

### C.   Tie-Up Back Reference to Introduction

This technique gives the impression of unity, of having come full circle, and thus providing a sense of complete-
ness.   Recall the oration "Taps and Reveille," mentioned
several pages back.   In the next-to-last paragraph of that
oration, its speaker summarizes its main points, and then
concludes with an allusion to the title and the first paragraph.

> My friends, taps is not, must not be the end of all
> our striving.   After this dark night of war, we
> must hear and heed the challenge which reveille
> brings.   Listen! ... Can't you hear it? ... that
> stirring note which heralds the dawn of a new and
> better day?[5]

In Chapter VII, reference was made to the introduction of the speech by Guy Vander Jagt concerning his meeting with "Lizi," a German girl, his counterpart in the Experiment in International Living.   Here are the two closing
paragraphs of that speech.

> I cannot help contrasting my hateful image of
> stereotyped masses of goosestepping Germans ac-
> quired during the war with today's feeling of bro-
> therhood with German people learned through the
> warmth of one human personality in times of peace.
> The train was in motion.   As I looked out the win-
> dow, I saw a charming, attractive German fraulein,
> the same girl who had said "Hello ... is your name
> Guy? ... There's been a terrible blunder."   Only
> this time there was no uneasiness in her approach.
> No, she was running, completely oblivious to the
> danger of lamp posts and baggage carts; running
> with reckless abandon as fast as she could to keep
> up with the train as long as possible.   Her arms
> were over her head, her hair was streaming out
> behind and tears down her face as she cried, "Auf
> wiedersehen! Auf wiedersehen!"[6]

### D.   Narrative Illustration

A narrative illustration is probably the most frequently used type of oration ending.   Examples abound.   Narrative illustrations involve people, movement, emotions, and
the audience is interested in all three.   Some are of the kind

I call "goose-pimple" conclusions, in that they arouse the listeners, lift them out of themselves, make them momentarily forget they are present as auditors at a contest situation. Whether or not his happens depends in a large measure upon the ethos, the personal proof, of the speaker as the audience detects this from the speaker's manner of delivery. For you cannot transmit a feeling which you yourself as the orator do not feel.

In Chapter IV, I mentioned that oratory is by no means outmoded, is being practiced all around us every day. My first two examples come from other than contest orations. Philip T. Rutledge, Director of the Bureau of Health Education in Michigan, closed a speech to an audience of college administrators in this way:

> In the colleges and universities of this state are some of the greatest minds in this nation, if not the world. Within walking distance of many of these institutions each day sits a boy in a slum, completely oblivious to all the knowledge and wisdom near him and to his responsibility for its proper use. Two hundred forty thousand miles away is the moon. With the help of the minds in those institutions, we will probably reach the moon before we reach that boy.
> I hope not.

In ending a sermon, Dr. David H. C. Read, pastor of Madison Avenue Presbyterian Church in New York City, used this illustration on the National Radio Pulpit:

> John Baillie in his book And The Life Everlasting tells a story of a doctor who was talking to a dying man and fumbling for something to say. Just then there was a scratching at the door. "Do you hear that?" he said, "That's my dog. He doesn't know what's in this room. But he knows that I am here--and that's all that matters to him." That, in the end, is all that matters to us. We don't know what is ahead for us tomorrow, next year, or when our days here are ended. But we know whom we shall meet all along the line. We see Jesus. He is already there. That is enough.

Bruce Van Voorst, currently Bonn-Berlin bureau chief for Newsweek Magazine, delivered an oration in 1954 entitled

"The Clock." It dealt with the possibility of atomic annihilation, based upon a solemn warning in The Bulletin of Atomic Scientists: "Only a few more swings of the atomic pendulum and from Moscow to Chicago, atomic explosions will strike midnight for western civilization." Bruce had spent the summer living with an Austrian family as the town of Holland's community ambassador. In the closing paragraphs of his oration, he recounts a narrative illustration aboard ship upon his return.

This role of individuals was crystalized in my thinking by an incident on our ship coming back from Europe. On the ship were hundreds of students, including Germans coming to study in the United States. One time several of the fellows began to talk about the war, and as they talked it became apparent that a couple of them, both German and American, had fought in North Africa. Suddenly a startling thing happened. The American turned to the German and said, "Where were you on March 26, 1942?" The German showed immediate signs of recognition and replied, "Why, that is the date of our big surprise raid on the American airfield at Oran." The American was shaking visibly when he said: "You know, I was there that day. I was shooting at you and you were shooting at me, but you won. I spent three years in the hospital and almost died from wounds suffered in that battle."

No one said anything; we just sat thinking. These two men, now the best of friends, sitting together on a deck in the middle of the Atlantic, had a few years before been deadly enemies, striving to kill each other. What the history books had described as a war between nations, we now saw as war between individuals. With the crisis of the atomic age looming inevitably before us, the alternatives were made clear. Either each of us must be ready personally to participate in fighting a suicidal war, or each of us personally must join in the struggle for peace.

Clock-conscious America. The clock points to two minutes to twelve. As we hesitate, it is ticking off those final, fateful minutes. Tick-tock! Tick-tock! _____ ! _____ ![7]

A final example of narrative illustration in conclusions is really two illustrations in one. To appreciate fully the motivation behind the speech, you should know of its background. At about Thanksgiving time of 1941, Nola Nies' brother returned home from his basic training, and told of the shocking moral conditions in the army camp where he was stationed. Thereupon she read everything she could on the subject, including much material in newspapers and especially in church magazines, for it was a live issue at the time. To speak about this subject was rather a delicate matter for a young woman but she handled it with the finesse one would expect from the charming woman she was and is. Her oration "The Warrior and the Woman," won her a SUPERIOR rating at the biennial convention of PKD at St. Paul in 1942.

> In one of our western cities stands an heroic figure in bronze. It is a woman, not in the frills of yesteryear, but somber in the garb of toil. In her hand is the hand of her small son, and her eyes look far into the future. It is the Pioneer Mother, symbolic of the earnest endeavor, the faith, the courage of womanhood that has made America great. She represents the struggles and aspirations of parents who ever seek to secure a nobler heritage for their children than they themselves have known.
> Her eyes gaze steadfastly through the mists of time and space ... and the distant scene reveals a group of soldiers standing idly on a street corner. They look this way and that; the movie houses are filled to capacity, the officers must have some place to take their wives; there's a supervised dance at the Service Club, there are but fifty girls and three hundred boys, and no chance for a private. The group finally disperses to the taverns nearby--one remains standing on the corner. One more hour until it's time to go back to camp. So young, so trim in his uniform, so alone. A car glides slowly up to the curb and he hears a soft voice, "Lift, soldier?" A moment's hesitation, the door opens invitingly and he steps in. The car moves swiftly toward the outskirts of town. The Pioneer Mother still looks--past the warrior and the woman--far into the future. What shall it profit a nation to win the whole war and lose its own soul?[8]

In addition to the four kinds listed, there are of course other ways of concluding an oration. Just as opening with a question or questions is sometimes effective, so, too, closing with questions is sometimes good. In his oration, "The Lamp of Freedom," John Hains asks: "Will you help keep that lamp burning? Will you?"

Another way is: having previously dealt with evils in the status quo, one could herald the coming of a better day by a prophetic vision into the future.

## V.   KINDS TO AVOID

There are two types of conclusions which suffer from over-use in the past. I recommend that you avoid them. The one is the "cross-roads" conclusion, as: "We stand at the cross-roads; the one path leads to doom and destruction; the other (yours) leads to bliss and happiness." The other overworked conclusion is the hortatory homily, facetiously called the "vegetable ending": "Let us ... Let us ... Let us ..."

## VI.   SHOULD A PROBLEM-SOLUTION ORATION REQUIRE A SPECIFIC SOLUTION?

Some may feel that an important type of conclusion has been omitted--the solution to the problem discussed. In my view, the solution itself, explained, expounded, and defended, more properly belongs in the body of the oration rather than in the conclusion.

However, this does raise the interesting and often-discussed question, Should every problem-solution type oration require the orator to provide a specific solution? There are differences of opinion among experts on this question. Away back in 1916, Andrew T. Weaver, for many years Chairman of the Department of Speech at the University of Wisconsin, wrote, "Let us get our students away from settling in fifteen minutes problems which have baffled minds through ages."[9] Some 36 years later, William Norwood Brigance echoed essentially the same thought:

> Remember that we really "solve" few problems in life. Through the centuries we have never "solved" the problems of marriage, divorce, crime, taxes,

>    war, tolerance, and equal justice under the law.
>    Instead we keep at solving them.  In real life,
>    sometimes the only solutions open to us are to
>    "Watch this problem carefully," or "Act with cour-
>    age," or "Be tolerant," or "Make these few ad-
>    justments."   There are times when even the Presi-
>    dent and the Congress and the Courts can advise us
>    only of the general direction we should go in sol-
>    ving pressing political questions.  It comes with
>    ill grace, at such times, for a college student to
>    point the way out in a five-minute speech with a
>    patent-medicine remedy.  It brings to mind
>    Winston Churchill's apt retort to free-lance advi-
>    sers:  "It is easy to give advice if you have not
>    got to carry it out."[10]

The perennial nature of this problem is indicated from this
excerpt in 1969 from Malcolm O. Sillars, Professor of
Speech at San Fernando Valley College:

>    A primary example of our oversimplification is the
>    emphasis we so often place on the problem-solution
>    analysis.  In the public speaking classroom and in
>    intercollegiate forensics we tell our students that
>    for every problem there must be a solution.  There-
>    fore, the logical order of speech is to explain the
>    problem and then provide the solution for it.  But
>    life is not this simple.  There is no one answer
>    to a given problem.  There are multiple solutions,
>    all with advantages and disadvantages.  It is im-
>    possible to select a single answer and then set a
>    neat pattern into action to persuade an audience of
>    its rightness.  Our students must, therefore, be
>    taught that their job is to weigh competing solu-
>    tions and lead the audience to think about, and
>    choose, the one that entails the fewest hazards.[11]

Some highly respected colleagues in the profession,
on the other hand, believe a specific solution should be provided.  Theodore F. Nelson of St. Olaf College, a former
president of PKD maintains, "Listeners have a right to expect a reasonably plausible solution to a problem."[12] Glenn
Mills of Northwestern University writes:

>    After a speaker presents a problem that he alleges
>    to be serious, he should propose an adequate solu-
>    tion and advise the audience precisely what to do

> now.  Do not leave unanswered the individual lis-
> tener's question, "Where do I come in?"  ...
> [T]his is a familiar weakness of problem-solution
> speeches, including college orations. [13]

How do I feel about this controversy?  Frankly, I
have ambivalent feelings on this matter, and I don't mean to
straddle either one!  On the one hand, I do feel a kinship of
spirit with those who say that the questions in the minds of
the audience at the end of the oration should be answered:
what now, specifically, do you want me to do as a result of
your speech? sign a petition? write my Congressman?  But
on the other hand, I definitely lean in the direction of not
requiring a specific solution.

For one thing, there is a saying:  "To state a problem correctly is half to solve it."  An orator could speak on
the complexities of a problem, the need for urgency in solving it, and seek to enlist the aid of the audience in the
search for a solution.  That enticement could in itself be
considered to be the solution.  Herbert L. Curry, of Central
Michigan University, believes an orator may mention a number of possible solutions and advocate that "some action be
taken along the lines of one or more of the solutions that
have been noted."[14]  I am inclined to believe that in some
types of problems, it is just too much to expect a high
school or college orator to come up with a glib solution.
And that not only because the problem has defied solution by
experts, but also because of necessary time or word limitations.  To my certain knowledge, this belief on my part,
judging both from written critiques and oral comments from
judges following a contest, has been a factor in some of my
orators receiving a lower ranking than they might otherwise
have received.  But, in keeping with my attitude toward winning contests, this has never particularly disturbed me.

Perhaps I could pin-point the exact time when I came
to this view about not in every case needing to provide a
specific solution, and with that I bring this chapter to a
close.  In the depression era, Willard Wilson, first-place
winner in the 1936 IOA contest, representing Nebraska Wesleyan University, spoke on "unemployment and the degen-
eracy bred of poverty," and the resultant crime among youth.
What he said at the close of his oration has always struck a
responsive chord with me:

Solution? I don't know what the solution is. You
can condemn me for this. Perhaps I should figure
out a pretty answer and offer it to you in terms of
high-sounding verbiage. Shorter working day to
provide for an equal opportunity in industry! Wise
use of leisure time! Education as a means of
crime prevention! But for an immature orator to
administer to himself or to an audience the opiate
of such an idealistic, theoretical solution would be
to rob our discussion of realism and integrity. We
don't ignore the findings in a study of cancer because the research scientist hasn't found the cure.
We no longer demand of the novelist that he substitute sentimentality for actuality. The characters
in a modern drama need not live happily ever after.
Why must the orator <u>always</u> save the world? The
youth problem is baffling sociologists and statesmen. I repeat, as an undergraduate, I don't know
the answer. But I do know this! Before my generation can make a contribution to any other problem it must deal with this problem. We are a
lost generation, on relief, jobless, homeless. We
commit nearly 60 per cent of your crime; nevertheless we must not put on a black shirt or a
brown shirt and go out with a song of destruction.
You and I are responsible for the intelligent leadership of this--our own--generation. [15]

## Notes

1. Robert Winter, "This I Believe," <u>WO-1957</u>, p. 75.

2. <u>WO-1962</u>, pp. 54-55.

3. <u>WO-1938</u>, pp. 33-34.

4. <u>WO-1935</u>, p. 15.

5. <u>WO-1944</u>, p. 46.

6. <u>WHCO</u>, p. 164.

7. <u>WO-1954</u>, p. 68.

8. <u>WHCO</u>, pp. 13-14.

9.   "The Interschool Forensic Contest," QJS, April, 1916,
     p. 145.

10.  Speech, Its Techniques and Disciplines in a Free So-
        ciety, Appleton-Century-Crofts, Inc., New York,
        1952, p. 217.

11.  "The New Conservatism and the Teacher of Speech,"
     in The Rhetoric of Our Times, ed. by J. Jeffery
     Auer, Appleton-Century-Crofts, New York, 1969,
     p. 188.  Students are encouraged to read also the
     article in the same volume by Thomas R. Nilsen,
     Associate Professor of Speech, University of Wash-
     ington, entitled "Liberalism, Conservatism, and the
     Teacher of Speech."  Note this excerpt from p. 197:
     "Specifically on oversimplification, are there really
     teachers of speech who tell their students that for
     every problem there must be a solution?  Are there
     teachers who do not teach their students to weigh
     competing arguments?  Are there teachers who are
     unaware of the elementary fact that problems are
     complex and that there may be several solutions to
     a problem?  If so, they should be relieved of their
     positions on the grounds of incompetence.  We doubt
     whether it would help them to become more conser-
     vative."

12.  "On Oratory," WO-1950, p. 4.

13.  Message Preparation:  Analysis and Structure by Glen
        E. Mills, copyright 1966 by Bobbs-Merrill Co.,
        Indianapolis, pp. 87-88.  Reprinted by permission.

14.  Herbert L. Curry and Emil R. Pfister, Fundamentals
     of Forensics, Central Michigan University Press,
     Mount Pleasant, p. 29.

15.  WO-1936, p. 46.  The paragraph quoted is the next-
        to-last paragraph of the oration with the unusual
        title "Willard Wilson," the orator's name.  The fi-
        nal paragraph represented a tie-up back reference
        to introduction in that a W.P.A. worker by the
        same name had been sentenced to ten years in pri-
        son for robbing a student of two dollars and fifty
        cents.  The orator tells of using his Pi Kappa
        Delta key number 13837 to interview the prisoner
        number 12486.  The orator concludes with these

words:  "His number stands for maladjustment and consequent crime.  My number and your number stands for privilege and consequent responsibility."

Chapter X

## THE LANGUAGE OF THE ORATION

An oration requires both good composition and delivery. It is idle to speculate which is the more important. The aspiring orator will strive for excellence in both areas. This chapter concerns the language in which you express your thoughts and feelings.

## I.  IMPORTANCE

Writing the oration constitutes one of the many values of participation in oratory. Such training in speech composition is of inestimable value not only during your student days, but throughout adult life. Make no mistake about it, the road to authorship is not easy; it has many ruts and pitfalls. Much heart-breaking toil and effort takes place between the birth of an idea and its final flowering in understandable and picturesque language. Much writing and rewriting is required. When writing, imagine the audience you will be addressing, just as you would do in a private delivery rehearsal with your coach.

The process of writing a contest oration may sometimes take three weeks or more. After a preliminary outline is prepared, my usual advice is to write freely in a first draft, preferably at one sitting, and to ignore contest word limits, but to try to stay within 2300 or at most 2500 words for an 1800 word-limit oration. There may be times when you write five or six versions of the oration. By all means, keep all your copies; you just never know when you might want to salvage some excerpt from an earlier version. In cutting the expanded oration, there comes a time when you must get ruthless and make deletions, not because the deleted portions are no good, but because what you retain is better.

## II.  TWO PRIMARY REQUISITES
### A.  Instant Intelligibility

The contest oration should possess two primary re-
quisites characteristic of all persuasive speaking:  instant
intelligibility, and interestingness.  The first means just
what it says, that the words spoken must be comprehended
at first hearing.  An auditor should not blink mentally and
say inwardly to himself, just what does he mean by that?
Speech is fleeting, ephemeral, evanescent, which hi-falutin
words translate to mean--here one moment, gone the next.
Listeners have just so much attention value to give and if
they are occupied trying to figure out what you mean by
what you just said, they cannot be giving undivided attention
to what you are saying at this moment.  All of which is
just another way of restating a part of Herbert Spencer's
admirable essay on "The Philosophy of Style."  Says he:

> A reader or listener has at each moment but a
> limited amount of mental power available.  To
> recognize and interpret the symbols presented to
> him, requires part of this power; to arrange and
> combine the images suggested by them requires a
> further part; and only that part which remains can
> be used for framing the thought expressed.  Hence,
> the more time and attention it takes to receive
> and understand each sentence, the less time and
> attention can be given to the contained idea; and
> the less vividly will that idea be conceived.

Using simple words, short sentences, frequent summaries,
and many coherence connectives (hence, thus, moreover,
therefore, consequently, then too), are all common ways of
securing this all-important Instant Intelligibility.  Here is
an illustration of simplicity:

> During World War II, the Office of Civilian De-
> fense ordered federal buildings to secure "obscu-
> ration either by blackout construction or by termi-
> nation of the illumination."  President Roosevelt
> grinned and rephrased it, "Put something across
> the window, or turn out the lights."[1]

### B.  Interestingness

Interestingness goes a step beyond having the kind of
material that is immediately understood.  It refers to lan-

guage that grips and compels attention.  Therefore, you
should become familiar with and apply tested techniques for
interesting an audience.  Fortunately, many textbooks are
already available on ways and means of doing that.  However, this handbook would not be complete without mention
of some of the compositional high lights in the language of
the oration.


## III.  FACTORS OF ATTENTION

Any stylistic device for securing immediate attention
and interest, indeed, every figure of speech, could be called
a factor of attention.  Quite arbitrarily, I have selected
and placed in alphabetical order an eclectic list of techniques and stylistic devices and called them Factors of Attention.  Some relate to the whole of the oration, some to
paragraphs within it, and others more specifically concern
word-choice.  The items in the list are not mutually exclu-
sive--many of the examples cited will exemplify these techniques in combination.

Our selected list of factors of attention follows:  Ac-
tivity, Alliteration, Antithesis (Contrast), Concrete-Specific,
Direct Discourse (Colloquy), Epigrams (Paradox), Euphony,
Familiar (Principle of Reference to Experience of Audience),
Figures of Speech, Humor, Illustration, Novelty (Unusual),
Questions, Quotations, and Repetition.


### A.  Activity

Activity means just what it says:  movement, motion,
activity in terms of the mental images evoked by the language employed.  Here is an explanation of it from the pen of
William Norwood Brigance:

> Activity ... commands our attention.  As we go
> down the street it is the rotating barber sign, rath-
> er than the still one, that attracts our attention.
> Or perhaps we see a crowd before a shop window.
> It is a safe guess that there is something animate
> within the window--a girl demonstrating a gas
> stove, a man operating a stamping machine, or a
> mechanical dummy displaying the latest sport suit.
> You will note the psychology of the front window
> kitchens now used by many restaurants.  Now in

the same way a speech which describes activity, that summons before us living characters and animated scenes will hold our attention.

Thus from the standpoint of arousing interest, rather than say: "When Congress declared war on Germany people everywhere became interested in what the next step would be--" we should make the picture animate, should let our listeners see the people displaying interest and hear them talking, as this:

Before people were out of bed, newsboys along the streets were crying out "War declared with Germany! Congress passes resolution!" The noise awakened sleeping citizens; men in bath robes signalled the newsboys at their doorways to purchase the extras. By eight o'clock no other topic of conversation could be heard. Along the streets and in places of business were clusters of men discussing the situation and asking one another, "What will be the next move?"[2]

I have chosen this old example from World War I days because it struck a responsive chord with me. Radios were not yet widely used at the outbreak of World War I, and most people in small towns and large learned of the war from "extras" of their daily newspaper. I well remember the hawking of the newsboys and the men in bath robes buying the extras. This example, therefore, was also for me a case of the use of the familiar, as well as activity, and thus shows the overlapping of these factors of attention.

### B.   Alliteration

Alliteration is the repetition of the same sound at the beginning of two or more consecutive words or of words near one another. Its use makes us attentive because the alliterative words have a pleasing effect upon the ear and are easily remembered.

One of my own orators, now the Reverend Harland Steele, said of some Christian evangelists: "They were interested in the men in the alley but forgot the man on the avenue."[3]

In the context of Christian pacifism and the church, Culbert G. Rutenber, Professor of the Philosophy of Religion at Eastern Baptist Theological Seminary in Philadelphia, avers: "It wants God, but it wants guns, too. It's for Bibles, but it is also for bullets. It trusts in Jesus, but also in jets."[4]

Returning to his pastorate after three years of service as an army chaplain, the Rev. Renwick C. Kennedy began his article "To the Victor the Spoils," by the use of alliteration. "The United States Army tacitly accepted the theory that loot, lust, and liquor are the rewards of the victorious soldier."[5]

### C.   Antithesis (Contrast)

Antithesis means, by dictionary definition, "an opposition or contrast of ideas, emphasized by the positions of the contrasting words." It is often found in the form of a balanced sentence such as Patrick Henry's familiar "Give me liberty or give me death!" or in the more recent utterance of President John F. Kennedy in his Inaugural Address: "And so, my fellow-Americans, ask not what your country can do for you: ask what you can do for your country." When E. Stanley Jones, world-famous missionary, said: "Fifty percent of sick persons need prayer more than pills, aspiration more than aspirin, meditation more than medication,"[6] he was using both alliteration and antithesis.

In the intellectual type audience you are most likely to face in high school and college oratory, there is almost an indefinable aesthetic appreciation upon hearing antithesis. For one thing, it immediately captures attention and for another, it is by that token easily remembered. Of course, over-use of this or any other rhetorical device, should be avoided.

Consider the contrasts in titles such as: "My Friend the Enemy," and "The Failure of Success." Or these representative examples of sentences from college orations. In an oration against pornographic literature, "Beware of the high cost of low reading";[7] in an oration on alcoholism, "Every man is a possible drunkard and every drunkard is a possible man";[8] in a speech against yellow journalism, "The slogan 'All The News that's Fit to Print,' has been subverted to 'All The News that's Print to Fit.' "

### D.   Concrete-Specific

Both concrete and specific language add vividness in expression and their use should be encouraged.   Such terms are frequently, but incorrectly, used as synonyms.   A concrete term denotes something that can be perceived through the senses; the opposite of concrete is abstract, a quality. The opposite of specific is general.   A word is more or less specific (or general) in relation to what word or words it is being compared to.   Paper, printed material, newspapers, American newspapers, the New York Times, the Times Sunday edition are concepts arranged in order of increasing specificity.   A generous use of both concrete and specific words and phrases brings imagery to the audience and aids in their comprehension and appreciation of your oration.

Asked in my class to convert the statement "Our great men had but meager schooling" into more concrete-specific language, one student wrote:   "The world's Ibsens, Sandburgs, and O'Neills obtained most of their schooling in the University of Hard Knocks."   Another changed "Not a breath of air was stirring" into:   "The air was as quiet as a butterfly doing push-ups on a lemon meringue pie."   Ralph Brooks, Superintendent of McCook, Nebraska, public schools, delivered his speech simply titled "Nebraska" over 300 times throughout that state.   It no doubt contributed to his being catapulted into the governorship in 1958, the first Democratic governor in 18 years.   In describing the magnitude of Nebraska's cattle industry, he used this picturesque language:

> If all the beef raised in Nebraska were contained
> in one cow, she could plant her front feet in
> Texas, her hind feet in Canada, drink water out
> of the Gulf of Mexico, and with her tail flick the
> frost off the North Pole. [9]

Note this vignette of a career girl in Jean LeVander's oration, "Brains or Brooms?":

> Career girl.   You only have to say the word out
> loud to notice what an odd even sinister label it
> denotes.   Career girl: a tall thin semi-shapeless
> woman, wears brown or gray tweed suits and dark
> framed glasses that she can hang pensively on her
> hip while making an important decision.   She lives
> in an immaculately well-kept apartment abounding

> with original touches.  The career girl gets along
> better with men than women and is quick to criti-
> cize her own sex.  But underneath her carefree
> exterior she is basically unsure of her femininity
> and ability to meet the challenges of motherhood
> so therefore has been forced to join the competi-
> tive man's world. [10]

And note the contrast in effectiveness in these two sentences.

> The Western United States are engaged in a strange
> course of self-destruction.
> In the plains and mountain regions of the Western
> states, too large cattle herds bankrupt the land,
> destructive farming squanders the precious topsoil,
> and the saws of the lumbermen bite deeper and
> deeper into the last great heritage of pine and fir.[11]

### E.  Direct Discourse (Colloquy)

Dialogue, real or imaginary, is a way of dramatiz-
ing your oration.  Auditors tend to pay added attention, for
we are interested in people talking with each other.  The
same principle operates when you are picking out a library
book for vacation reading.  You are likely to be more interested in one with many paragraphs sprinkled with dialogue
than in a forbidding heavy tome with solid unindented pages.
Direct discourse (He said: "...") is preferable to the indirect (He said that ...).  To avoid monotony, it is well to
use synonyms for "said," such as "replied," "whispered,"
"exclaimed," "pointed out."  With extended dialogue, you
can omit the prefatory verb altogether.  Sometimes you may
introduce a form of direct discourse between yourself and
your audience, as when you say "But you may ask ... ?"
"And I answer ..."  Note in the example which follows a
combination of a personal reference with the use of direct
discourse.

> "Jane, do you consider yourself to be a Christian?"
> A friend asked me this question as we were drink-
> ing tea and munching shortbread in a brightly lit
> cafe in Edinburgh, Scotland.  I thought that per-
> haps the minister whom we had heard preaching
> on Princess Street, the Hyde Park of Edinburgh,
> had prompted this question.  But when I answered

yes, he quickly said, "Then tell me something.
Why are you feverishly hurrying in and out of the
shops of Edinburgh in an attempt to find a skirt to
match the green sweater you bought in England? I
thought Christians were not supposed to be so concerned with the material aspects of life." It
wasn't until later that I began to realize the pene-
trating nature of this question. It haunted me:
"Jane, do you consider yourself to be a Christian?"
Evidently my friend could not tell by my actions
that I was a Christian. [12]

The example just cited appeared in the opening paragraph. I recall a winning MISL oration by Judi Swanlund of
Western Michigan University, Kalamazoo, where it occurred
throughout the speech. We were taken on an imaginary trip
to Europe, the Middle East, and the Far East. At each
stop, the orator would pose a question to and receive an
imaginary reply from world leaders such as Willy Brandt,
Dag Hammarskjold and others. Most oratory league consti-
tutions set a 10% limit upon direct quotations from others
but also provide that "Direct discourse, dialogue or other
stylistic devices within quotation marks created by the orator shall not be included in the 10% total."

F. Epigrams (Paradox)

Epigrams, by dictionary definition "bright or witty
thoughts tersely and ingenuously expressed," are effective
attention-getters. So, too, are paradoxes, "tenets contrary
to received opinion; also, assertions or sentiments seeming-
ly contradictory or opposed to common sense, but that may
yet be true in fact." Gilbert K. Chesterton, the English
master of the paradox, once called it "the truth stood on
its head to attract attention." Frequently, striking contrasts
are found in epigrams and paradoxes. Like a slogan, these
devices not only are attractive to an audience, but are easy
for them to remember.

The poet Carl Sandburg once said: "The Civil War
was fought about a verb. The United States IS, not ARE."

Dr. Ralph W. Sockman, the famous radio preacher,
pointed out: "We see Americans using ever more stimulu-
lants to cheer them up and ever more tranquilizers to calm
them down." [13]

Journalist Henry R. Luce said: "Today the Scopeses, and the Bryans and Darrows too, understand that they do not have to make a choice between knowing the age of rocks and the Rock of Ages."[14]

Many besides Bishop Ralph Richardson may have found that "Christmas presents can obscure the Christmas Presence."[15]

### G.  Euphony

Euphony refers to sounds that are pleasant to the ear. What we mean here is that we should avoid its opposite, cacophony--sounds which grate harshly on the ear.  For example, a sudden rhyming effect should be avoided, such as "We must not paralyze transportation and thereby jeopardize the public interest," or "Then Robert E. Lee began to make history."  Such expressions tend to distract thought away from the ideas sought to be conveyed and call attention to themselves.  Sometimes violations of euphony occur from an over-use of an otherwise good quality, alliteration.  Samples from class-room speeches: "the steaming ships that sail the seven seas," and "the fretful furor over finance."  Repetition of similar sounds should be avoided, such as "I can candidly say," "agree to a degree," "very varied," "the subjective perspective dare never overrule the objective value."  This last sentence also suffers from lack of instant intelligibility.

My earlier suggestion of thinking of the audience as you struggle with composition, even to the point of talking the words out loud, will most likely avoid cacophony.  If such expressions should escape detection, they will most likely be caught and corrected in the first delivery rehearsal.  This category in our list is not earth-shakingly important.  But it is worthy of mention for you should never be satisfied with anything less than perfection.

### H.    Familiar (Principle of Reference to Experience of Audience)

If this listing of language qualities had been arranged in order of importance or frequency of use rather than alphabetically, the familiar would occupy a place near the top. The principle itself has been in operation since antiquity, but

it got this particular name probably from the pioneer speech
teacher, Arthur Edward Phillips.  Here's his explanation:

> Reference to Experience means reference to the
> known.  The known is that which the listener has
> seen, heard, read, felt, believed or done, and
> which still exists in his consciousness--his stock
> of knowledge ...  Reference to Experience, then,
> means coming into the listener's life.[16]

Lionel Crocker has pointed out that Henry Ward Beecher was
himself well versed in this principle, and that in his Yale
Lectures on Preaching he urged its use by others.  Crocker
noted that Beecher knew

> ... the apostles were successful in their preach-
> ing because they began with the experience of the
> audience and addressed their remarks to the wants
> of the audience.  Beecher states that he went
> through the Scriptures and found about forty of
> these, what he terms, "you all knows" [sic].[17]

Since slang is so obviously a form of the familiar, a
few words about it.  Some slang is very expressive and effective, gains wide usage and even later gets included in
dictionaries.  However, much of it is in bad taste.  I would
suggest using it sparingly in an oration.  While the nature of
your oration subject may occasionally justify its use, what
you gain in audience response from some, you may lose
from others by their failure to take you or your subject
seriously.  Then too, there's no accounting for taste in
slang and what you may consider to be exceptionally amus-
ing and relevant to some point in the oration, may offend
others.  (My disapproval of slang is mild, however, for I
am just dying to say here that in the usual case, slang's a
"no-no!")


I.   Figures of Speech

Figures of speech--simile, metaphor, personification,
and many others--deserve a place as a factor of attention.
Their purpose is not only to assist in clarifying ideas but
also to stir the imagination, thus evoking in the auditor an
aesthetic sense of appreciation.  However, like all good
things, their use too can be overdone.  The idea must always remain primary.  If any figure of speech causes the

listener to be enamored of it for its own sake to the point of losing the idea you are trying to convey, skip the figure!

There are so many different figures of speech that one hardly knows where to begin or end in providing examples. By the way, I got a chuckle when a patriarch of our speech profession, James Albert Winans, wrote: "Even if some student says he will 'leave such flowery stuff to the wind-jammers, and hot-air artists,' he is using metaphors, and mixing them too."[18] You should not mix your figures. It may amuse but it distracts when you say, "this has all the ear-marks of an eye-sore," or, "before the chickens come home to roost, it will be a horse of a different color," or "with Nixon at the throttle, the Ship of State will move forward with leaps and bounds."

The authors Lew Sarett and William Trufant Foster present us with some interesting figures of speech.

> A speaker might say, "the day was drawing to a close," or "it was growing late." In neither case would anybody remember his phrasing, but when George Brooks said, in Collier's, "The clock hands were closing like scissor blades on midnight, snipping off another day," 234 men and women in 40 states and Canada wrote the editors of Reader's Digest about it.[19]

Note these examples of personification: "The admonishing finger of a church steeple ... Piers wading into the ocean on centipede legs ... A lie can travel round the world and back again while the truth is lacing up its boots."[20] And note how these figures stir the imagination: "Fig-leaf phrases used to cover naked ignorance ... Speeches as long as roller towels ... He talks like a dictionary on its best behavior ... The man's personality was as cold as an unlighted candle.[21]

In reference to death, two clergymen used these expressions: "For over this frontier the path contracts and all must travel Indian file,"[22] and "Some are proud of wealth, though there are no pockets in a shroud."[23]

A newspaper report in 1961, referring to Russian space exploration, read, "If successful, the space probe might be likened to standing in New York with a rifle and hitting an apple in San Francisco."[24]

My dear friend Father Michael Beahan, who conducts
a weekly "Fifteen With Father" TV broadcast, said this of
our first moon landing: "To appreciate the true significance
of our flight to the moon is like trying to paint the Washington Monument with a toothbrush."[25]


## J.  Humor

In our alphabetical listing, humor belongs here.  We
have already made some comments about it in Chapter V,
urging it as a category for your filing system.  Humor is
an attention-getter of the first rank.  For probably the first
60 years of intercollegiate oratory, the use of humor was a
rarity.  But increasingly, with a change toward more informality of style, one encounters more of it.  However, oratory is and remains serious business.  Don't over-use humor.
In an oration, the witticism, the clever turn of a phrase, the
sort of thing that evokes a chuckle rather than a belly-laugh,
is preferable to the funny story.  In deciding whether or not
to use a bit of humor, you should ask yourself, would this
gain support for my SPS or detract from it?


## K.  Illustration

By this caption, we mean an anecdote, a narrative incident that comes out of your own experience, or one that
you have heard or read about.  The use of this device not
only captures attention, but helps to clarify and impress i-
deas upon your auditors.  Thomas Babington Macaulay says:
"Logicians may reason about abstractions, but the great
masses of men must have images."  Illustrations provide
those images.  They involve people, and we are interested
in people, and what happens to them.  Narrative involves action, and we are interested in that.  Suspense is created,
and we are made curious as to the outcome.  Whenever a
speaker says "for instance," or "to illustrate," an audience
perks up.  As a member of a luncheon club, I have noticed
that interest is quickened when a speaker appears with slides.
Since these are not allowed in contests, you can do the next
best thing and have word-pictures.

The importance of illustration cannot be exaggerated.
Henry Ward Beecher in his Yale Lectures on Preaching, de-
votes an entire lecture to it.[26]  Russell H. Conwell, noted
preacher and founder of Temple University, delivered his

famous chautauqua lecture "Acres of Diamonds" about 6,000
times. His basic plea--that we should not go to far-away
places to seek happiness but find in in our own back yard--
consisted mainly of a series of illustrations. Dr. Halford
Luccock, Professor of Homiletics at Yale Divinity School,
writing one of his weekly contributions to the Christian Century, under the pen name of Simeon Stylites, gave some good
advice which young orators might well take to heart.

> Many speeches go "klunk" because of a lack
> of narrative. That is part of the unfailing power
> of the parables of Jesus. Narrative has kept Aesop
> very much alive for many centuries. Take that
> most gifted speaker of all times, the Ancient Mari-
> ner. Notice how he begins a speech: "There was
> a ship, quoth he." That gave him a half-nelson on
> the audience. He did not begin, "Now let us con-
> sider the principles of navigation." He knew a
> trick worth two of that. He held his audience by
> narrative. Look at the record:
>
> > He holds him with his glittering eye,
> > The wedding guest stood still,
> > And listens like a three years' child,
> > The Mariner hath his will.
>
> Go thou and do likewise,
> > Yours,
> > > SIMEON STYLITES.[27]

If a teacher wishes to test the value of an illustration,
let him try this experiment. Read the following excerpt as
I have done for a number of years to my classes. Read it
expressively, act out the part--and note the perfect attention
--it has never missed!

> We know speakers who say that they have no time
> to be interesting. This is the same as saying
> that they have a message which is so important
> that they can't take time to make it effective. They
> say, "We are not going to tell anecdotes and use
> illustrations, because to do so takes time which is
> needed for more important matters." They feel as
> one of the ancient Greek orators is reported to
> have felt on one occasion when he had been address-
> ing the people of Athens concerning the dangers
> surrounding their national life. The day was warm,

the argument was dry, and the audience had become inattentive--that is to say, the audience had become attentive to something else, namely, to feelings of fatigue and bodily discomfort induced by stimuli in the situation, other than those emanating from the speaker.  Suddenly the speaker broke off abruptly and said, "There were once two travelers who were going down from Athens to Piraeus to take ship.  One of them, having a great deal of baggage, rented a donkey to transport it for him. At the noon hour the two travelers paused for rest and refreshment.  The one who had rented the donkey took the beast to one side of the road and lay down in its shade.  The other traveler rudely suggested that he would like to share the shade of the donkey.  A heated argument ensued.  The man who had rented the donkey contended that with it he had rented the shade.  The other man denied this." Here the speaker stopped suddenly and walked off the platform, whereupon the multitude began to shout vociferously, "Come back, come back and finish your story."  After a few minutes he reappeared and said, "O men of Athens, when I tell you the things which concern the salvation of your city you fall asleep, and when I tell you the silly story of two men and an ass you are all ears." This speaker evidently knew how to interest his audience.  He should have been making use of his ability to interest them in the discussion of his theme.  Had he done this he would have had no occasion to scold them for what was, of course, his own failure.[28]

The preceding illustration establishes the effectiveness of an illustration.  We next proceed with two examples, one from a sermon delivered on The National Radio Pulpit series, and another from a college oration.

Once, during the hostilities in China, when men were lying untended in improvised hospitals, a visiting journalist found a nun spending her days in cleansing the terrible gangrenous wounds of the mutilated soldiers.  "I wouldn't do that for a million dollars," he remarked.  She looked up and answered quietly:  "Neither would I."[29]

A story is told of one of the South's greats which
points out both sides of this--[first] the way whites
do think basically, and [second] the way they should
be... Shortly after the close of the Civil War, a
Negro entered a fashionable church in Richmond,
Virginia, one Sunday while communion was being
served. He walked down the aisle and knelt at the
altar. A rustle of shock and anger swept through
the congregation. Sensing the situation, a distinguished layman immediately stood up, stepped forward to the altar, and knelt beside his colored brother. Captured by his spirit, the congregation followed this magnanimous example. The layman was
Robert E. Lee.[30]

Dr. Harry Emerson Fosdick tells us

Samuel Goldwyn once remarked that he wanted "a
film which begins with an earth-quake and works
up to a climax." He rightly assessed the popular
attractiveness of the colossal.[31]

All of which is a way of introducing a special kind of
illustration which in my oratory class I refer to as the
"super-duper" type. It is of course merely a matter of degree, but I mean the kind which particularly grips the heart,
and which is particularly useful as a climax at or near the
end of the oration. For example, there is the incident of
the four chaplains, two Protestant ministers, a Catholic
priest, and a Jewish rabbi. They gave their life-jackets to
soldiers and hand in hand went down to a watery grave into
the icy waters of the Atlantic when their cargo transport
Dorchester was sunk by a Nazi torpedo in World War II.[32]
Another example is that of the errant son who, repentant,
like the Prodigal Son, wondered if he would be welcomed
home by his parents. He had written them to ask that if so,
the parents should fly a white flag on the apple-tree in the
yard of his old home. Not daring to look himself, he asked
the motorist with whom he had hitched a ride, to look for
him. Whereupon the motorist reported, "Why, son, there
are white flags fluttering on every branch of the tree!"

The winner of the 1923 University of Michigan Oratorical Contest was Gerrit Demmink, with his oration entitled "The Mind In Thrall." From its title, and the context
of the following excerpt, we discover what a powerful example of a "super-duper" illustration this is.

We see this servitude deep laid in centuries of
tradition, steeped in the doctrine of ancient times.
People were not supposed to be intelligent. Reason
was stunned from the shock of a brutal intolerance.
Man was haunted by visions of a watchful ruler
standing guard over his ideas. If some thinker,
in advance of his times, dared to fly in the face of
accepted belief, he was silenced with arguments of
blood and iron. Such is always the tyranny of
might. To us, the spectacle of ancient torture is
so remote that we can scarce perceive it. It is
cloistered and sequestered in the dim passages of
long, long ago--a thing faded and forgotten. But
if we can accustom our eyes to the darkness, we
shall see men utterly broken in body and spirit,
drooping in tearful agony under the lash; we shall
see them torn limb from limb or crushed in joint-
ed armor; we shall see the rack, the wheel, the
gibbet and the collar of torture: those creatures
of ingenious cruelty. Under the soft Italian skies,
the martyr Christian lifts his face to heaven, to
catch the dying solace of his faith, untouched by
human vengeance. And what is that which lights
the Appian Way, those intermittent, ghostly, crack-
ling flames; they are but fagots--aye, fagots, but
fagots burning men--men--Christians burning! Oh,
God, that man should be so cruel! Such was might
in the olden days; such was the kingdom of fear
which sought to hold the mind in thrall. [33]

L.  Novelty (Unusual)

Many people, perhaps most, lead drab, humdrum routine lives. We are so constituted that we seek escape and
relief by reading or hearing about extraordinary people and
places. This trait accounts for the success of the "Believe
It or Not" cartoons of John Hix and the late Bob Ripley. It
explains the large attendance at the travelogue series sponsored by our local Kiwanis Club. It explains the avid interest in TV programs such as "Wild Kingdom" and "The
Undersea World of Jacques Costeau."

One might raise an eye-brow and think, how is it
that the familiar and the unusual can both be factors of attention? Recall that I mentioned the overlapping nature of
them. Here is an example of it. Back in May 20-21, 1927,

when Charles Lindbergh flew the Atlantic, it was not, as now,
an everyday occurrence. It was a novelty. A few weeks
thereafter, many of my faculty colleagues at the University
of Colorado incorporated references to the flight, and drew
moral lessons from it, in their commencement speeches of
that season. In so doing, they were also applying the familiar, for the event had the element of recency and had been
constantly in the news. J. Jeffery Auer, Chairman of the
Department of Speech and Theatre at Indiana University, says
of this quality of novelty that it is:

> ... familiarity's counterpart, and equally important
> in maintaining interest because too much reliance
> upon one stimulus may wear out its effectiveness.
> Listeners want enough novelty to offset monotony,
> just as they want enough familiarity to maintain
> stability. In supporting his arguments, for exam-
> ple, the speaker can employ unusual illustrations
> of familiar principles, and novel ways of phrasing
> traditional ideas. [34]

As the preceding sentences indicate, novelty may refer both to the content of the idea, as well as to the novel
way of putting it. Note for example:

> If you were invited to dine at the home of a rich
> man in certain sections of China, it would be pro-
> per to toss chicken bones and olive seeds over
> your shoulder onto the floor. You pay your host
> a compliment when you do that. You show that
> you realize that he is wealthy, that he has plenty
> of servants to tidy up after the meal. And he
> likes it. ... Have you found these facts about
> Chinese life interesting? If so, do you know why?
> Because those are very unusual aspects of very
> usual things. They are strange truths about such
> commonplace events as dining out and bathing.
> That is what interests us--something new about the
> old. [35]

M. Questions

Questions require answers. Thus, when the speaker
asks them, he compels the attention of the audience. He involves them. He challenges their thought-processes. In a
sense, he courts mental dialogue, except that the response

is not oral, but visceral. When Patrick Henry implores,
"Is life so dear, or peace so sweet, as to be purchased at
the price of chains and slavery?" he is compelling auditors
to answer inwardly, before he provides his own stirring answer.

Questions may be of two kinds, the ordinary and the
rhetorical. The ordinary question is useful to indicate transitions between major divisions of the speech, introduction,
body, and conclusion. "You ask, what are the main ingre-
dients of this problem?" "What, you may ask, can we do to
solve this problem?" are typical questions used as transitions. In effect, you are orally asking the auditors and
speaking in their behalf the very questions they are thinking.
Psychologically, too, you are inviting them to join you in
going cooperatively in search for the answer to the problem,
as contrasted with dogmatically telling them. And since oration subjects are mostly highly controversial, this approach
is particularly effective when the audience is hostile to your
ideas. The question aids in removing barriers of antagonism and disarming their prejudice.

In the rhetorical question, you do not answer it yourself but unmistakably imply the answer. Shylock in "The
Merchant of Venice" asks: "Hath a dog money? Is it possible a cur can lend three thousand ducats?"

Or consider Christ's questions: "What doth it profit
a man to gain the whole world and forfeit his life? Which
of you by being anxious can add one cubit to the measure of
his life?"

Psychologically, as contrasted with direct and dogma-
tic assertion on your part, the rhetorical question assists
the auditor in making him feel that he is convincing himself,
making up his own mind, is being led, not driven. In passing, while we will come at the matter again in the chapter
on delivery, frequently a pause is in order following the
rhetorical question, in order to allow the auditor time to
answer before you proceed.

### N.   Quotations

Recall that in Chapter V, quotations were suggested
as a worthy category for inclusion in your filing system.
There are two primary reasons for including them in your

oration. First, when the prestige of the person quoted is
high with the audience, it aids in securing acceptance of your
ideas. Second, his "way of putting it" may be exceptionally
attractive and compelling. If used for this latter purpose,
but the person making the statement is either unknown or not
favorably known to the audience, it would then perhaps be
best to have him remain nameless, and to introduce the quotation by some such expression as "As some one has so aptly said." But do be sure to acknowledge that the material
is not your own. In my examination of thousands of orations,
sometimes in manuscripts students submit to me for inspection and correction, I have found quotation marks, but with
no indication given that the material is quoted. Without that,
how in the world would an audience be expected to know the
words are not your own?

Which leads to saying a word about plagiarism, the
direct use of the words of another without acknowledgment.
It is literary theft--avoid it! Of course, all of our ideas
have come from some outside source. I rather like the
idea behind what a top-notch newspaper columnist, O. O.
McIntyre, said of someone many years ago: [He has] milk-
ed many cows, but the butter is [his]."[36]

A word about the manner of introducing quotations. I
have a personal dislike for the method coming into more common use, of saying "quote" and "unquote" at the proper spots.
Especially if the person quoted is not generally known, be
sure to identify him. It is a way of establishing his creden-
tials and right to be heard. Try to avoid the rather prosaic
"Mr. Bigshot said: ..." Here are a couple of examples of
quotations which are brought in unobtrusively:

> It is as true as it was when the psychologist
> William James said it, that "what holds attention,
> determines action."[37]

> Why does an audience laugh? Professor Edwin R.
> Guthrie has suggested a reason: "We speak of
> laughing things off or of having a good cry. Both
> actions are capable of erasing a pattern of ten-
> sion ..."[38]

This final word of advice on quotations. They ought
to be used only if they bring to the audience the persuasive
impact of a well-known personality, or if the person being
quoted has expressed an idea in a way that you could not

improve upon. But I now suggest that, with all due deference
to your individualized filing system with its many quotations,
in which I strongly believe, you nevertheless do not down-
grade the majesty of your own mind. What is to prevent you
from racking your own brains, stirring up your imagination,
and to come up with expressions so effective and original
that others may want to quote you? It's worth thinking about!


### O.   Repetition

Repetition of words, phrases, sentences are effective
means of enlivening attention and securing emphasis. It is
often a delight to the ear, and creates almost a hypnotic effect. Bill Nye in one of his chautauqua lectures used to say:
"I will belave anything if ye will tell me aften anough." In
Lincoln's Cooper Union speech in 1860, he referred 15 times
to the phrase: "our forefathers who framed the government
under which we live." After the retreat at Dunkerque,
Winston Churchill galvanized the British people with these
words:

> We shall defend our island, whatever the cost may
> be. We shall fight on the beaches. We shall fight
> on the landing grounds. We shall fight in the fields
> and in the streets, and we shall fight in the hills.
> We shall never surrender. [39]

Notice the magical effect of the Twenty-third Psalm:

> He maketh me to lie down ...
> He leadeth me beside the still waters.
> He restoreth my soul.
> He leadeth me in the paths of righteousness.

In summation, we reiterate what was said earlier in
this chapter. The attention of an audience ought never to
be presumed or commanded. It must be wooed and won.
Each of the language techniques we have considered, and
many others that we have not, is a means of doing that. A-
gain, a reminder not to use too many in a single oration, to
the point where the audience becomes so intrigued with your
manner of expression that they forget about the matter, your
message! Used to excess, any one of these devices, good
in themselves, may alienate your audience. Like a good
quarterback, you should become adept at mixing up your
plays!

Notes

1.  Milton Dickens, Dynamic Communication, Harcourt,
    Brace and Company, Inc., New York, 1954, p. 176.

2.  The Spoken Word, F. S. Crofts & Co., New York,
    1927, p. 122.

3.  Temple Time broadcast, Reformed Church in America,
    Pamphlet.

4.  The Dagger and the Cross, Fellowship Publications,
    New York, 1950, p. 3.

5.  Reprinted by permission from The Christian Century,
    July 31, 1946, p. 936. Copyright 1946 by The
    Christian Century.

6.  Time, December 6, 1948, p. 77. Reprinted by per-
    mission.

7.  Kenneth Erickson, South Dakota State College,
    Brookings, "Procurers of Pictorial Prostitution,"
    WO-1953, p. 89.

8.  Bernard W. Crocker, Wittenberg College, Springfield,
    Ohio, "Matriculating in Alcohol," WO-1953, p. 82.

9.  Rotarian Magazine, December, 1952, p. 62.

10. Pi Kappa Delta Winning Orations, National Convention
    and Tournament, Southern Illinois University,
    Carbondale, March 19-23, 1963, p. 48.

11. Mark Hanna, Public Speaking Without Fear and Trem-
    bling, The Macmillan Company, New York, 1956, p.
    68.

12. "An Echo or a Voice?, WHCO, p. 115.

13. "Allies in Faith," National Radio Pulpit, October, 1959,
    p. 13.

14. Pamphlet, A Speculation About A.D. 1980, p. 18. (Re-
    print from December, 1955 Fortune Magazine). Used
    courtesy Fortune Magazine.

15.   "Light of the World," Christian Advocate, December 14,
      1950, p. 8.

16.   Effective Speaking, The Newton Company, Chicago, 1908,
      p. 28.

17.   "The Rhetorical Training of Henry Ward Beecher," QJS,
      February, 1933, p. 24.

18.   Public Speaking, rev. ed., The Century Company, New
      York, 1921, p. 149.

19.   Basic Principles of Speech, rev. ed., Houghton,
      Mifflin Co., Boston, 1946, p. 428.

20.   Ibid., p. 428.

21.   Ibid., p. 561.

22.   Douglas Steere, On Beginning From Within, Harper and
      Brothers, New York, 1943, p. 127.

23.   Bernard Iddings Bell, God Is Not Dead, Harper and
      Brothers, New York, 1945, p. 74.

24.   UPI Report, Holland Evening Sentinel, February 13,
      1961.

25.   TV "Fifteen With Father" broadcast, August 3, 1969.

26.   Lectures on Preaching, J. B. Ford and Co., New York,
      1872, p. 157.

27.   Like a Mighty Army, Oxford University Press, New
      York, 1954, pp. 114-15.

28.   James Milton O'Neill and Andrew Thomas Weaver, The
      Elements of Speech, Longmans, Green and Co.,
      New York, 1926, p. 302. Used by permission of
      David McKay Company, Inc.

29.   David H. C. Read, National Radio Pulpit, November 22,
      1964.

30.   Pat Rickert, Grove City College, Grove City, Pennsyl-
      vania, "The Other Side of the Story," PKD Provin-
      cial Convention, Charleston, W. Virginia, April 9,
      1958.

31.    "A Faith For Tough Times," Reader's Digest, Decem-
       ber, 1952, p. 86.

32.    An account of this incident appears in "Strong Men of
       God," by Daniel A. Poling (father of Clark Poling,
       one of the four) in Reader's Digest, May, 1945, p.
       85.

33.    One can well imagine how this example came to mind
       as I traveled along the Appian Way en route to the
       Rome Airport during a European visit in 1960.

34.    "The Persuasive Speaker and His Audience," The Rhet-
       oric of Our Times, J. Jeffery Auer, ed., Appleton-
       Century-Crofts, 1969, pp. 260-61.

35.    Dale Carnegie, Public Speaking and Influencing Men in
       Business, Association Press, New York, 1935, p.
       419.

36.    O. O. McIntyre's column, Grand Forks Herald, Janu-
       ary 19, 1936.

37.    Ralph A. Micken, Speaking For Results, Houghton
       Mifflin Company, Boston, 1958, p. 76.

38.    Lionel Crocker, Public Speaking For College Students,
       2nd edit., American Book Company, New York,
       1950, p. 350.

39.    Lew Sarett and William Trufant Foster, Basic Princi-
       ples of Speech, rev. ed., Houghton Mifflin Company,
       New York, 1946, p. 431.

Chapter XI

MEMORIZING THE ORATION

After the composition of the oration, the next chronological step in preparation for competition is to memorize it.
However, it would be highly unrealistic, even begging the
question, to presume that memorization is the best method
of delivery. That would fail to consider the many objections
to it, and would bypass consideration of alternative methods
which have been proposed, including extemporaneous speaking and reading from a manuscript. The latter method particularly has been growing in popularity in recent years.

Recall that in the opening chapter I mentioned that
oratory contest procedures were very properly under constant
review. I do not believe the survival of oratory hinges upon
the retention of the requirement of memorization. Nevertheless, risking the charge of being an "Old Fogey,"[1] I hereby
assert my belief that memorization, liberally interpreted, is
still the best method of delivery in contest oratory. This
chapter, then, aims: 1) to state in considerable detail my
reasons for this belief: 2) to offer some hints on mastering
the fear of forgetting; 3) to offer some suggestions on how
to memorize; and 4) to make a bold suggestion on methods
of delivery.

I.  A LONG-STANDING CONTROVERSY - MEMORIZATION

As early as 1951, a questionnaire of college coaches
revealed that "the chief objection, with respect to the type of
speaking taught for the oratory contest, concerned the requirement of memorization."[2] For some, memorizing the
oration is not difficult. When it has been written and re-
written many times, the memory process is already pretty
well along. Accordingly, many orators hardly have to sit
down or pace the floor consciously to try to memorize.
Prior thorough preparation in composition, coupled with
youth and a facile memory, makes the memory chore com-

paratively easy.   Others are not so fortunately endowed.
Memory is a problem for many speakers.   Note these two
extreme examples from textbook writers:

> Memorizing a speech places a terrible burden on
> the memory.   We all know that our memory will
> play tricks on us.   Ministers have been known to
> forget the Lord's Prayer or the benediction. [3]

> No matter how hard they try to memorize speeches
> or outlines, people actually do forget.   A success-
> ful business man-- and one without any quirks in
> his mental makeup--was asked his name.   He could
> not answer.   He had forgotten!   An actor may go
> through a hundred performances without missing a
> single cue.   Then, suddenly and with no apparent
> reason, he forgets!   Surely every speaker of wide
> experience, whether he uses verbatim memoriza-
> tion or an outline, has many times been appalled
> to find that his mind is blank.   Professional speak-
> ers have this difficulty in common with beginners.
> The difference is that the professional knows how
> to "cover up" without the audience's realizing he
> has been plunged into a mental vacuum. [4]


II.   ADAPTATION NOT APPLICABLE TO CONTEST ORATORY
     A.   Unfair Competition

        The 1951 Diem Report on oratory practices said some
coaches object to the necessity of following a script because
it "precludes any opportunity to adapt to a speaking situation."[5]
It is difficult to know exactly what is meant by that.   It hardly seems likely that proponents of extemporization could be
referring to the failure of contest orators to make references
to one another's orations.   Yet this is one possible interpretation.   The matter came up for discussion at the last annual business meeting of the IOA that I attended in 1967; I
was asked for my opinion, and repeat here substantially what
I said then.

        A contest situation does not, and ought not to, lend
itself to that kind of adaptation.   Suppose one speaker were
to plead for an extension of our country's global responsibilities, and another for a return to isolationism.   Or suppose succeeding speakers presented opposing viewpoints on
our Vietnam involvement.   In such cases, it would not be

proper for the second speaker to allude to the difference.
That would turn the oratorical contest into a debate, and an
unfair one at that, since the first speaker would be at a dis-
advantage in that he would have no opportunity to reply. Even
such an innocuous statement as "Apparently my friend and I
see this matter differently" would be superfluous, for that
would be apparent to all.

### B.   Adaptation Possible - Off-Campus Audiences

Where orations are delivered to off-campus audiences
in other than contest situations, however, such adaptations
to the speaking situation as making allusions to contrasting
viewpoints, are not only possible, but highly .recommended.
Indeed, in line with my view of using oratory to provide en-
lightenment upon public questions, it is a splendid idea, by
deliberate intention, to arrange appearances for orators with
opposing viewpoints.   Suppose, for example, two orators appeared at a Rotary Club, one favoring and one opposing our
recognition of Red China.   Here, references to one another's
speeches would be perfectly in order, provided each had an
opportunity for further reply.   Moreover, in such appearances, nothing would stand in the way of each making such
other adaptative references as he wished which were relevant to the audience and to the occasion.

While it is difficult to intersperse memorized with
extemporaneous remarks, it is by no means impossible.   The
degree of success varies with the individual orator; some are
more capable of adaptation than others.   Those who are not
adept at doing this should make an effort to cultivate that
ability.   Not to have adaptation would severely limit one's
effectiveness in persuasion both in their student days and
thereafter.

My orators usually welcome outside appearances as
another opportunity to expand the influence of their ideas.
The orator should be so thoroughly conversant with his subject that he can not only make adjustments in presentation
to an outside audience, but also hold his own in a question-
and-answer period following his talk.   I recall two orators
of mine who did just that on a rather extensive scale.   One
is now serving in his fourth term in the U. S. House of
Representatives, and the other is serving in his second college presidency. [6]

III.   DEFENSE OF MEMORIZATION, <u>LIBERALLY</u>
       <u>INTERPRETED</u>
       A.   Reference to Current Events Permissible

The underlined words are not a quibble.  It is entirely possible that we who favor memorization are not too far
apart from the advocates of extemporization.  In my article,
"College Oratory As I See It," in the January, 1954 Forensic,
I wrote:

> The Diem Report [on oratory 1951] reported that
> some coaches object to the necessity of following
> a script because it "precludes any opportunity to
> adapt to a speaking situation."  Of this, Mr. Diem
> said:  "This prompts an editorial question.  Do the
> rules forbid extemporization, adlibbing?  If the
> rules do not forbid it, why should the judge penal-
> ize it, so long as it is effective and keeps within
> the time limit?"  This comment makes sense.  The
> rule requiring that the oration as delivered should
> conform to the manuscript can be and is being
> liberally interpreted.  For example, if a relevant
> news release came out on the day an oration was
> delivered, no judge of my acquaintance would be
> likely to penalize an allusion to that fact.  Such a
> reference might violate the letter, but certainly not
> the spirit of the rule.

Thus, as early as 1954, interpreting as I did the expression
"precludes any opportunity to adapt to a speaking situation,"
to mean a reference to a timely current event, which was a
reasonable interpretation, I favored a liberal interpretation.
Since this was written, such an allusion to a current event
no longer violates even the letter of the law.  For the closing sentence of the first item of the AFA "Code For Contests
in Oratory" specifically reads:  "Extemporaneous reference to
timely events is permissible."  (Emphasis mine)  Thus, depar-
ture from rote memorization at least to that degree has already been liberalized by as prestigious an organization as
the AFA.

       B.   When Memory Falters, Extemporization
            Permissible

In theory, the memorization of an oration is best if it
is word-perfect.  But most often in practice, it is not memo-

rized word-perfectly. What of the situation when the memory
falters? What does the orator do? He does just what any
other speaker would do. He tries to prevent the audience
from knowing that he is floundering and has forgotten, and
most of the time, he succeeds. Who would want to fault
him for that? For this presence of mind, he deserves com-
mendation, not condemnation. The criteria of judging the
contest should hinge upon the orator's communicative ability
and not upon his memorizing ability. If such memory lapses
are detected and noticeably detract from his communicativeness, he should be penalized for that, but not for his loss of
memory per se. If it is so slight that it is not noticed,
more power to him, and why should he be penalized at all?

   Let us take a specific example in the case of an extemporaneous substitution of words in a prepared, memorized speech. We do so from the book by two men who are
acknowledged experts in oratory, Professors Harold A.
Brack and Kenneth G. Hance. Brack took part in IOA oratory, and is now Associate Professor of Speech and Homiletics in the Drew Theological Seminary; Kenneth G. Hance,
now Professor of Speech at Michigan State University, is
not only a successful coach of orators, but served for many
years as Executive Secretary of the IOA, and in 1960 served
as president of the SAA.

> ... [T]he speaker should rephrase ideas when he
> cannot remember particular words or phrases ...
> For example, let us suppose a preacher wishes to
> make the point that we should not just mouth words
> of the Apostles' Creed, but he cannot recall "...
> mouth the words of the Apostles' Creed"; so he re-
> states, or says the same thing in another way, by
> saying, "When we say the Apostles' Creed we
> should not hurry through it without paying atten-
> tion to its meaning."[7]

In this particular example, if you ask me, I prefer the second extemporaneous wording above the original, planned
memorized and forgotten one! But in any case, again, such
a transposer deserves credit for his presence of mind, and
not rebuke. It is a permissible example of what I mean by
favoring memorization, liberally interpreted.

   I do not wish to be misunderstood at this point. I
am referring to allowable slight substitutions and alterations,

not to wholesale insertions of new material.  I recall an instance of wholesale insertions in the State Peace Contest in
Michigan in 1967.  A foreign student had rather belatedly
brought his oration in compliance with the 1200 word limit,
and had submitted a written copy of it.  He survived preliminary eliminations.  In the finals the student's memory became shaky and it was obvious to many that much new and
additional material was included which was not in the submitted copy.  A protest was made, not by me, and his director very properly recommended that his entrant be disqualified.  In his letter to colleague coaches, he explained:

> During the final round, he "blanked" and struggled
> to find his place within the speech.  In so doing he
> inadvertently added much of the material which had
> been cut as well as other material that had never
> been included within the oration.

### C.  When Short Substitutions Come Spontaneously, Extemporization Permissible

Now what of the situations where departures from the
manuscript are made, not so much from loss of memory,
but because at this particular moment in time, a better extemporaneous wording occurs to the orator?  Such changes
no doubt occur in every contest, and are not likely to be detected by the audience, which includes the judges.  But even
if they were, should that be frowned upon and penalized, so
long as the orator does not exceed the word or time limit?
I think not.  Such a thing would be "Picky! Picky!"  Here
again, a liberal attitude--one might combine the two words
and call it "latitude"--should prevail.  And why shouldn't it?
After all, as has been said before, the contest element
should center in, revolve around, the ideas and the manner
of expressing them, not upon how well they are memorized.
Thus, another example of memorization, liberally interpreted.

Through both of the allowable departures from memorization in the B and C captions, memorization still remains
as the desideratum, the goal.  For this particular way of expressing your thoughts has previously been decided upon as
the best and most exact way to express them.  By the latest
IOA definition of an oration, if an orator is exceptionally
gifted in extemporaneous speaking, and prefers that method,
there is no prohibition against it.  Whether extemporization
or memorization is preferable is a matter of opinion.  Pres-

ently we shall compare the two methods.  I just happen to
believe, upon the basis of my experience with orators, that
memorization is best.


## IV.  OBJECTIONS TO MEMORIZATION - NOT VALID

John E. Gow, Director of Forensics at Elmhurst College, Elmhurst, Illinois has written a brilliant, stimulating
and very provocative article critical of memorization in oratorical contests. [8]  It is one of the best I have seen, and
therefore, I would like to use his criticisms as a spring-
board for continuing this examination of memorization.  Two
of his arguments against it are:  "Contemporary speech peda-
gogy emphatically favors the extemporaneous method," and
"Memorization is neither required nor often possible in public speaking as actually experienced."  The first of these
statements is quite correct.  I would have a few reserva-
tions about the second, remembering that the Rev. Harry
Emerson Fosdick practically memorized his sermons, and,
incidentally also used a manuscript in the pulpit.  But in my
view, the assumption that memorization in oratory, to be acceptable, must meet those two tests, is not.  They are non
sequiturs.  They are not proper criteria to determine whether or not we should memorize an oration for a contest.

We must take into account the differences in temperament and memorizing ability among oratory candidates.
Speech teachers in class do stress extemporaneous speaking
as the preferred and more commonly used type of speaking,
for both within and out of the classroom.  I do myself, and
strongly so.  In none of my fundamentals of speech classes
do I require a memorized speech.  I warn students against
it, and spend at least a half class hour in an early session
extolling the virtues of extemporaneous speaking.  I advocate it as the most useful not only during their school years,
but in the years beyond.

But it does not follow that, therefore, memorized
speaking should be avoided for an oratorical contest.  Memorized speaking is not for everyone; it is for superior students who wish to take part in a specific, time-honored
form of persuasive speaking known as an oratorical contest.
Undoubtedly, there are many speech students in college who
do not "come out for oratory" either because they feel in-
capable of memorizing, or simply because oratory is too
much hard work and does not appeal to them.  What is

wrong with retaining both kinds of contests, the extemporaneous speaking contest with extemporaneous speaking, and the
oratorical contest with memorized speaking?    Each has its
distinctive advantages and disadvantages.

        Gow's alternative recommendations to memorization
in oratory are:   extemporaneously-prepared persuasion, and
manuscript speaking.   It is admitted that in memorized speaking, one must guard constantly against the fear of forgetting,
against thinking ahead of wherever one is in the actual delivery, with a resulting lack of spontaneity.   For this to happen to the orator with a memorized oration is an ever-pres-
ent possibility.   In fact, it is an open secret among oratory
coaches that the thing to strive for in delivery is to have
the oration, although memorized, appear to be extemporaneous.   That can be done; that is being done.   An orator can
deliver a memorized speech without merely repeating words.
He can be thinking of what the words mean as he speaks
them.   He can create "the illusion of the first time."

        How do I know?   A simple pragmatic test--all my
life I have seen it done.   The dangers can be overcome because they have been overcome.   True enough, occasionally
a contestant forgets, noticeably hesitates, even stops.   But
within my experience, such cases are rare.   I have noticed
very few total memory breakdowns.   With my own orators,
I have had only one case of an orator forgetting in a major
oratorical contest.   No oral indication was given by him
that he had forgotten, but his more volatile and almost rau-
cous delivery plainly indicated it to all.


V.   COMPARISON OF EXTEMPORANEOUS AND
     MEMORIZED ORATORY

        In spite of the undoubted value of extemporaneous
speaking, which is conceded, let us not get carried away
with extemporaneously-prepared persuasion.   It, too, has
its disadvantages.   Let us compare the situation facing the
extemporaneous and the memorizing orator.   We'll call the
one Mr. E and the other Mr. M.   Both E and M, it is a-
greed, ought always to be thinking of the meaning of the
words as they speak them.   It is alleged, and most likely is
true, that E is more apt than M to do that, because E
doesn't have the added burden of keeping the memorized
words in mind.   But M does, and while at times he may be
able to speak effectively, at other times M may say the

words in a desultory, mechanical, rote fashion.  While E is cerebrating every minute, M may be diverting part of his energy to remembering his oration.  Chalk one up for E!

On the other hand, M has prepared a speech with prior planning in composition, with precision of language in word-choice and illustrations, saying exactly what he wants to say.  Moreover, he has practiced and rehearsed many times over the exact way he will deliver the oration.  E, however, does not have that advantage.  There will be variations in the content and delivery among different renditions of the speech; in fact, that is one of the virtues claimed for it.  Without a script, he has to depend upon the inspiration of the moment for his words.  At one time, he may be perking on all six cylinders, his ideas come flowing fast and free without hesitation, and he speaks them with vim and vigor.  But not always, for sometimes the mood may not be upon him.  Chalk one up for M!

M most usually has a word limit. [9]  His words are all selected, and he does not have to worry about timing. E, however, without a pre-planned speech, necessarily has to have a time limit.  By reason of the virtue of flexibility claimed for extemporization, there would be variations in the content and wording from one time to the next, with the different renditions consuming different amounts of time.  He is confronted with the added hazard of staying within the time limit.  He has no assurance that he will always reach the most effective climactic portions of his speech within the allotted time.  Sometimes he does, and that's good.  But even when he does, he no doubt has been worried about it.  Sometimes he doesn't, and that's bad.  Chalk up another for M!

Incidentally, if E in such a case went over-time, unless there was a clear-cut prior provision for penalties for over-time, it could result in ill-will among contestants and coaches which I think we should avoid at all costs.  For myself, I am inclined to be charitable for I believe timing to the split second is terribly artificial.  Perhaps a grace period of at least one full minute should be allowed.


## VI.    COMPARISON OF MANUSCRIPT AND MEMORIZED ORATORY
### A.   Popularity of Reading from a Manuscript

The second alternative to memorization suggested by Gow is manuscript speaking.  Let us take a look at it.  One

is tempted to dismiss it peremptorily as a suitable substitute
for memorization upon the simple ground that it is reading,
and not speaking. But it is undeniably true that the practice
of reading from a manuscript has been frequently done in the
past, and is being done in the present, even in contest oratory. An early textbook on oratory revealed that

> Those tremendous sermons of Jonathan Edwards,
> which moved his Puritan hearers to cling to the
> pews and pillars of the church and cry out for
> mercy, were read without a gesture and almost
> without a glance of the eye away from the manu-
> script .... Lincoln's Gettysburg speech was, like-
> wise, carefully written out and read from the man-
> uscript. [10]

Reading from a manuscript came into more common usage
with the advent of radio and television where there is need
to observe exact time limits, and where frequently a prior
script needed to be submitted for examination. The practice is also the expected thing in the addresses of a President, whose every word must be weighed lest an inadvertent
slip of the tongue or an ambiguous expression which is mis-
interpreted, should set off a global war.

Robert Scott, Director of Forensics at the University
of Minnesota, and author of the section "Oratory in Interscholastic Contests," in the Contest Speaking Manual, [11] as
early as 1954 wrote "Most carefully worked out and worded
speeches in our society are delivered from manuscript."[12]
He argued convincingly for the use of that method in oratory.
In a survey conducted by Donald W. Klopf, of the University
of Hawaii, involving 39 oratorical or manuscript speaking
contests examined, 66% permitted use of the manuscript,
28% expected no notes or manuscript but memorization only,
and 6% allowed reading only. [13] This indicates a considerable decline in the popularity of memorization, and a cor-
responding rise in the popularity of manuscript reading.
There is a possibility that this may in part be due to the
fact that it allows participation of orators in early-season
tournaments. My own time-consuming method of preparing
for contests is such that we have rarely taken part in such
early-season tournaments.

B.   Reading from a Manuscript - Advantages and
     Disadvantages

One good quality reading from a manuscript and the
memorized speech have in common.   Both have prior preparation in composition which can achieve the kind of literary excellence which evokes appreciation from the audience.
The chief objection to a speech that is read is that it most
usually sounds as if it were.   That is to say, the "reading"
speaker, perhaps by reason of needing to keep his eyes
glued to the manuscript, often speaks in a desultory, life-
less fashion.   It just doesn't sound like talk.   There is lack-
ing a flexibility and range in the pitch and rate of the voice,
resulting in an ineffectiveness in oral delivery.   All too often, the reading fails to recreate, in voice and attitude, the
full emotional impact the words possessed when first composed.   It must be acknowledged that some readers can and
do surmount these handicaps, and that, therefore, reading
from a manuscript is not to be avoided at all times by
everybody. [14]

However, the manuscript speaker is further handicapped in his lack of appropriate gestures.   Let's face it--
is not the first reaction of an audience to a written manuscript a groan?   Note how the attention and interest perks
up when the speaker departs from his manuscript to interpolate some remarks.   The improved directness of the speaker is immediately favorably detected by the audience from
his manner of speaking.


C.   On Balance, Memorization Preferred

The memorized oration does permit eye- contact, more
so than the manuscript speech.   It is true that memorizing
is difficult for some, but this is remediable.   Assiduous application of the seven suggestions presently to be made for
overcoming that difficulty, will help.   In that connection,
Professor Henry L. Ewbank, University of Wisconsin, President of the SAA in 1934, asks a pertinent question, "Did you
ever hear a play director object to memorized lines?"[15]
Note, too, this excerpt:

Many will object to my statement that oratory at
its best is written out and learned by heart.   And
yet this is obvious from the fact that speeches of
great orators have been preserved to us through-

out history.  There were no stenographers in
Athens to take down what Demosthenes said.  And
Cicero himself declared that "careful and assiduous composition ... is the true source of the admiration and applause that is bestowed on eminent
speakers." ...  To jump a long way across the
ages, Mark Twain said the same thing: "A person
who is to make a speech at any time or anywhere
on any topic whatever owes it to himself and to
his audience to write the speech out and memorize
it."16

The primary charge leveled against memorization is
a lack of directness.  There is an expression which has
stayed with me all my life since my first foray into forensics in 1916 as a high school debater: "plausible at first
sight, but ill-founded upon close inspection."  It seems so
apropos of this charge of a lack of spontaneity.  On the one
hand, it would appear that memorization could result in a
tendency to be indirect.  But my experience with my own
orators does not indicate it has been a major problem.  In
such few cases where it has occurred, the evil is not an
inherent one which is not remediable by much practice and
rehearsal.  So my answer to that allegation must be: "'Tain't
necessarily so."  Perhaps I have been influenced by the writings of a pioneer in our profession, James Albert Winans,
Professor of Public Speaking at Cornell University, one of
the founders and second president of SAA, and have subconsciously transmitted those views to my orators.  On this very
point of spontaneity, Winans writes:

Some hold that a speech committed to memory cannot be delivered with spontaneity; but observation
proves that this is not true.  It has been said concerning the practice of George William Curtis, one
of the best speakers of the last generation: "He
practised that perfect memorization which has the
virtues of extemporization without its faults."
Higginson tells this story of Wendell Phillips:
"I remember that after his Phi Beta Kappa oration,
in which he had so carried away a conservative and
critical audience that they found themselves applaud-
ing tyrannicide before they knew it, I said to him,
'This could not have been written out beforehand,'
and he said, 'It is already in type at the Adverti-
ser office.'  I could not have believed it."
It is all a matter of re-creating the thought, and

it is a poor thought that cannot be thought more
than once ... The lecturers of the Lyceum and
Chautauqua platforms may repeat their addresses
hundreds of times, and yet deliver them with
freshness.[17]

But it may be said that the foregoing testimony is
ancient history, and does not take into account that times
have changed. Consider, then, this following excerpt from
a recent publication by Donald W. Klopf and Carroll P.
Lahman, both of whom have written extensively in the field
of forensics. While the reference is to a memorized debate
speech rather than to an oration, the point of it is not thereby invalidated.

This essential element of communicativeness can
be had even in a memorized speech, provided the
debater does not perform parrot-like but thinks vitally while he is speaking.[18]

In summation, then, because competent authorities
agree that memorized speaking has been effectively done in
the past, and is being done in the present, but mostly because this has been confirmed by my own experience during
a 40-year period of working with orators, I cast my vote
for the retention of memorization in oratory.

VII.   FOUR HINTS FOR MASTERING THE FEAR
       OF FORGETTING

Recognizing that some memory lapses are inevitable,
I feel it is only proper that I should present a few hints on
how to act, feel, and conduct oneself when they do occur.

Hint #1 - Keep cool, calm, and collected. In contest
situations, many of your fellow contestants, and certainly the
judges, are likely to be sympathetic. They have no doubt at
some time or other been in your situation. I commend to
you particularly this helpful and reassuring sentence from
Professor Horace G. Rahskopf, of the University of Washington: "Forgetting may be an embarrassment but is no crime."[19]

Hint #2 - Many textbook writers, writing on memory
lapses, agree that the pause which to you may seem an eter-
nity, is not so thought of by the audience. For all they know,
you may be pausing deliberately for effect. Keep that in

mind.

Hint #3 - Indulge in physical activity. Changing the stance and moving often reestablishes lines of communication and will get you on the right track again.

Hint #4 - Repeat some of your last sentences deliberately. If you have observed the first hint, the lines of association may be reestablished. As far as the audience is concerned, they may well think the repetition is deliberate for the sake of emphasis!

## VIII.   SEVEN SUGGESTIONS ON HOW TO MEMORIZE

Here are some suggestions on how to memorize. These may also be of help to those who take part in high school Oral Declamation contests.

1.   Tackle the task of memorizing only when the mind is fresh, never when fatigued.

2.   Start memorizing early and spread the time over several days.

3.   Memorize your speech as a whole, never sentence by sentence. Memory is a matter of association. The last word of every sentence, like the cues in a play, should suggest the first word of the next.

4.   Concentrate hard on the meaning of the words and ideas as you memorize.

5.   Do your reading and repeating of the material to be memorized out loud. Thus, you employ the use of both the eyes and the ears.

6.   In your reading and repeating, always imagine an audience present.

7.   Finally, this is the most important and an exceptionally good bit of advice which should be taken to heart:

The best insurance against forgetting is "overlearning," or "learning beyond the point when it can barely be reproduced." The best way to forget is not to review." (Italics mine)[20]

## IX.   METHODOLOGY VS. MESSAGE - A BOLD SUGGESTION

These closing personal words are to my young readers and aspiring orators.  The fact that you are reading these words is an indication you must be interested in oratory.  Do not ever lose that interest.  This chapter concerned methodology, by what method an oration can best be delivered.  But always remember that the message of the orator, what he has to say, is far more important than by what method it is delivered.

In this chapter, I have argued for memorization, liberally interpreted, and presented reasons.  Not all readers may be convinced.  That is not too important.  I make no pretense of having said the final word.  We ought all to be agreed upon the value of a continuation and expansion of oratorical contests, whatever method is used.

I now venture to make a bold suggestion.  In any kind of forensic contest, so that all contestants may perform under uniform conditions, we shall always need some rules and regulations, such as time or word limits, and limitations on quoted matter.  But I wonder:  do we really need to impose any limitations at all on methodology of delivery?  We do not do so in the companion forensic activity of debate.  Would perhaps more students be attracted to oratory if each orator were permitted to choose his own method of delivery--speak from memorization, extemporaneously, or reading from a manuscript?  Except for impromptu speaking, which is wholly unsuited to oratory, these three methods are after all the only other methods of delivering any speech.  Already extemporaneously-prepared oratory and reading from a manuscript have been experimented with.  Because memorization has been the predominant method used in the first century of educational oratory is no reason it need always remain so. Who knows what the future holds?  Perhaps in the next century reading from a manuscript may become the more acceptable method.

We should be under no illusions that removing all restrictions on the methodology of delivery will solve all our problems.  During the experimentation period, judges may be inclined to harbor a prejudice favoring the method they now think is best.  Even so, the experiment is well worth trying:  first, because winning should not be all that impor-

tant and, for the orator, should be offset by the satisfaction
of having gotten across a message that just had to be said,
and by the method in which he preferred to say it; second,
because I have enough faith in the intellectual maturity of
educator-judges to be open toward changing their minds about
methods of delivery.   Any person who has not upon occasion
in life changed his mind upon some important matter lacks
the rudiments of education, and has no business being a teacher. [21]   So, let us abandon all restrictions on methodology
and let each orator "do his own thing."

## Notes

1.     A favorite exam question in my University of California
       Far East Program classes was taken from one of
       their textbooks, which said: "We are Old Fogeys
       from the moment when we become unable to accept
       any new fact, any new idea, which would necessitate
       changing our established habits of thought." [The
       question:] "Name and explain at least one example
       from your own life within the past two years, to es-
       tablish that in your judgment, you are NOT an Old
       Fogey in that sense of the term!" I received some
       illuminating answers.   A. E. Mander, Logic For
       The Millions, Philosophical Library, Inc., 15 East
       40th Street, New York, 1947, p. 47.

2.     W. Roy Diem, Ohio Wesleyan University, "Factors of
       Effectiveness in Oratory," WO-1951, p. 6.

3.     Howard L. Runion, Essentials of Effective Public Speak-
       ing, Longmans, Green and Co., New York, 1948, p.
       85.   Used by permission of David McKay Company,
       Inc.

4.     Donald Hayworth, An Introduction to Public Speaking,
       rev. ed., The Ronald Press Company, New York,
       1941, pp. 245-46.

5.     WO-1951, p. 6.

6.     Representative Guy Vander Jagt, and Arend D. Lubbers,
       former president, Central College, Pella, Iowa, pre-
       sent president, Grand Valley State College, Allendale,
       Michigan.

7.  Harold A. Brack, and Kenneth G. Hance, Public Speak-
    ing and Discussion For Religious Leaders, Prentice-
    Hall, Inc., Englewood Cliffs, N. J., 1961, p. 42.
    By permission of Prentice-Hall, Inc.  This example
    struck my fancy because my memory is atrocious.
    In reciting the Apostles' Creed in church, I find my-
    self mumbling along a syllable or two after others
    and would probably falter in a solo rendition of it.

8.  "Re-examining Contest Speaking," Forensic, January,
    1968, pp. 3-5.  See also Donald N. Dedmon, "The
    Extemporaneous Method and Speech Contests," CSSJ,
    November, 1964, pp. 279-84.

9.  True in MISL, IOA, and PKD contests.

10. Clark Mills Brink, The Making of an Oration, A. C.
    McClurg Co., Chicago, 1913, p. 197.

11. Dr. William E. Buys, Western Michigan University,
    editor, and others.  National Textbook Corporation,
    Lincolnwood, Illinois, 1964, pp. 1-32.

12. "Is Oratory Dead?" Forensic, March, 1954, pp. 74-75.
    An answer to this article appeared later, suggesting
    that better and more personalized subjects was a
    greater need than to change the type of speaking in
    oratory.  E. L. Pross, Texas Christian University,
    "More Probing of the Cadaver," Forensic, January,
    1955, pp. 53-54.

13. "Tournament Competition in the Individual Speaking
    Events," JAFA, January, 1966, p. 35.

14. Practical Public Speaking, The Macmillan Company,
    New York, 1954, p. 305.

15. Platform and Laboratory Projects For Speech I, Harper
    & Brothers, New York, 1929, p. 35.

16. Max Eastman, "The Lost Art of Oratory," Saturday
    Review, March 6, 1954, p. 11.  Copyright 1954 by
    The Saturday Review Associates, Inc.

17. James Albert Winans, Public Speaking, rev. ed., The
    Century Co., New York, 1926, pp. 35-36.

18.   Coaching and Directing Forensics, National Textbook
      Corporation, Skokie, Illinois, 1967, p. 157.

19.   Basic Speech Improvement, Harper & Row, New York,
      1965, p. 208.

20.   Giles Wilkeson Gray and Waldo W. Braden, Public
      Speaking: Principles and Practice, Harper & Bro-
      thers, New York, 1951, p. 470.

21.   "Sometimes I suspect that many who boast too loudly
      of having the courage of their convictions in reality
      may have little more than the cowardice of their
      prejudices." William Schrier, "Decalogue For an
      Ideal Citizen," Vital Speeches, January 1, 1963, p.
      189.

Chapter XII

# THE DELIVERY OF THE ORATION

An effective oration requires not only excellent composition but also superior delivery. One should strive for perfection in both areas. For there is no point in having nothing of real importance to say, and saying it superbly. Nor of having a fine composition with challenging ideas and delivering it lackadaisically.

I. OPENING IMPRESSIONS
   A. Wearing Apparel

In one sense, the delivery of your oration begins before a word is uttered. Your wearing apparel should not be gaudy or in any way draw attention to it. For men, a dark suit, white shirt, dark tie and socks and well-shined black shoes are acceptable. For women, excessive make-up, jewelry or anything likely to distract attention away from the speech, should be avoided. If you are seated on the platform, you should be aware that at all times you are under public scrutiny. Do nothing to draw unfavorable attention to yourself. Auditors just cannot keep from sizing you up, forming impressions about you. Your job at this point is to see to it that the impressions are favorable rather than otherwise.

   B. Poise - Control

It is quite understandable that you may be a trifle on edge. To say that you are not likely to be a bit nervous is highly unrealistic. The best of speakers testify to a bit of apprehension in facing an audience. After all, it is almost a sacred act you are indulging in--having the opportunity of leading the thought of fellow human-beings and soliciting their undivided attention during the time you speak. But try to avoid giving the impression that you are unduly worried or ill-at-ease. And the best way to do that is not to be. Avoid

169

an "I'll do this if it kills me" attitude. Your concern at
this stage is not the total elimination of fear, which may be
too strong a word, but rather to get that "fear feeling" under
intelligent control.

One way to do that is to be thoroughly "sold" on the
worth of your message. Richard Storrs, a brilliant preacher
of the latter part of the nineteenth century, writing almost a
century ago, said, "Always carry with you on the platform a
sense of the consequence which may depend upon your full
and faithful presentation of the truth."[1] The look on your
countenance should be a pleasant one of joyous anticipation.
Now, at long last, after all the hard work of the last few
weeks in composing and rehearsing your speech, all that is
now about to bear fruit. The opportunity to get others to
feel as strongly about your subject as you do, has now arrived.

Friends and well-intentioned well-wishers may have
approached you just prior to the contest, and in effect, urged
you to do your very best to win. They mean well, but take
these remarks in stride. Do not let them disturb or distract you. Your mind should be upon your message and the
audience, not upon the contest. Sit with an air of pleasant
eager anticipation until the chairman calls your name. If
you are not on the platform, but must come up from among
the audience, walk deliberately, creating neither the impression that you are going to a fire or a funeral. Acknowledge
the chairman orally, or by a nod. Saying "ladies and gen-
tlemen" is optional, depending upon the degree of formality
of the occasion. Poise, control are the key words at this
stage.

All of us are creatures of moods. There may come
times when you have to deliver your oration, but you just
are not in the mood for it. That happens to everyone in
public life who does any speaking. What do you do then?
That's easy--just force the mood. Apply the time-tested
James-Lange theory of emotions which in essence says, in
layman's language, that if you go through all the physical
motions that accompany a psychological mood, that mood
will come.

C. Pause

You should pause slightly before beginning your oration. To do so will allow your audience to observe your

real, not feigned, self-possession and poise. A pause gains
attention and gives both you and your audience a chance to
size each other up. Those opening words of your oration
are very important. Your oration may have that special
kind of attention-catching introduction which requires undivided audience attention. In a judged situation, if you are not
the first speaker, you should wait quietly until all known
judges are through sorting their notes and critiques, so that
each gives you attention. During such an interval, do not
look petulant, nor be a "sober-sides." By all means, avoid
the fight image. Even though your oration subject may be a
"shocker," one in which you may have to win over a hostile
audience, your attitude toward them should never be bellig-
erent. During this pause, you should take the attitude of
Thurston, the magician, and say inwardly to yourself, or
think it: "I love my audience! I love my audience!"[2] And
believe mightily at the same time that they love you, too.
For the average audience, and the judges as well, want you
to succeed and to do well. Noticeably to do less than your
best is really an embarrassment to them as well as to yourself.

I have lingered on this caption of opening impressions
because in oratory especially, "first impressions last." Delivery has many aspects, and many excellent texts are on
the market treating of it. It is beyond the scope of this
work to cover all details. I shall content myself with covering four Fundamentals of Delivery, and relate those to the
oration. Let's categorize them under the headings of: 1) distinctness; 2) directness; 3) alertness; and 4) earnestness.


II.   FUNDAMENTALS OF DELIVERY
      A.   Distinctness

By distinctness, is meant primarily that the utterance
be loud enough to be heard. This is elemental. Something
not heard cannot possibly be understood. In many orations,
especially in climactic portions, you may want to get considerable contrast in the voice, from a loud orotund tone to
an aspirate whisper. But never so low as to become inaud-
ible.

While "distinctness" may not be the exact term, we
include here impeccable pronunciation and enunciation. Oratory is speaking at its very best, a model of perfection in
the art. There is simply no excuse for a mispronounced

word in an oration.   For the pronunciation of a word can be
looked up ahead of time, and improper pronunciation preven-
ted.   Nor is there any excuse for mumbling or sloppy enunciation such as the use of "kin," "git," "gonna," "becuz,"
nor for swallowing of syllables as in "prob'ly," "guvment,"
nor for being imprecise in hitting consonantal sounds, as in
"awwiz," "hunnert," "dint," or for running words together
as in "innisway," and "zhawlno."   Of course, overenuncia-
tion, a pedantic over-precise type of speech is equally bad,
and for the same reason.   It calls attention to itself, and
by that token away from the thought being expressed.   Enunciation should not intrude upon the consciousness of the audience from either direction.   It should be neither too sloven-
ly nor too pedantic.   The average person, not wanting his
enunciation to appear stilted, allows himself to become care-
less, and goes to the opposite extreme, and makes it sloppy.
But the speech of the high school or college orator should
be above average.   In a contest particularly, the conscious
concern of the audience should be exclusively focused upon
the speaker's message.   It should not be distracted by the
improper manner of delivering it.

If an orator wins a local contest, and is guilty of
these enunciation faults, some good stiff drills are in order
before he goes on to further competition.   New habit pat-
terns need to be formed, and that takes time.   For example,
a "becuz-gonna" type person should be made to say, at different times during the day, and at least 100 times a day:
"I am going to say 'because' 'because' 'because' is correct."
One who habitually says "are" when he means "our" would
profit from repeating "Are our oars here?"[3] until he is a-
ware of the distinction.

## B.   Directness
### 1.   Eyes

Directness manifests itself primarily through the eyes
and the voice.   It requires direct eye-to-eye contact between
speaker and hearer.   Notes or manuscript break the circuit.
A furtive, hurried look at them is like turning a light switch
on and off.   Eye contact serves a double purpose: first, to
see to it that the orator talks directly to his audience as opposed, let us say, to looking out the window; second, to permit the orator to search out the eyes of the auditors to determine how what he is saying is registering with them.   Anyone who has ever addressed an audience of blind students

realizes how dependent a speaker is upon the answering light
in the faces of his hearers.  Speech is communication--that
implies two parties.  It is not a soliloquy, but a colloquy.

Each person must seek out his own best method of
attaining eye directness.  In giving high school commencement speeches, I made it a practice, while seated on the
platform, to seek out some especially friendly faces--proud
parents and fond grandparents--and then made a special effort to "contact" them during the talk.[4]  In an oratorical
contest, where it is known who the judges are and where
they are seated, I advise orators to contact them particularly.

## 2.  Voice

By directness through the voice, we mean a conversational, communicative quality.  Unfortunately, this expres-
sion--"conversational"--is often misunderstood.  Sometimes,
it may mean on the level of a friendly chat.  But not always.
Conversation does not preclude animation and vigor.  James
H. McBurney, for many years Dean of the School of Speech
at Northwestern University, laid this misunderstanding to
rest rather well.  In his early years as manager of the
Michigan High School Forensic Association, he wrote:

> Much has been written in recent years about "the
> conversational basis of public speech" and many
> people, I find, understand this to be an endorse-
> ment of a quiet, greatly restrained, inhibited type
> of speaking in which any show of emotion or ac-
> tivity or force is very much tabooed.  Nothing is
> farther from the real meaning of this conception
> of public speech.  The conversational basis of pub-
> lic speech is meant to emphasize the importance
> of directness, communicativeness, and naturalness
> in vocal intonation and inflection in public speech.
> A speaker can be perfectly conversational and make
> the auditorium ring with forceful, enthusiastic ut-
> terance [Emphasis mine].  He can be perfectly con-
> versational and yet very much alive and animated
> in public speech.[5]

On the matter of voice and directness, it is best not
to give conscious attention to the use of your voice while
you are speaking.  What needs attention in improving the use

of your voice should be worked on in rehearsals prior to delivery, before the contest.   By that time, the suggestions
which follow should have become so much a part of yourself
that they are acted upon subconsciously.

By all means, don't "play with" your voice. It thwarts
directness, calls attention to itself.  Remember, the voice is
merely a vehicle for stirring up thought.  We have all heard
orators with excellent sonorous tones who seemed to be saying to us: "See how beautiful and mellifluous my voice is!"

Strive for variety in voice-- in pitch, time, quality--
in keeping with the exact shade of meaning you are attempt-
ing to convey.  In rate, for example, one aspect of time,
avoid going so fast as to create the impression you are
much more anxious to "get your oration over with" than to
"get it over."  Adjust the rate to the meaning of the words
being uttered.  Some words may require impressive prolongation of vowel sounds; others may need to be said "tripping-
ly off the tongue."  Adjust the loudness to the size of the
room.  In contests, the size of the room often varies between preliminary and final rounds, and this requires voice
adjustment.

Keep in mind the principle of reserve power. Remember, "All force is no force."  Anyone who creates the impression that he is using his maximum amount of force does
not make a good impression.  Make us as auditors feel that
you have not completely lost control, and that you are still
in charge.  Better to have the audience think: "Wow! what
if he had really let out!" than to have them say: "He just
ranted and raved!"

Do not overlook the importance of pause in oratory.
In rehearsing with orators, I often say: "Pause is more
than the mere cessation of utterance--you are still talking
while you are pausing." And you really are.  You ask a
question toward the end of an oration--you pause while a-
waiting an inward response from the auditors-- all the while
with your eyes directed piercingly toward them as if seeking
out their answer.  Let one idea sink in, especially if it's
an important one, before starting another.  Leonardo Da Vinci
is reputed to have said:  "When I pause longest, I make the
most telling strokes with my brush!"[6]

C.  Alertness

In this caption, we include such matters as posture, movement, and gesture.  Those who take part in oratorical contests already possess some gifts in public speaking so that a coach does not have to start from scratch.  But if you as a coach have a "passion for perfection," and imbue your charges with the same zeal, there are few students who do not need any further work in delivery.  So we make a few observations on three subdivisions of Alertness.

### 1.  Posture

Posture is the first thing an audience notices.  It may seem like a contradiction in terms, but the best posture is that which is not noticed at all.  For when an audience does notice posture, it is usually an improper one.  For example, when you slouch, or stand awkwardly with feet wide apart, weight equally distributed on the two feet, then as the orator you are in trouble.  For to the extent that your audience pays attention to that, by just that extent are they kept from giving full attention to what you are saying.

There is no one single correct way to stand for everybody.  For some, it's the hardest thing in the world just to stand in front of an audience with both hands hanging loosely at their sides.  I often joke about this in fundamentals of speech classes and say that measurements have been taken of a person's hands, from the wrists to the finger-tips, while seated, and of that same person's hands while speaking.  And the astonishing result is that the measurements are identical!  In other words, your hands aren't really tennis racquets, they just feel that way!  Practice, practice, practice, and more practice, standing in a comfortable position for you, hands at your sides, can get you to feel perfectly at home.  President Richard Nixon, even from periodicals in general opposed to many of his policies, receives plaudits for his ability to stand in a good position, and without resort to notes, in his press conferences.[7]

### 2.  Movement

The most usual movement in oratory occurs between paragraphs.  Just as there is an indentation at the beginning of each paragraph of a written composition which is helpful to the eye-appeal of a reader, so too, for the auditor you need "oral punctuation" at changes of thought.   To allow for such forward movement, I usually advise an orator to begin about a yard and a half back from the first row of seats in a classroom to allow for it, and slightly farther back when speaking from a raised platform.   The purpose is to allow room for the needed forward movement at important points in the speech.   Incidentally, I do not go along with those who say the speaker should never retreat.   Some spoken material readily lends itself to a backward movement.

You are a human being, not a statue.   Aside from between paragraphs, you should move wherever in the speech you sense the urge to do so.   But be sure the impulse is there and that it is not just a mechanical, planned movement. That would be exhibitionistic and distract from the message. One secret of proper, meaningful movement is to <u>move and talk simultaneously</u>.

I was amused at what Max Eastman said in an article "The Lost Art of Oratory": "The amount of energy wasted trying to keep awake at public meetings would turn all the dynamos in the country."[8]   It may be that it is because I love oratory, but I cannot believe this is true of oratory contests.   For an oration is chock-full of vigorous ideas which need and usually have the accompaniment of physical vigor and movement.   We as auditors need to be kept awake. If there is no movement, we become apathetic; if there is movement, we empathize.   We tend to act as the speaker does.   Have you not found yourself in the football stands, trying to help out the fullback when it's fourth down and inches to go?   Of course, a speaker can use too much movement.   In that case, you go away from the speech saying: "He just wore me out."

### 3.   Gesture

By gesture, we mean any movement of the head, hands, shoulders, in fact, any part of the body, even the lift of an eye-brow, which emphasizes, re-enforces an idea in the oration.   Occasionally a student in speech class will say: "It is not natural for me to gesture."   Often the protest is accompanied with vigorous head-bobbing and arm-waving which belies the statement.   Any person in life, wholly apart from a public speech situation, who is gripped with an idea and engaged in animated conversation, cannot keep from gesturing to reenforce his thoughts.

Most contest speakers already have an acquaintance
with the various kinds and purposes of gesture so that it is
not necessary to go into specific details here.   The impulse
to communicate is the basis for the use of gestures.   For
without that impulse, the gesture has nothing to justify it.
My experience in working with orators, as differentiated from
those in required speech classes, is that they just can't talk
without gesturing.   In that respect, they are like the man
that Professor Robert Oliver, for many years Chairman of
the Speech Department at Pennsylvania State University, writes
about:

> A story is told of two ordinarily voluble gentlemen
> who were walking in the park one 'cold winter eve-
> ning without exchanging a word.   Finally, one of
> them said, "Well, let's talk."   "No," replied the
> other, snuggling his hands deeper into his pockets.
> "Too cold."[9]

However, occasionally one does encounter an orator who has
picked up some awkward habits of gesture technique.   In such
cases, some good stiff drills and plenty of practice usually
succeed in overcoming the bad habits and forming good ones.
In our treatment of delivery rehearsals in the next chapter,
we shall indicate some of the methods used in working on
gestures with an orator.

### D.   Earnestness
#### 1.   Supreme Importance

One hesitates to make choices as to the most important item in the delivery of an oration.   But if compelled to
make a choice, I would rate first by a wide margin the quality of earnestness.   That's why I saved it for last!   It is
truly the sine qua non ("without which there is none") of oratory.   You should have a message, believe in it thoroughly,
welcome every opportunity to get others to share that belief.
And all of this motivated primarily, not to win a contest or
a medal, but to advance the cause of human betterment for
the life of all of us on this planet.

### 2.   Absorption in Message

Earnestness is truly the one indispensable ingredient
of an orator's power.   Absorption with your cause will tran-
scend your fears.   The most effective orator just has no
time to think of them.   He is too absorbed with his message,
and with his effort to have his audience share his concern.
Student orations deal with political reform, social injustice,
religious concerns, and international problems of the first
magnitude.   These subjects should grip him to the point
where he has no energy left to think of himself and his fears.

In a contest, if an orator is fired up in this way and
has that motivation, the audience may well find that feeling
transmitted to them.   Since the audience includes the judges,
they are likely to be too entranced to be on the lookout for
a list of things to criticize.   Many times when serving as a
single critic judge in oratory, I have said in orally reporting results to the audience:   "This person won because I was
just too absorbed and thrilled to take notes," and then pro-
ceeded off the cuff to cite its many excellencies.

All these matters of voice, gesture, and others, are
simply means to the grand end of conviction, and not the end
itself.   Compared to earnestness, they are mere peccadilloes.
In fact, while it is by no means recommended, the earnest
student orator may even at times violate accepted rules of
pitch, force, emphasis.   For as Sam Walter Foss, the author of the well-known "The House by the Side of the Road,"
and the Edgar Guest of his day, says in one of his rhymes,
"The Big Four and the Little Man":   "The man with genius
in his soul, All formulas o'er-reaches."   This may sound
like heresy coming from a coach of oratory, but they're my
sentiments.

### III.   CLOSING ADVICE
####    A.   Feel Your Speech

In my own coaching, when all our work together in
composition and delivery rehearsal is over, and we begin to
taper off, my usual last words to the contestant prior to a
contest, are:   "Now remember some of these points we've
worked on if you can, but above all things, remember to
feel your speech and to get it over at the moment of utterance.   Compared to earnestness, all these other little points
about posture, poise, and pause don't amount to much."   I

frankly like to get the orator to the point where he makes his listeners totally oblivious to their surroundings, making them forget that they are present at a contest. Of course the likelihood of that happening often is remote. But if that is your aim, you <u>will</u> achieve it on occasion.


### B.   Leave-Taking

There are no doubt many equally good methods for taking leave of the audience when the oration is over. For what it's worth, here is what I recommend to my orators: 1) indicate by a genial, sincere smile that you are through; 2) draw back whichever foot is forward, and at the same time coordinate that movement with a slight nod of the head from the neck, not from the waist which would be more appropriate for an artist's performance; and 3) draw the other foot back also, and then move to your seat.


### C.   "Forget It"

You, the orator, have now finished delivering your oration. If you have really had the quality of earnestness, you are probably mentally and physically exhausted. You may possibly think of some things about the delivery which could have been improved. Don't brood about it. Forget it; that's now in the past and the past is like sawdust, and you can't saw sawdust. Remember that earnestness, like charity, "covers a multitude of sins."


### Notes

1.   Richard Storrs, Speaking Without Notes, Dodd Mead and Co., 1875.

2.   "Thurston had a genuine interest in people .... He declared he never stepped in front of the footlights without saying to himself over and over: 'I love my audience. I love my audience.' Ridiculous? Absurd? You are privileged to think about it anything you like. I am merely passing it on to you without comment, a recipe used by one of the most famous magicians of all time." Dale Carnegie, How To Win Friends and Influence People, Association Press, 1935, pp. 86-87. Copyright 1936 by Dale Carnegie--

renewed (c) 1964 by Dorothy Carnegie. Reprinted
by permission of Simon & Schuster, Inc.

3.    "The minister of a church in Wyckoff, N. J. told the
      sexton to put on the bulletin board his sermon topic
      for the following Sunday: "Are Ministers Cracking
      Up?" The sexton looked puzzled but did as he was
      told and put up the letters to announce: "Our Min-
      ister's Cracking Up." Reader's Digest, June, 1967,
      p. 108; contributed by William W. Bowyer.

4.    For an example of teaching eye-contact, see my article
      "A Goodwill Visit to Six German Universities," CSSJ,
      Autumn, 1961, pp. 37-38.

5.    Pamphlet, A Collection of Public Speeches for Declama-
      tion, with a chapter on Declamation, prepared by
      J. H. McBurney, Department of Speech and General
      Linquistics, Manager, Michigan High School Forensic
      Association, University of Michigan, p. 5. See also
      Harold A. Brack, "Is Effective Public Speaking 'Con-
      versational?'," ST, November, 1965, pp. 276-78.

6.    Raymond H. Van Dusen and Howard Van Smith, The
      New Speech-o-gram Technique for Persuasive Speak-
      ing, Prentice-Hall, Inc., Englewood Cliffs, New
      Jersey, 1962, p. 89. By permission of Prentice-
      Hall, Inc.

7.    T.R.B. from Washington, "Ticket to a Sinking," New Re-
      public, combined December 20 and 27 issue, 1969, p. 4.

8.    Saturday Review, March 6, 1954, p. 36. Copyright
      1954 by The Saturday Review Associates, Inc.

9.    Robert T. Oliver, Training For Effective Speech, The
      Cordon Company, New York, 1939, p. 453.

Chapter XIII

COACHING THE ORATION

In working with orators--at both the
high school and college levels--we soon recognized a paucity of practical literature on
directing oratory.[1]
> Phillip K. Tompkins
> Eldon E. Baker

The preceding statement is very true. This entire
book, and this chapter in particular, is an effort to remedy
this situation. Note that in the chapter title and in the sentence quoted above, the terms "directing" oratory and "coaching" it are used as synonyms. I believe this is proper. In
some circles, the term "coach" may have acquired some e-
vil connotations, some stemming from an excessive stress
upon winning contests. But merely changing the name from
coach to director would not of itself remove them. I don't
scare easily; the term "coach" is good enough for me.

In this chapter I shall consider the many duties of a
coach. It will necessarily involve an explanation of my own
methods in coaching as they have evolved over a period of
40 years. There is no one correct way of coaching. Size
of schools, numbers interested in oratory, past oratorical
traditions, the population of the community, whether small
town or large metropolitan area--all these and many other
factors vary from school to school. These may very well
require different approaches and procedures. Nevertheless,
this expository account of "one man's way" may be suggestive and helpful to others, particularly to beginners in coaching.

At Hope College, oratory activity is centered in four
local contests, two for men and two for women. Winners of
the Raven (men) and Adelaide (women) contests, go on as
school representatives in the MISL contests, and if success-

181

ful in winning first place there, go on to represent Michigan
in the annual IOA contest.  Local Peace contest winners likewise go to the State contests where all the speeches are tape-
recorded.  Tapes of the winners of first place in both the
men's and women's contests are then judged by a board of
judges under the auspices of the IPSA.  At Hope, the "old-
line" contests are usually held on campus just before the
close of the first semester, to coincide with the end of the
oratory class, about which more will be said later in this
chapter.  The Peace contests are usually held shortly after
the beginning of the second semester.  Most usually they
have been held off-campus, for the last ten years at a public
dinner meeting of the men's club of the local Methodist
church where the wives were also invited.

## II.   DUTIES AND METHODS OF COACHING -
### THROUGH LOCAL CONTESTS
#### A.  Personnel

        To gain and sustain an interest in having students
"come out for oratory" is one of the duties expected of a
coach.  It is frankly a selling job.  I have no particular a-
version toward enticing promising high school orators to
come to our college by proffers of loans or scholarships.  I
do not indulge in the practice myself.  Understand, I have
no strong feelings against it; it just doesn't happen to be my
"cup of tea."  I have never felt the need of such inducements.
Hope College had an enrollment of 600 in 1939 when I came
and over 2,000 thirty years later.  With either of these numbers, it would be most surprising not to have potential prospects present.  Such students are there; they just need to be
found.  We make do with such prospects as are here.  This
is the only consistent attitude I could assume in the light of
my life-long feeling that winning is not the primary purpose
of oratory.

        Interest and number of personnel taking part in ora-
tory will fluctuate from year to year.  Four comparatively
simple methods are used at Hope to locate and interest prospective orators.  They are: 1) fundamentals of speech classes,
and interviews; 2) a "Speech 11" contest; 3) a speech rally;
and 4) an advanced class in oratory.

        Obviously, an oratory coach talks briefly to his sec-
tions of required fundamentals of speech classes, telling
them of the advantages of oratory participation.  He keeps

an eagle's-eye lookout for those in his own classes with vigorous ideas and obvious talents in delivery, and calls them in
for a personal interview.  He asks his colleagues in other
sections (usually about 12 sections in all) to report to him
the names of his especially talented students.  Each semester a Speech 11 contest is held, consisting of a six-minute
conviction-type speech.  The winners of each section, chosen
by the class members themselves, compete in preliminary
and final contests.  Competitors in these contests, especially the finalists, are interviewed and often become interested
in taking part in the college oratorical contests.

In the early years at Hope, when I was in complete
charge of all forensic activities, a well-publicized speech
rally would be held early in the fall.  At this affair, past
participants in forensics would tell of their experiences and
point out the many advantages of participation.  The individual's development of competence in speech, the pleasure
and profit from meeting the talented speakers from other
schools, the medals and prizes available, would be mentioned at these meetings.  In the usual case, I would wind up
the meeting with a short talk.  At no time would I assume
an attitude of wheedling, coaxing, urging them to come out
as if they were doing me a personal favor.  Rather, I would
point out the grand opportunity for personal development
which they could ill afford to overlook.  I would especially
stress the opportunity of appearing before public audiences,
as contrasted with strictly contest situations.  Such appearances would provide for them the opportunity to influence
audiences "for real" on issues about which they had strong
feelings.

When at my request, my extra-curricular work was
reduced to just coaching oratory, I had a similar meeting
for oratory prospects only.  At the close of the meeting,
those present would be invited to leave their names, and to
indicate any past experience they may have had in high school
forensics.  It was made clear to them that having no such
prior experience was no handicap so far as our interest in
them was concerned, that we welcomed participation from
many on a broad base and the avoidance of the "star" system.

When other teachers in the Department notified me of
their top-notch students, I would send these students a mimeographed letter during spring registration, telling them of a
special course in oratory in the fall.  Here is a copy of it:

Dear _____

You know of Hope's remarkable record in oratory. Unfortunately, this affects only a few individuals and is not on as broad a base as I would like to see it. Many more persons should avail themselves of the opportunity to study this specific phase of persuasive speaking. From my personal knowledge of you, or upon the recommendation of other teachers in the Department, I'm certain you could profit by taking part in this activity. Even though this is mimeographed, I wish you would consider this a personal invitation to take part in this activity next year.

I'm aware of the multiplicty of school activities which sometimes keep people from taking part. May I therefore call your attention to Speech 71, a two-hour credit course which makes it possible to do oratory work and at the same time receive academic credit in doing so. It is offered in the fall on Tuesday the 8th and 9th hour.

Believe me, as a general rule it is against my nature to solicit students to take a course of mine, and I'm a little old to begin that now. But in this case, I have no hesitancy in making an exception. Give the matter some thought, will you?

Sincerely yours,


Wm. Schrier, Chairman,
Speech Department, and
Director of Oratory


The two-hour credit of the course is not repeatable. At its close, participation is required in either the local "old-line" or Peace oratorical contests. As a text, we use Winning Orations of the IOA of the preceding year, and, since 1966, Winning Hope College Orations, 1941-1966. We require a notebook in which students record the gist and outstanding qualities of a selected reading list of excellent past college orations. This list varies from year to year. Many possible subjects for orations such as those mentioned in Chapter VI, are explored in depth. Shortly thereafter, an early assignment in the oratory class I conducted for 20 years, was: Hand in three possible subject areas, complete

with a Specific Purpose Sentence, and a brief statement of
reasons for your choices. I would look those over, return
them with a commentary on each. In a following class session or two, the students were asked to come prepared to
defend their choices in a class discussion. Exploratory research and planning is done in each of the three areas, and
class discussions are held on periodic reports on them. Just
before mid-semester, each narrows the three choices down
to one. Obviously, a teacher urges each student to get a
subject suited to his personality, one he is absorbingly interested in, and wants to communicate to an audience.

The students next proceed to the writing of the orations, following these mimeographed instructions with which
they have been previously supplied:

> WRITING THE SPEECH. My suggestion is that
> you "write yourself free," even though you may exceed
> the word limits (1800 for "Old-line" contest, 1400 for
> Peace contests). It is far easier to cut down than to
> build up. I'll be happy to see a copy of your written
> speech, and to write a commentary upon it within 48
> hours, or to consult you about it in an interview. In
> connection with the writing, there are some important
> technical details to keep in mind:
> a. Count the words and indicate the number on the
>    ms., so that as I read it, I can correct it with
>    compression or expansion in mind.
> b. Count and indicate the number of quoted words.
>    In final copy, this number must not exceed 10% of
>    the total words.
> c. Write either double or triple space so that there
>    is room for me to make penned suggestions.
> d. Write on one side of a page only.
> e. Page the sheets.
> f. It is a help to number the paragraphs with arabic
>    numerals.

At the end of the semester, a completely revised and corrected "file copy" of the oration of each student is required.
I believe the value of the study and practice of oratory is
such that it is worthy of academic credit and highly recommend such a course in high schools and colleges.

Eligibility to compete in local oratory contests is not
restricted to members of the oratory class. Prior to the
contest, this notice is inserted in the Daily Bulletin:

A Pi Kappa Delta ruling of some years back, still
in effect, stipulates: In order to insure adequate
preparation, and to determine whether or not preliminary eliminations are necessary, and to check
that rules (for length and quoted matter) are com-
plied with, contestants must submit a copy of their
oration to the Director of Oratory one week prior
to the contest.

## B.  Getting Audiences

If we invite auditors to come and listen, there is an
obligation to provide a program worth listening to.  That
should be true for any audience upon all occasions.  Since
we instituted the oratory class, whose members come up
with quite acceptable orations, there's no problem on the
score of not getting good orations.

## 1.  Publicity Media

The orators likewise have the right to expect an audience to hear their orations.  The event is publicized in the
Daily Bulletin, college and local newspaper, and sometimes
is announced by some professors in their classes.  Usually
the attendance does not exceed 60, but many times we have
approached the 100 mark.  Increasing the size of audiences
remains a perennial problem.  The subject of audience attendance will be discussed in detail in Chapter XV.

## 2.  Required Attendance?

Perhaps one answer to larger attendance lies in requiring attendance from all enrolled in fundamentals of speech
classes.  Requiring such attendance and a report on the orations can no doubt be defended pedagogically.  It would provide actual laboratory study of a speaking situation, the very
thing being studied.  But I do not require such attendance because of what one might call almost a revulsion against a
"captive audience."  I cannot wax enthusiastic about forced
attendance for three reasons.  First, since such students
are a "captive" audience, many also may be slightly hostile
rather than receptive, on account of the captivity.  Second,
to sit with pens or pencils poised to take notes for their
reports, which many are likely to do in spite of admonitions

not to, imposes an added distracting element upon the orator.    Third, a compulsory audience for the purpose of a report places an undue emphasis upon the orations as "exhibitions" which at all costs we should avoid.    I usually call the
attention of class members to the contest, urge upon them
the value of attending, assure them that no one will be in
any way penalized for non-attendance, but say, with a twinkle
in my eye, that if I see them there, it will be kept "favorably in mind."

### C.   Getting Judges

As coach, I have always taken upon myself the task
of selecting the judges for the local contest.    In so doing,
competence is the criterion.    I most usually select a panel
of five, recruited both from townspeople with some special
claim to competence, and from the faculty.    I do not assume
that merely being a member of the faculty renders one competent to be a judge.    There must be some special reason
for competency beyond that, such as past identification with
forensics as either participant or coach.    The identity of the
judges is never disclosed to the contestants until the beginning of the local contest, nor are the ratings of each individual judge revealed to them afterwards.    It is made clear to
the judges they are free if they wish, to compare their ratings with one another.    If the judges, as sometimes happens, have taken notes and care to discuss these with the
competitors or to leave their notes for the contestants' benefit, the judges are free to do so.    The practice is neither
encouraged nor discouraged.    If the judges themselves wish
to reveal how they rated a student, that's their business.
The student is not encouraged to inquire into this, but if he
is sincere in wanting to know how he can improve, the kind
of judges I get will no doubt be willing to proffer helpful advice.

This method has worked satisfactorily for me.    It is
a matter of pride that at no time in my entire period of oratory coaching has my selection of judges been challenged upon the grounds of unfairness--not once!    I am truly, as I often say in announcing results, "charmingly impartial, well,
impartial if not charming!"    Of course I do have some prior
knowledge of the political leanings and interests of the judges.
This knowledge may often be one criterion of the selection.
That is, if I know a crime subject will be discussed in an
oration, the sociology professor, if otherwise qualified, is a

"natural"; so too, with a moral problem, the Department of
Religion and Bible has some well-qualified judges who would
be interested in hearing such an oration.   At no time do I
"stack" the judges, although admittedly the opportunity for
doing so is there.   Even if I were so minded, there would
be no point in it because my job as coach of most of the
contestants (excepting those not in the oratory class) is to
have gotten them to the point where I would be satisfied with
any contestant chosen for me.   I love them all,  have helped
them all equally in preparation for the local contest,  and usually have no preferences.

### D.   Choosing the School Representative
for State Contest

I always accept the winner of the local contest, as de-
termined by my panel of judges, as the school's representative in the state contest.   I have no special case for that
practice.   My acceptance of the winner probably arose from
the fact that a president of an institution I served prior to
coming to Hope frowned upon the practice of directors of an
activity serving as a judge.   I know that at many other institutions, the directors of oratory feel free to make their own
choice of representatives from among those who competed in
the local contest.   One of the late greats among oratory
coaches, I. M. Cochran of Carleton College, for many years
secretary of the IOA, wrote me a letter February 9, 1932,
in response to my inquiry about his practice, in which he
said:

I have your letter inquiring about how the College
Orator is chosen at Carleton College.

Our college orator is chosen in what is known as
our Home Oratorical Contest in which a first prize of
$40 and a second prize of $10 is offered.   The contest
is open to the entire school.

There are five judges, usually chosen from members of the faculty, who sit in judgment upon the orators.
They decide who is to get the prizes.

It is my privilege and duty, however, to select the
College Orator.   He may be the man who won the first
prize or he may be any other man in the contest.   I always pick the man I think will develop into the best ora-

tor by the time of the State Oratorical Contest, regardless of his present attainments.

With cordial good wishes, I am,

Sincerely yours,

I. M. Cochran

I believe this may be the more common practice. But I have
experienced no difficulty in following my method of abiding by
the selection of the judges.

III.  DUTIES AND METHODS OF COACHING -
      STATE AND PKD CONVENTION CONTESTS
      A.  The Role of the Coach
          1.  Need for Rapport - Preliminary Interviews

Assume that we now have our four orators (two men
and two women) selected. We are about to proceed to coach
them for further competition in the IPSA and "old-line" state
(MISL-IOA) contests and in alternate years for the provincial
and national PKD convention contests. Usually, but not always, the local winners are from the oratory class, and a
good rapport has already been established between student
and teacher. They have written an oration under some supervision, one good enough to be worthy of being heard by
a public audience. Still, we are never satisfied to rest on
the laurels of winning a local contest. For further competition, we assume the vehicle needs change and improvement,
sometimes much and sometimes little.

It is at this point that I have a good preliminary interview with each individual orator. I tell them that anything worth doing at all is worth doing to the limits of one's
capacity, and that I expect them to "give it all they've got."
I remind them of the values of oratory, and that to get the
maximum benefit from oratory participation, they should be
prepared to devote considerable time to both composition
preparation and delivery rehearsals. I ask them to plan
their work and study schedule to allow for such time.

The contestant should have confidence in the coach as
one who knows his business. The coach should be mature
and astute enough to respect the individuality of the contest-

ant when differences of opinion arise. That may occur on
decisions as to the inclusion or omission of an illustration
in composition. It may come in delivery on the exact shad-
ing of stress and emphasis to be given a key word. In such
cases, we just take time out frankly to discuss the pros and
cons. The final decision is always left to the orator for the
piece is, after all, his oration.

Obviously, on the part of the coach, the utmost of
tact is required, defined as "the art of making a point without making an enemy." This morale-rapport problem is not
a frequent occurrence, but it does come up occasionally. Individual contestants obviously differ in temperament and have
to be handled differently. Most students are aware of their
limitations, and are eager for suggestions and help. But on
occasion one comes down the pike with an exaggerated and
inflated ego, one who "knows it all." The area of criticism,
both in composition and delivery, is one of the most delicate
in the field of speech. Orators, by reason of being superior
students, most often already have a wholesome attitude toward it. Coaches, too, should not forget that criticism, properly interpreted, includes praise and favorable comment as
well as blame and admonition.

### 2.    Coach-Contestant Disagreement on Subject

Occasionally, it may happen that the subject, or, more
properly, the SPS, is one that the coach cannot fully subscribe
to, and may even be one he positively disbelieves. The likelihood of that occurring is rather remote if the winner has
come from the oratory class. For in that case, there has
already been some collaboration between teacher and student
during the time of selecting the subject. But if the winner
is not from the oratory class, the question may arise, how
should a coach conduct himself if he does not agree with the
thrust of his contestant's oration?

I raise the point only because I want this handbook to
be comprehensive, not because it has ever happened to me.
In fact, it never has in any situation where we had to work
together with a local contest winner to go on to further state
competition. It did happen once at the University of North
Dakota in a freshman oratorical contest. One entrant spoke
in favor of capital punishment although I am opposed to it.
At that time, North Dakota, like my present State of Michigan, had a law prohibiting it. A particularly gruesome mur-

der had aroused the state to white heat, and there was a
widespread clamor for the restoration of the death penalty.
I found no compunction at helping this entrant, as well as
his competitors, in preparation for the contest.

I can defend that position upon the simple ground that
the oration should represent the work and views of the orator, and not be merely a parroting of the views of the coach.
Capital punishment surely is a subject upon which reasonable
men may differ. I am fully committed to the statement of
Wendell Phillips, the noted abolition orator, who said at the
centennial anniversary of Phi Beta Kappa of Harvard College:

> Men are educated and the state uplifted by allowing
> all--everyone--to broach all their mistakes and ad-
> vocate all their errors. The community that will
> not protect its most ignorant and unpopular mem-
> ber in the free utterance of his opinions, no mat-
> ter how false or hateful, is only a gang of slaves.[2]

In the Preface to my 1966 publication, WHCO 1941-1966, I
wrote:

> The ideas expressed [in the orations] bear my im-
> primatur in the sense that I believe they deserved
> public expression, having assured myself that the
> sentiments expressed represented the sincere con-
> victions of the orators at the time of delivery.

I worded this precisely that way for two reasons: to disa-
buse readers from the idea that everything said in the orations represented my views; and to protect the few orators
whom I suspect since the delivery of the orations may have
changed their minds, which is everyone's right.

On the other hand, I must hold out for the right of a
coach to seek to influence, but not coerce, his young charges,
and to seek to have the orator change his mind. I believe
he has that right, and even obligation, upon the simple ground
that any citizen has the right to try to influence another citizen, be he young or old. I do recall, for example, that in
an oration on the student rebellion, I was instrumental in
persuading an orator to delete a favorable reference to that
annual bash of young people at Fort Lauderdale which I never
held in high esteem. I do have a feeling that a teacher always teaches himself as well as his subject. I am reminded
of the story of an alumni re-union where a wealthy industri-

alist accosted a class-mate rather condescendingly and almost sneered: "So you teach Greek, eh?" "No," replied the
venerable teacher, "I teach men and women--Greek is what
I start with."

For many years, my fundamentals of speech classes
contained a current events unit.  For the years just prior to
my retirement, the "black-white" and "peace-war" problems
were discussed.  Upon occasion, after four or five class
discussions by the students, I have taken a 50-minute class
hour to expose them to my ideas.  My attitude is expressed
in the opening paragraph of one of the last of these occasions:

> In 1939, an article appeared in the Christian Cen-
> tury by Carlton L. Wood, Professor of Political
> Science at William and Mary College entitled: "What
> Do You Believe, Professor?"[3]  He contends that
> teachers should express their views on controver-
> sial matters but that many are either too lazy, or
> more often, too fearful to do so.  Neither charge
> applies to me--no one has ever accused me of
> lacking the courage of my convictions.  Both pri-
> vately and in public speeches, I've spoken my mind
> on the subjects you have been discussing.  I'll pre-
> sent today the high spots of some things I have
> said.  My immediate intent is not to make converts
> to my point of view.  If you proceeded to believe
> as I do simply on my authority, without the same
> environmental influences impinging upon you that
> bore upon me in my lifetime, you would be doing
> violence to the majesty of your intellect.  I mere-
> ly want to expose you, as one such influence, to
> my ideas.  Of course, ultimately, if together with
> other such environmental influences, in the form
> of what you read, what you hear from others you
> talk to, you later come to share my views, I shall
> not of course be unhappy about it.

It should be noted that in the discussion of this problem, there is implicit the assumption and my firm belief that
what young people say in their orations has in it the power
to influence public opinion.  To believe otherwise is to assume that they are engaged solely in a contest, merely play-
ing a role, with no real concern for the consequence of the
words they speak.

I am certain that students in all my classes thoroughly understand my position on the question raised in this caption.   The result of a quiz administered to some 600 of my
students during six semesters confirms this.   We used
WHCO 1941-1966 as a supplementary text.   One quiz question asked was:

> In the article and speeches in Appendices to WHCO
> 1941-1966, as also in "Decalogue For an Ideal Citizen"
> are statements of what one might call my philosophy to-
> ward controversial questions and intercollegiate compe-
> tition.   As a matter of curiosity, I am anxious to check
> on how well you have absorbed it, not whether or not
> you agree with it.   On that basis, then, check two plus
> marks (+) and two minus marks (-) in the left hand mar-
> gin, on what you believe I would do in this hypothetical
> situation.
>
> You have a student entrant in the local oratorical
> contest with tremendous ability in delivery, one who is
> almost certain to win the local contest and to become
> the school's entrant in the State Contest.   But his pro-
> posed subject and views on it are diametrically opposed
> to yours.   As a coach, what procedure do you believe
> I would and would not follow prior to the local contest
> which he is almost sure to win.
>
> ( )   A.   Talk with him, show him material from my files
>            on the opposite side from his present beliefs, seek
>            to have him change his subject altogether or the
>            side he takes on the present subject.
> ( )   B.   Ask him not to enter the contest.
> ( )   C.   Tell him if he wins, he can expect no help from
>            me and he's "on his own."
> ( )   D.   Tell him if he wins, I'll do my best to help him
>            in both composition and delivery, and to help him
>            attain the highest possible rating in what I still be-
>            lieve to be an unworthy cause.

The proper answers require a plus mark in the A
and D space, and a minus for B and C.   By a margin of
98% all answers were correct; of the remaining 2%, some
who had made wrong checks told me they had misunderstood
the question.

And yet, having said all that in defense of a coach's
helping someone with a subject in which the coach does not
believe, I must confess that I would probably be rather in-
effective in coaching someone who wanted to expound on the

virtues of the Ku Klux Klan or the John Birch Society. However, as I have said, for me the question is largely hypothetical since I have never had a single instance of where this
has occurred in a contest in intercollegiate competition.

Consideration of the subject of the oration led us to
comment upon the role of the coach, especially in regard to
coach- contestant disagreement on subject. Since first and
foremost the coach is a teacher of speech, we therefore turn
next to consider the joint work of the coach with the contestant on matters of speech composition and delivery.

### B.  Composition Revision

There are times when the work of composition revision will begin with additional reading in depth in an expanded bibliography. If my own personal files contain anything
of value on the subject, the orator is allowed free access to
them. It may be that he may find there, for example, a
more effective illustration than one he already has in his
oration. At times, two, three, or even four weeks are occupied by the work of composition revision. Some winning
orations in the local contest are better in composition than
others. How much revision is done depends upon how much
needs to be done, keeping always in mind the goal of perfection. There is no "typical" case; each orator and each
oration is different. Hence, it is not possible to write of
this phase except in general terms. The joint coach- contestant sessions are covered by the material mentioned in Chap-
ters VII, VIII, IX, and X.

One procedure in our compositional work together
may be of interest. Since "instant intelligibility" is the sine
qua non of all good oral discourse, this sometimes happens.
I say: "This sentence, Jim, just doesn't register with me.
I don't know exactly what you mean. Now tell me, just what
are you trying to say?" Thereupon he tells me and I immediately say: "Quickly now, grab a pen or pencil and write
that down just as you said it, and we'll use those exact words
in the script!"

There are times in composition work where the original copy gets so interlaced with arrows, brackets, dele-
tions-- so undecipherable, that we sometimes need to make
as many as six re- typed copies. But, as has been said before, we do not immediately destroy the old copies for one

never knows when the orator will want to recapture an expression or phrase from an earlier script.

Some years ago in a speech to our faculty when it was
wrestling with the problem of counseling, I had occasion to
say:

> I have a definite feeling that the seat of many of
> our difficulties is a violation of the fundamental
> rule that, in the process of maturing students, the
> best procedure to follow is to treat them as adults.
> ... I don't believe in doing anything for the stu-
> dent which he can reasonably be expected to do for
> himself.

I carry that philosophy over into my training of an orator.
For I draw the line on writing the speech for him! I agree
with my friend Dr. Herbert L. Curry of Central Michigan
University, when he writes:

> ... some supervision of the writing of a good ora-
> tion is essential, but that supervision should show
> the student how something should be written and
> then permit the student to do his own writing. ...
> One of the very common sins found in the language
> of orations is that the language is not that of the
> speaker. Some so-called "coach" has reduced the
> oration to a sort of ventriloquism; the speaker is
> little more than a Charlie McCarthy who is mouth-
> ing the words produced by an Edgar Bergen. This
> is not only reprehensible from an ethical and mo-
> ral point of view; it is also a perversion of good
> education, for it has placed the goal of winning a
> contest over and above the intellectual development
> of the student. [4]

### C.   Delivery Rehearsals - General

Once the composition revision has been completed,
the next step is a period of delivery rehearsals. The time
devoted to rehearsals varies, depending upon the needs of
each orator. It may take anywhere from three to six weeks.
I profess to have a standing rule not to rehearse until the
orator has thoroughly memorized his oration. To do so
wastes his time and mine. The matter of memorizing should
not take too long. After all, he has already memorized the

basic speech for the local contest, and now, with revisions
made, it is more a case of "unmemorizing" the earlier
draft, and familiarizing himself with the wording of the revised one.

### 1.  Variety in Needs of Orators

A coach must recognize that each orator differs in
temperament and in delivery attainments.  We must start
with where the orator is in delivery ability, and work from
there.  Individual differences should be detected early, and
respected.  It is impossible, and in any case unwise, to try
to make every oratory student use the same delivery technique.  Most local contest winners are already likely to be
reasonably self-assured.  Others may need to have their
confidence built up.  In a case of the latter type, I give
them to read a written copy of a ten-point talk on "Nervous-
ness, Stage-fright, Fear and Confidence" which it takes me
a class hour to deliver in a fundamentals of speech class.

### 2.  Planning Rehearsals

What is done in each rehearsal should be planned in
advance by the coach.  At the close of each session, the
orator should be informed what to work on prior to the next
meeting.  In delivery rehearsals, there is just no substitute
for drill, drill and more drill.  It may involve overcoming
deep-seated bad habits, and the establishing of new and improved habits.  All this at times may become monotonous.
Assure the orator, however, that no more of his time will
be taken than is necessary to achieve the goal of perfection.
A little note of levity at this stage helps.  For example,
"That's very good, Jim, and so much better, but let's try
it once again and see if we can't make it a wee bit 'gooder.'"

### 3.  Imagining Audience Present

As the rehearsals begin, ask the contestant to imagine that an audience is present in the small class-room in
which first rehearsals are usually held.  Later, as the state
contest nears, we practice in a larger auditorium.  Sometimes at this stage, we appear at some off-campus audiences
prior to the state contest.  Usually, a coach is rehearsing
with a man and woman entrant in both the state "old-line"

and Peace contest, and often the rehearsals take place during the same time span. If the needs of some of the four entrants are similar, it conserves the time of both the contestants and coach to have some of the other orators present during the rehearsals of their companions.

### 4. Methods Used

As I listen, I never use a printed or mimeographed correction sheet. I use a blank 8.5x11 inch sheet of paper, and jot down by Arabic number plus and minus comments as the oration is delivered. I ask the orator please not to be distracted by my writing and joshingly, but truthfully, as he finds out later as I go over the comments, say that for all he knows, it is a favorable comment I am recording. The first rendition is to hear the oration in its entirety. Later, I may hop up and interrupt to demonstrate a point just when the need for it occurs--on posture, movement, gesture or whatever is needed. We take up little matters as well as big ones: the tilt of the head, the lift of an eye-brow, and such elemental matters as sloppy enunciation such as "becuz," "git," "gonna," and "prob'ly."

All rehearsals begin with the orator sitting in a classroom seat. This is the kind of situation he will be confronted with in the preliminaries of the state contest. Thus, even his walk to the front of the room is part of the rehearsal. His manner of approaching his task is part of what the judges and audience will observe.

Circumstances alter cases, of course, but ere too long, we dispense with going over the entire oration. Rather, we go over the speech by blocs, sometimes stopping in the middle of the speech and the next day, or day following, resuming where we left off. Usually, a rehearsal lasts a little over an hour, rarely two hours. There may be times when we skip a day or two, with the understanding that the orator works privately on some specific assigned parts of the oration.

After about four or five rehearsals, to avoid repetitive ones, we put the speech on tape, and may spend an entire hour in a play-back and discussion. If there is a tendency to be indirect, that old stand-by, of inserting the name of some person at certain places, may help to attain a greater degree of conversational directness. If, on account of our

stress upon the importance of earnestness, the orator over-
does the vigor, he may need reminding that "all force is no
force."

Earlier, I said I "profess" to refuse to rehearse until the revised composition has been thoroughly memorized.
In actual practice, however, I do relent. I find that a few
orators would like their copy of the oration available on a
nearby desk during the first few rehearsals. I myself refuse to hold the script. After the first two or three rehearsals, however, even the presence of the manuscript is positively forbidden. He must then "sink or swim" and continue
with his speech, doing exactly what he would do if loss of
memory happened in the contest itself. After all, these rehearsals are partly a preparation for that possibility. He
should think fast, try to keep composed, possibly move, and,
if possible, keep the audience from detecting that he has
forgotten.

It is not customary to have a prompter in an oratorical contest. Some organizations may positively forbid their
use. But even if allowed, I would not be in favor of using
one. There would be an inevitable tendency to rely upon
him. There would need to be, and rarely is, a thorough
understanding between orator and prompter at just what point
the prompting should be done. But the fact of prompting
would be a clear indication that the words being spoken were
just that - words, words, words, - and not living ideas coming from the heart. Briefly to extemporize in getting back
on the main track is better.

A few words about interruptions by the coach during
a rehearsal. The purpose of delivery rehearsals is to get
the maximum effective presentation of the ideas. That requires interruptions. The best time to point out a fault either of commission or omission is at the moment it occurs.
It may involve, for example, a failure to make a smooth un-
obtrusive change in position of the feet at a change in thought.
Occasionally, from one rehearsal to the next, I find the orator has marked his script with a notation "move here." This
practice I discourage. The need for the movement, "oral
punctuation" I call it, should have become so apparent that
such reminders are not necessary. Any movement resulting
from such memos may tend to become routinized and mechanical. Movement should result from a natural impulse from
within.

Repeated interruptions can obviously become discon-
certing to the orator.  It is difficult to maintain a high level
of earnestness in going over a portion of the oration a second or third time following an interruption.  But with a little
common sense on when and how often to interrupt,  an astute
coach can call a halt before boredom sets in.  Interruptions
should be kept to a bare minimum.

        D.   Delivery Rehearsals - Specific
           1.  Gesture - Visualization

Thus far I have written of delivery rehearsals in general terms.  Perhaps it would be more helpful to give specific examples from my past experience.  First, let us consider the areas of gesture and visualization.  Charles Leng
had an oration entitled "The Man Who Comes Out," dealing
with the problems facing the discharged prisoner.  At its
close he said:

> Regardless of what you believe the purpose of im-
> prisonment to be, surely you cannot believe that
> society has the right to destroy the hope of a man.
> If so, then let us not hide the fact.  Rather, let
> us inscribe upon the gates of our state penitentia-
> ries, Dante's flaming inscription upon the gates of
> hell, "All hope abandon, ye who enter here."

At those words in the inscription, coach and contest-
and had agreed to direct the attention of the audience with a
descriptive gesture toward the right, and to read each word
slowly as spelled out in an arched semi-circle.  The problem is to get the orator actually to see those words in his
imagination.  Only as he sees them can he expect the audience to see them also.  I can recall interrupting abruptly to
say: "Wait a minute, Charlie!  Do you really see those
words?  Tell me more about them; how big are they?"  This
is the sort of thing we have previously referred to as a
"goose-pimple conclusion."  In such cases, it is my studied
and deliberate practice never to rehearse such things many
times at any one rehearsal.  The subject-matter is too
solemn, serious, one might almost say sacred, to be rehearsing it to the point where it becomes stagey and mechanical.

Another example in this area of gesture and visualization:  Harland Steele's oration, "The House That Sam

Built," pleaded that, following World War II, we do not a-
gain retreat into isolationism as we did following World War
I. To appreciate the picture, and comment upon it, here
are the last three paragraphs of the oration:

> Soon he [Uncle Sam] will stand at the banquet table
> of peace, with places set for more than victors on-
> ly. As he looks around, may he see that now is
> the time for him to be more than a hinting toast-
> master; here is his chance to be one of the main
> speakers. And pray Heaven, when Sam does get
> up there to make that speech, may the unadulte-
> rated wisdom of ages pour forth with every word
> he utters.
> Can't you see him standing there--tall, dignified,
> gazing into the expectant faces lined up before
> him. Over there sits Holland and all her little
> cousins, with eyes silently begging for help. And
> ragged Poland and Czechoslovakia, their desire for
> revenge softened by his persuasive power. Over
> here, battle-scarred John Bull wonders how he fits
> in. Next to him a weary Russia, still gasping for
> breath. And shattered Italy, solemn and waiting.
> Yes, and even Germany is there, head slightly
> bowed, penitent we hope, scarcely daring to look
> up, yet gazing with pleading eyes at Uncle Sam.
> These faces present problems. The shadows that
> flitter across them remind Sam of that time years
> ago when he was confronted by the same faces,
> saw the same problems. That time, you remem-
> ber, he wavered and faced about. This time he
> does not - turn his eyes - away![5]

At this banquet scene, which was practiced many many times,
there was many an interruption, with questions darted to the
speaker as to just what each of the nations really looked like.
Did the eye-shifts indicate exactly where they sat? It is my
feeling that the audience simply cannot vicariously enter into
this scene unless the orator really is seeing the scene himself.


## 2.   Pause - Voice

The closing sentence of the Harland Steele selection
illustrates the delivery device, "pause" (where the dashes
are). We turn to two additional examples of pause, which

we have earlier said is a neglected art. It is often used at the dramatic close of an oration. If the orator can master this device, without being "arty" or over-dramatic, it is powerfully effective. Take, for example, the oration by Bruce Van Voorst, "The Clock," dealing with the possibility of atomic annihilation.

> Clock-conscious America. The clock points to two minutes to twelve. As we hesitate, it is ticking off those final, fateful minutes. Tick-tock! Tick-tock! _____! _____![6]

Those two blank spaces at the close are intended to represent a pleading palm gesture with both hands, pleadingly extended, stroking the last two times without vocalization.

John Hains, speaking on "The Lamp of Freedom," closed with these words:

> Let us eliminate class injustice, racial antagonism, and hysteria-born hatreds. Then when the dawn of some distant day flames in the sky, it will light a new America, a strong America, truly a "sweet land of liberty." Ours is today the last great lamp of freedom, shining through the twilight of dictatorship. Will you help keep that light burning? Will you?[7]

The timing here at the close, after many interruptions and much practice, was well-nigh perfect.

One could not possibly mention all of the problems encountered by a coach in conducting delivery rehearsals. They are almost as numerous and varied as the orators themselves. Each orator has his special problems. Some may need help in getting variety of rate within a single sentence, saying dependent clauses tripplingly off the tongue, slowing down and lingering a bit longer with prolongation of vowel sounds, on the independent clauses. Sometimes I go to the blackboard to make that graphic, to make sure it sinks in, thus:  .

The coach should become adept at detecting little telltale signs of the orator going stale. It is well then to declare a halt for a few days. Who has not at times caught himself reading pages of print with our minds on vacation? Analogously, an orator sometimes says words without really

thinking about them.

Quite frequently, as the rehearsal period draws to a close, we seek out opportunities to have the orator speak to off-campus audiences before the contest event, as well as after.  After all, why shouldn't he?  He has something to say which deserves a public hearing beyond mere participation in a contest.

### E.   The Dress Rehearsal

We wind up delivery rehearsals with a dress rehearsal, literally that, at least two days before the event.  The orator is dressed at his best, preferably in the same suit he will be wearing at the contest.  I never rehearse the day before a contest.  Anything I might criticize of an adverse nature could probably not be corrected and fully mastered in a day.  Hence, this kind of comment could only depress, and not impress, the orator.  In the final rehearsal, I keep my comments to an irreducible minimum.  I again remind him of the over-riding importance of earnestness.  Following the dress rehearsal, I have a rather extended heart-to-heart talk with the orator, with some parting words of advice.

## IV.   PARTING INSTRUCTIONS
### A.   General - On Details

From my recollection of my work with orators, I have compiled a list of items which I usually discuss following the dress rehearsal.  The list may have some value, especially for novice coaches.  I remind the orator that I am not a "baby-sitter," that he is of age, that he should take care of these matters, and not rely upon me to do them for him.

1.   Be sure you are well-groomed: shoes shined, trousers pressed, hair combed.

2.   Be prompt at the general meeting, on hand and available when and where drawings for places are held.

3.   It is your job, not mine, to check where you are to report for preliminary and final rounds, and to be there on time.

4.  At State, Provincial and National Conventions of PKD, class-rooms are at a premium, and contests may often be held in chemistry labs or in small rooms not the most suitable for speaking.  Avoid wherever you can standing behind a desk or lectern, if space is available for your entire body to be seen.  It is always best to speak with "all of yourself."

5.  The title of your speech may well be significant. It should preferably be spoken by the presiding officer, and not by you.  The chairman may be a speech major from the host school, and may not have been properly briefed on his duties.  Check with him to ask that he mentions the title orally, or writes it on the blackboard.

6.  Often "No Smoking" signs may appear, especially in some church-related colleges.  Where they do, be a good guest and observe them.

7.  If at all possible, be at your assigned place for preliminaries early, to gain some acquaintance with the size and general lay-out of the room.

8.  A friend of mine once wrote some simple words which struck a responsive chord with me:  "The writer has been in speech situations where for sheer improvement of attention one raised window would have been worth five striking illustrations."[8]  If the student chairman or custodian has been remiss in attending to the ventilation, assume the initiative and raise the window yourself.

B.  Specific - On Attitude

This second list of last-minute instructions following the dress rehearsal is even more important than the first. As a matter of fact, he is not deluged with this list all at one time following the last rehearsal, for hints on many of them have been made from time to time during the rehearsals.  But I do try to see to it that all of these points on attitude are covered, and most do come following that last rehearsal.  I shall write these just as if I were talking to the orator.

1.  Remember, the result, win or lose, is not too important.  You do believe in your subject, and you have every right to.  You have examined the evidence, and come

to your conclusion. You should realize that others in your audience may also have done so, and come to opposite conclusions. That is partly what makes life so interesting. You may not succeed in converting your audience fully to your point of view, but, judging from my work with you in rehearsals, you will have done some good by exposing them to it. Of course, do your best to try to win them over. Be reconciled, however, to the idea that you may not succeed, and don't let it worry you.

2. Be unconcerned as to which place you draw in the order of speaking. Especially do not "jinx" or "psych" yourself into thinking first place is a bad position. Scores of examples can be cited, many from our own school, showing where the first speaker in a contest with as many as eight speakers in a contest, emerged with a first place in the ratings.

3. We have worked hard in preparation. Remember, however, that others have also done that. Other speakers will be good. They will have good subjects. And even as you hope to win the approval of the audience, and that includes the judges, other speakers will be seeking to do the same. In fact, you yourself may be tremendously impressed by the speeches of others in the contest. You may be especially impressed by the speaker who immediately precedes you. In that connection, I have two bits of advice: 1) Do not let this weaken your faith in your own subject - that should remain firm and unshakable. Don't mentally sit in judgment on that excellent speech, and figure you don't have a chance. There are judges for that purpose, and you are not one of them. Your job is to get your speech over; 2) Do not allow the climax of the immediately preceding speech to tempt you, as a means of trying to combat its effect, into starting on the same high emotional plane on which the previous speaker ended. Be calm and deliberate in the opening, as we have planned in the rehearsals, so that later the audience can see, from your calm beginning to your "rousements" at the close, the wide range of your talents.

4. Pause before beginning to speak until you have the full attention of everyone. Remember, sometimes the chairman may not realize that the judges have considerable "busy-work" to do, viz., writing critiques, filling in names on a ballot. The chairman may not allow enough time between speakers for the judge to give you his undivided attention. I am convinced in my own mind that a contributing

factor in Jacob Ngwa's first place in the 1964 IOA contest
was his calm self-possession, poise and pause, all the while
accompanied by a pleasant and not a petulant facial expression, awaiting the attention of one of the judges.  In a small
room in preliminaries, do not conspicuously direct your attention to the judges, but at the same time, do not neglect
them.

　　5.  Be prepared for distractions.  If people come and
go during orations, wait until the commotion has subsided.
Do not allow a late-comer to distract you.  The Boy Scout's
motto "be prepared" is a good one to observe as to distractions.  They may come at any time--the loping down the
aisle of a lost dog, the clacking of a malfunctioning radiator,
the humming of air-conditioning equipment, the passing of a
train, the rehearsal of a choir in an adjoining room.  If a
disturbance is likely to cease soon, it would be well to stop.
If the disturbance is not major, at least combat it to the extent of raising your voice.  This advice applies primarily to
provincial and national PKD conventions rather than state contests.  At conventions, you may "expect the unexpected."

　　6.  As you know, in our state contest, I will be elsewhere judging the preliminaries and will not hear you.  If
you survive and enter the finals, I will be there under the
coach-judge system.  I promise to remain impassive, and
not sit with pen or pencil poised.  Don't worry about me--
think about your speech.  At conventions, I may have a free
round from judging, and may have a chance to hear you.  I
will leave it entirely up to you as to whether or not you
would be distracted by my being in the audience, and I will
abide by your decision.  I hope it will not disturb you.  I
had made no such prior arrangement with Jacob Ngwa at the
1965 PKD Tacoma Convention.  I shall always be curious
whether or not my dropping in on one of his rounds in oratory caused him to get a second place vote in that round,
when all other 11 votes in the four rounds were firsts!  He
had told me afterwards that my arrival there, after he had
begun speaking, did slightly "throw" him.

　　7.  This is a friendly contest.  You are dealing in
ideas.  Your competitors are friends, not enemies.  Be considerate and courteous to them at all times.  Get acquainted
with them, introduce yourself, and converse with them.  You
all have a tension-producing element in common.  Show at
all times elemental courtesy by listening attentively while
your friends are speaking.  Exude a genuine, and not feigned,

interest in the subjects of other speakers.  Be that way by
no means for the ulterior motive of making a good impression in order to win a contest.  Be it simply because that's
the way civilized and educated people should act toward each
other.  Should you not win, take defeat graciously.  Don't
complain about the decision, certainly not outwardly, and not
even inwardly.  It just isn't that important.  If you are sure
you got your message across, you should be satisfied.  In
Michigan, you know, we use the coach-judge system.  You
could roam all over the United States and nowhere find a
better spirit than among us in the MISL.  In a speech to the
Holland Rotary Club in 1958, "Behind the Scenes in Oratory,"
I bore public testimony to that when I said:

> While to the average person it might appear that
> the coach-judge system lends itself to abuse, in
> that one coach could rank very low a person he
> thought was giving his own entrant a close run, I
> really don't know of a single incident where the
> traditional cry of the defeated boxer was ever heard:
> "We wuz robbed!"

8.  Finally, my young friend, I have done all I can
for you.  You are now on your own.  It has been a real joy
working with you.  If this has been a "pep-talk," it is the
last and only one you will hear from me.  Not to give such
a last-minute pep-talk just immediately prior to speaking has
probably come as a result of my own recollection that it
hurt, rather than helped me as a competitor.  It would, I
suspect, get you tense whereas you should be cool, calm and
collected, relaxed.  The most that you next can expect from
me is an "easy does it" as you get up to speak.

## Notes

1.    "Coaching the Contest Oration," Forensic, January, 1961,
      pp. 12-14, by Mr. Tompkins, Kent State University,
      Kent, Ohio; and Mr. Baker, University of Montana,
      Missoula.

2.    "The Scholar in a Republic," James Milton O'Neill,
      Models of Speech Composition, The Century Company,
      New York, 1922, pp. 803-04.

3.    December 17, 1939, pp. 1601-02.

4.    <u>Fundamentals of Forensics</u>, The University Press, Central Michigan University, Mount Pleasant, Michigan, August 1959, p. 32.

5.    <u>WHCO</u>, pp. 28-29.

6.    <u>WHCO</u>, p. 78.

7.    <u>WHCO</u>, p. 9.

8.    Ralph A. Micken, <u>Speaking For Results,</u> Houghton Mifflin Company, Boston, 1958, p. 78.

Chapter XIV

JUDGING THE ORATION

## I. NEED FOR JUDGES

Chapter III indicates my belief that in contest oratory getting over the message should be paramount to the goal of winning. Such emphasis is often the best method of achieving victory. The desire to win, however, is always operative among the participants. Most of them have a natural desire to excel. The element of competition and rivalry also enhances the interest of the average audience in the contest. Thus, we need judges to sit in judgment to determine the winners.

Much controversy has centered around judges and judging. In this chapter, we group ideas under the 5 C's: 1) Competence; 2) Criteria; 3) Critiques; 4) Criticisms; and 5) Compassion.

## II. COMPETENCE
### A. Who Best Qualified

Who are best qualified to judge oratory contests? The AFA has served the profession well in the formulation of its "Code for Contests in Oratory." Section B-1 of the Code provides a good answer to the question.

B. Contests should be judged only by persons competent in speech evaluation.
1. Normally such competence will derive from speech education or from professional experience in public speaking ...

A coach of oratory should be the very best qualified person to judge oratorical contests. Any professionally trained teacher of speech, however, even though oratory may not be his specialty, should likewise be competent to judge. From his academic preparation, he is likely to be familiar with principles of persuasion and evaluation. This requirement is the key to competence. In local contests at Hope College, exceptionally talented speech majors have occasionally been pressed into serving on the roster of judges. So, too, have professional speakers among towns-people who have had previous training in evaluating speakers.

## B. The Problem of Incompetent Judges

The problem of securing competent judges does not usually arise in local or state contests or the IOA. In local contests, it is relatively easy to secure those who meet the required tests of a knowledge of persuasion and evaluation techniques. Nor is it likely to be a problem in state contests. I am not familiar with how other states choose their representatives for the IOA. In Michigan, for as far back as I can remember, we have employed the coach-judge system. We have been satisfied with it, and no proposal has been made at any time to abandon it.

There is a problem, however, in securing competent judges to serve in tournaments and in the provincial and national PKD conventions. At these affairs, there simply are not as many qualified judges in attendance as are needed. Unfortunately, in these situations, it is sometimes necessary to press into service some who are not qualified, and even some speech teachers known to have a positive dislike for oratory as a speech activity. Under the circumstances confronting the directors of oratory at conventions of PKD, I stand in awe and admiration at their fine efforts to supply as many competent judges as possible. As already mentioned in Chapter III, withholding announcement of winners following each round, the use of ratings (SUPERIOR, EXCELLENT, GOOD) rather than rankings (1, 2, 3), do have the effect, whether so intended or not, of diminishing the importance attached to winning.

## C. Disagreements - A Perennial Problem

Tastes differ. My tie is red, yours is blue. I disdain the professional rectitude of a cutaway, you dote on it. To me the Saturday Evening Post is a glorious habit, to you it is so much piffle. I am satisfied to own a Ford, you scorn the humble ani-

mal. I hate to be called Professor, to you it is
the breath of life. Yet we can measure a quart of
water, a foot of tape, an acre of ground, a cord
of wood, a ton of coal, and <u>agree</u> on the result.[1]

These are the opening words of Ralph Dennis, for
many years Dean of the School of Speech at Northwestern
University, in a paper entitled "The Oratorical Contest:  A
Shot in the Dark, " read before the convention of the National
Association of Academic Teachers of Public Speaking, over
55 years ago.  The words graphically illustrate that, even if
all judges in an oratorical contest met every test of competency, disagreements about judging would still remain.  Equally experienced coaches, all with unquestioned expertise in
judging, often differ widely in their judging of the same oration.  Recall, for example, the reaction cited in Chapter IV
to the oration "The Years Between" by Miss Jo Ann Westervelt, wherein she was awarded first place by many judges,
although another, whom I sincerely believe to be one of the
best in the business, said of it:  "It wasn't an oration!"

D.  Best Attitude Toward Disagreements -
A Charitable Spirit

There will always be disagreements about judges and
judging.  It is a fact of life.  It is one reason we should
not take decisions as seriously as many contestants and
coaches now do.  We ought to become reconciled to the failings and foibles of human nature, rather than being upset by
them.  To assume there will ever come a time when there
are no such disagreements is "a consummation devoutly to
be wished" but it will never happen.  A palliative--not a
remedy, for there is none--is a reduction of the emphasis
upon winning, coupled with a charitable spirit.  A good sense
of humor helps too!

III.  CRITERIA FOR JUDGING
A.  The AFA Criteria

Item 5 of the AFA Code begins with these words:
"The orator should be evaluated or judged by standards which
embrace the elements of content, composition, and delivery."
There is not likely to be disagreement on these three general items.  But each item of this trilogy must be further
broken down, each into various sub-divisions.  Judges may

well differ in what those sub-divisions should be, and what
weight to accord to each.   Perhaps it is just as well that
the code does not attempt to do this for them.   It does warn,
negatively, that "Critics should not be confronted with nebulous ballot items such as 'power of truth' or 'ability to thrill.'
Evaluation criteria should be clear and specific. "


        B.   Ballot Preparation
            1.   Requiring Percentages for Specific Items
                 Unwise

    Some ballots contain a list of criteria such as, for
example, suitability of subject to the orator, arresting style,
cogent reasoning and supporting materials.   These are helpful as reminders of criteria to novice judges, but hardly
necessary, although not harmful, for experienced judges.   I
do think, however, it is unwise to require giving a specific
percentage value for each such listed items.   A competent
judge should be allowed the latitude of making his own de-
termination of the weight to be given the criteria within the
general framework of content, composition, and delivery.
That is part of the judging function which should not be u-
surped by the preparer of the ballot.


            2.   Misunderstanding About Percentages

    Many ballots stipulate that the judges shall give each
contestant both a ranking and a percentage grade.   The latter is helpful as usually the first method to be used in
breaking ties.   In an effort to have uniformity for the judges
in using the same scale for percentages, it is often stipu-
lated that the lowest ranked contestant must receive 75%
and the highest ranked must receive 95%.   These were the
limits used for a number of years in the MISL.

    I have found a great deal of misunderstanding concern-
ing this provision for percentages, and particularly about the
requirement of arbitrary upper and lower limits.   Sometimes,
in a weak contest, a judge may hesitate to give the best
speaker 95%, as the rules specifically require, on the grounds
that even the best speaker wasn't that good.   Or, in a strong
contest, he may not like to give the lowest-ranked speaker
75% on the grounds that he was not that bad.   This is a
total misconception of what these arbitrary figures are for.
They are merely to assure that each judge uses the same

scale of measurement. In the latter case, for example, the
75% does <u>not</u> mean that the speaker is 3/4ths on the way to
100% perfection. I have known of a number of cases where
a judge has had to be called in to rectify his ballot to conform to the explicit instructions before a tie could be broken.
If he has disappeared from the scene, misunderstandings and
ill-will often result.


### C.  Recording Evaluations

Every judge has to "work out his own salvation" in
the matter of note-taking. From his notes, he arrives at
rankings, percentages, and the critiques he writes for the
contestants' benefit. I use either a 4x6 or 5x8 inch card,
and under each name put a plus sign (+) on the right hand
margin, and a minus sign (-) on the left, to note good and
bad points. I have my own set of Schrierian hieroglyphics;
for example, "gen" on the right hand side stands for "geni-
ality, poise, self-possession," and on the left "bkhd" means
the hands were awkwardly calling attention to themselves in
that the back of the hands faced the audience instead of being
at the sides. In this way, I can keep watching, observing,
listening to the orator with a minimum loss of contact with
him, as also a minimum of distraction to him. These little
memos to myself are consulted briefly between speeches to
arrive at rankings and percentages as the contest progres-
ses, and also later to jog my memory after the contest for
use in writing a short critique.

Now suppose there are six speakers in a contest. Let
us use capital letters for the speakers, and Arabic numerals
for the order of speaking, A-1, B-2, C-3, D-4, E-5, and
F-6. I usually record 85% for the first speaker (A-1), regardless of how good or bad he is. As B-2 finishes, I compare him to the first, A-1. Speaker B-2 is appreciably better than A-1, and therefore I rate him 90% I next compare
the third speaker, C-3, with the previous two. Knowing that
I am going to have to do that when he finishes, I may even
subconsciously be doing that while he is speaking. If C-3
was not as good as B-2 but a wee bit better than A-1, I
would give him, let's say, 87% From this point on, the
going really "gets tough." The secret, I have found, of doing a good, conscientious job in judging is to keep up-to-date
in your rankings at all times, and to have those decisions
made before the next, D-4, speaker begins. If you don't do
that, you will have to keep two speakers subconsciously in

mind without an evaluation and you will not give the succeeding speaker your full and undivided attention which is his due.
At a convention, if a speech student in charge as chairman
does not allow enough time for some deliberation before calling on the next orator, do not hesitate to speak up and ask
for a slight delay.  The D-4 speaker is far superior to the
first three, so tentatively we rate him 95%.  He is now first
in ranking until and unless the remaining two speakers sur-
pass him.  Let's assume they do - E-5 is even better than
D-4.  E-5 now receives 95% and D-4 must now be deprived
of that percentage and receive another.  But D-4 is still better than the first three, so his percentage rating must be
higher than any of theirs.  I now decide that D 4 must be de-
moted from 95% to 91%.  But his superiority to B-2 who now
occupies the 90% spot is more than one percentage point, so
I demote B-2 to--oh, about 85%.  But C-3 is occupying that
third spot with 87%, so he is juggled to 80%.  By this time,
the A-1 speaker, who started with 85% gets dropped to 75%
unless the last speaker should be less good than he.  F-6,
the last speaker, is a trifle better than A-1, but not as good
as the others.  I may settle on F-6 for 80%.  But C-3 is occupying that percentage, so I move C-3 in this game of musi-
cal chairs up to about 84%, and promote B-2 from 85% to
88%.  Let's make it graphic, in terms of percentages and
final rankings.

Final rank:

| | | | | | | | |
|---|---|---|---|---|---|---|---|
| A-1 - | 85% - | 85% - | 85% - | 85% - | 75% - | 75% - | VI |
| B-2 - | | 90% - | 90% - | 90% - | 85% - | 88% - | III |
| C-3 - | | | 87% - | 87% - | 80% - | 84% - | IV |
| D-4 - | | | | 95% - | 91% - | 91% - | II |
| E-5 - | | | | | 95% - | 95% - | I |
| F-6 - | | | | | | 80% - | V |

## IV.  CRITIQUES IN JUDGING
### A.  Absence of Critiques Indefensible

Item 6 of the AFA Code reads:  "There should be opportunity for individual criticism of speakers following the

event. This obviously enhances the learning value of speech contests to the contestants."

I believe the absence of critiques is indefensible. In many state contests, as in the MISL, written critiques of some sort are required. My recollection is that they have often been optional at provincial and national PKD conventions. To make critiques mandatory might not result in helpful ones if judges are reluctant to write them. It is difficult for me to comprehend the reasoning of the educators in charge of oratory contests where critiques are positively forbidden. I have personally never encountered such cases but apparently there are such contests. [2]

To omit critiques is to assume that the primary interest of the student is the answer to the questions, "Who was best? Who won?" That could well be the attitude of many. But it ought not so to be. Ideally, he ought to ask himself, and the critique should provide an answer to the question, "How well did I get over my message, and how could I have improved it?" I served in preliminary and final contests in oratory of the MHSFA in 1967. Even though that was "the end of the line" as far as further competition was concerned, interest in improvement should never flag. I was disappointed in the lack of provision for critiques as well as the apparent lack of interest of both contestants and coaches in receiving them.

At tournaments and conventions, it is said that:

> Lack of time usually prevents their [judges] preparing extensive written or oral evaluations. Tournaments operate on such tight scheduling that little time is available for anything but the contestants' performances. Many coaches and tournament directors deplore the lack of oral and written criticism. Nevertheless, few have done anything to provide more time for critiques. [3]

Critiques at conventions with a crowded schedule may necessarily have to be a bit more brief. But it is difficult to see why they should be omitted altogether. It should be possible for the judge to write a few helpful suggestions. My practice normally, where time allows, is to write critiques after the contest is over. But at conventions where both participants and I have to hurry away to a distant building for another speaking or judging assignment, I write the critiques following each speaker. I agree with Grace Walsh, of Wisconsin State University, Eau Claire, an outstanding coach of oratory and all other forms of forensics, when she writes, "At the national conventions of honorary speech fraternities, speakers have the right to expect helpful criticism."[4] It should not be overlooked that critiques also involve favorable comment. A few well-deserved compliments could well encourage the youthful orator as he goes on to the next round.

### B.   Content and Preparation of Critiques

As a nudge toward having judges write a critique for each orator, managers of contests might provide printed or mimeographed critique sheets, with a listing of a few major items to evaluate, with some space for comment and helpful suggestions. Such items should not be so detailed as to make of the judge a mere automaton and "glorified book-keeper," and thus keep a judge from giving 100% attention to the orator. A judge should be that, a judge, and not one wholly pre-occupied with "busy-work."

What to write on a written critique, where no form is provided, is a matter of individual judgment. Latitude should be permitted each judge to prepare his critique in his own way. I have already indicated my method of note-taking. I try to touch upon the main factors, the highlights, which contributed to my decision. Sometimes I add, and so label it, a "Triviata Department," listing mispronunciations, or enunciation lapses, such as "gonna," and "becuz." Of course they are not really "triviata" for, as Michelangelo says: "Trifles make for perfection, and perfection is no trifle."

In local and district contests within a state, I welcome, when serving as a single critic judge, the opportunity of giving an oral critique, with or without an audience present. It gives me a chance to be an educator, to "give an account of the faith that is in me," so far as this contest is concerned. It makes me in rapport with the orators and, hopefully, makes them feel I am their friend and a booster for their activity. They see a person rather than some impersonal marks on a critique sheet.

C.   Attitude of Judge Toward Further Discussion
     of Critiques with Contestants

The attitude of a judge toward the whole process of
judging the contestants should be that of an educational help-
er and friend.  He should not have the attitude of a stern,
critical, detached person sitting atop Mount Olympus.  That
attitude could only result in inducing in the contestant still
another tension- producing element.  He already has enough
of those to contend with.  Accordingly, if anywhere-- a local,
district, state contest, or at a provincial or national convention of PKD-- a contestant should approach you, the judge,
for further help and suggestions, what attitude should you
assume?  The first impulsive reaction ought to be a willingness to be helpful further with amplifications of his written
critique which is necessarily brief.  Many times at conventions I find myself at dining halls and during the social hours,
approaching a youngster to compliment him or her upon a
performance in a contest I judged.  Often I wind up by prof-
fering postage and telling them I would appreciate very much
their sending me a copy of their oration since I am a con-
noisseur and collector of orations.

But the determining factor here is always, is the person sincere?  Does he really want further help or suggestions?  Or is he inquiring merely to complain and wanting to
start an argument?  If I detect that in his attitude, I muster
as big a smile as under the circumstances I can, and change
the subject.  I may say something like:  "I'm sorry you were
disappointed.  I just try to be a good umpire, and call 'em
as I see 'em."

D.   Attitude of Coach Toward Critiques Received
     by His Own Contestant

Often critiques at a provincial or national convention
of PKD are withheld from the contestants by the officials in
charge until all rounds of oratory are over.  I think this is
sound practice.  On those occasions where they are given
directly to the contestants following each round, I do not encourage a conference between myself and contestants about
those critiques, in the hope of improving his performance in
the following rounds.  I believe it is unproductive.  Often the
advice in the critiques from the various judges is conflicting.
If the contestant tries to alter his method in ensuing rounds
in such cases, it just adds another tension- producing element

in the contest situation.  After all, coach and contestant have
worked out between them the best manner of delivering this
speech, and it is just as well, for this convention at least,
to adhere to it.  Then too, for the contestant to change his
mind would clearly indicate that the desire to win, to get a
higher ranking, is a motivating force with him.  He should
be interested at all times only in the desire to get his message across.

       This is not to say that we downgrade the critiques at
all.  Either enroute home, or at home, we have a scheduled
conference to look them all over again very carefully to see
what we can learn from them.  Especially if there is a pattern of uniformity in some comments, we assume the expert
judges must be correct.  I recall an occasion when a judge
of one of my contestants wrote that his gestures were "arty,"
somewhat artificial.  In the post-contest conference, I told
my contestant that I agreed 100%.  It happened to be something that I had detected in the final contest, but something
he had never before done in rehearsals.  So my main contributions here are:  Don't try to change renditions between
rounds, but do consider critiques carefully following the
contest and learn what you can from them.

## V.  CRITICISMS OF ORATORICAL JUDGING PRACTICES

       One deficiency of oratorical judging procedures, es-
pecially at conventions, has already been referred to:  the
failure to have critiques at all.  There are two additional
criticisms.

### A.  Judging the Same Contestant More Than Once

       Article V, Section 4, of the 1968-69 IOA Constitution,
reads:  "No judge shall hear any contestant twice."  This is
a good rule.  It is not universally observed; it ought to be.
In recent years, it has not always been observed in our own
MISL organization.  I believe that is a tragic retrogression
in a state which has pioneered and been in the vanguard of
promoting sound oratory practices.  In Michigan, we now
have two preliminary rounds of oratory before selecting finalists.  The reason given for two preliminaries is that it
provides still another speech appearance for all contestants.
Under this system, it is often necessary for a judge to hear
the same contestant twice.  In my judgment, the disadvan-

tage of having a judge sit in judgment upon the same person
a second time far outweighs the alleged advantage of a second preliminary round appearance, especially when the audience in these preliminaries is composed of judges and other
competitors only.

I believe it is simply impossible in a contest to ren-
der the same equally good judgment on a contestant a second
time as one can the first. An oration is an entity. Unlike
years ago, we do not have separate judges prior to the contest on thought and composition and another set on delivery.
We consider its total impact as communication, not exhibition. If you have heard the oration before, the element of
surprise is gone. You already know all the rhetorical devices, the unusual beginnings perhaps, the climactic close.
Subconsciously, the judge is comparing it hypercritically with
its first rendition. Thus, in a sense, we as judges are likely to engage in "exhibition" judging which is as bad as "exhibition" speaking. That is, we are looking for flaws and
imperfections rather than allowing the speech to "speak to
us."

Furthermore, it is entirely possible that the rendition
by the orator will vary between one time and another. But
the judge has already committed himself that this speaker
was inferior or superior to the others. For him to change
his judgment and reverse the relative positions of other con-
testants--which of course he should do if the one he is hearing a second time has measurably improved and surpassed
them--would nevertheless plant seeds of ill will and suspi-
cion. It could disturb the good will now prevailing among
coaches. This could very well happen under the two-preliminaries system when a coach judges the same contestant
twice. A number of years ago, before the two-preliminaries
practice was in effect, I sat in judgment upon a preliminary
contest where two were selected to go on into the finals. I
had not placed the winner among the first two. But at the
finals, which I heard but fortunately did not have to judge,
he did a superb job, so much better than when I had heard
him in the preliminary, and he was very properly awarded
first place. Had I been a judge, I too would have awarded
him first place, above the two I had in my earlier judgment
ranked above him.

In summation, then, I believe a judge should not judge
a contestant twice for two reasons. First, it is difficult for
him to judge fairly the second time. Second, for him to

change his rankings in any way on the second hearing could cause discord and disturb the harmony which should prevail in any forensic organization.

### B.  Judging and Holding Manuscript at Provincial and National PKD Conventions

It is customary at national conventions of PKD for the orator to be required to deliver a copy of his oration to the director of oratory upon arrival at the convention.  Presumably it is for the purpose of checking compliance with rules for length and quoted matter.  In the final of four rounds, one of the three judges is assigned the task of holding the manuscript, to check that the oration is delivered with reasonable conformity to the script submitted.  I have avoided that task whenever I could graciously talk myself out of it, but do remember doing so upon one occasion.  In my judgment, this is clearly bad practice, and should be discontinued.

### 1.  Holding Manuscript is:  Disquieting

To the orator, this practice is disquieting, distrustful, and discourteous.  Disquieting in that it introduces still another tension-producing element into a contest situation. If the orator's memory is already a bit shaky, it may probably result in his doing less than his best work to feel that he might be penalized or disqualified for inserting an extemporaneous reference now and then.  This apprehension may even become a cause of his forgetting.  Particularly if he has made some trivial extemporaneous substitutions in prior rounds, it may well increase his anxiety.  For he has no way of knowing how strict the "detective judge" is going to be.  I know of no directives ever spelled out from the director of oratory of how strict he <u>ought</u> to be.  No bases of disqualification have been agreed upon.  Without such agreement, different judges would have different standards as to when disqualification should occur.  Maybe there has never been a single such case.  All the more reason for abandoning the practice.  It should be pointed out also that there is nothing essentially wrong for an orator deliberately to make a few extemporaneous departures from his written script. [5]

## 2.  Distrustful

This practice needlessly accentuates the contest element.  It presumes the contestant may deliberately want to
"cheat." In effect, we as coaches are saying: "There is
always the possibility you may slip in an extra paragraph or
two from an expanded version of your oration-- we have to
police you to see that you don't."


## 3.  Discourteous

The practice of holding the manuscript is also discourteous in the extreme.  The orator deserves the undivided attention of a judge.  He cannot really give that when
burdened with this added duty of holding the manuscript.
There is no consistency in urging that contestants be courteous and considerate toward each other during a convention,
and then to have the students find that the judges are fla-
grantly discourteous to them by their inattention.  Besides,
so much stress has been placed in these latter years upon
the problem of listening.  Note, for example:

> For selfish reasons alone one of the best invest-
> ments we can make is to give each speaker our
> conscious attention.  We ought to establish eye con-
> tact and maintain it; to indicate by posture and fa-
> cial expression that the occasion and the speaker's
> effort are a matter of real concern to us. [6]

Of whom should this be more true than of a judge?

To all of this it may be said, "Anyone who criticizes
current practices should come up with a better plan." Touché!
If we have rules, they should be observed, and there should
be penalties as means of enforcing them.  Why not give the
honor system a try at PKD conventions?  Jimmie Trent,
Executive Secretary, writes me that there is no such checking in the finals of the IOA.  Where the competitive spirit
prevails to the degree that the honor system would not work,
perhaps some method of surveillance, by someone other than
a judge, could be worked out.  An alternative suggestion,
which would eliminate some but not all of objections to holding the manuscript, would be to have qualified persons act
as roving observers, appearing at any one of the four rounds
of oratory, unannounced.

## VI.   COMPASSION FOR JUDGES

This caption hardly lends itself to sub-divisions.   I should like to conclude this chapter with a plea for the much-maligned judges.   Their job is a hard one.   In a state contest, all orators are already local winners.   Thus, they are all likely to be quite good.   And this gets to be even more true as one goes to the top in regional and interstate eliminations.   Of course, all this is elemental, but we do tend to forget it.   Thus, there is not likely to be a big gap between even the first and last place speaker.   The situation is comparable to that of the finish of a 100-yard dash, with all runners well-bunched.   In a contest of eight, the fact that a person places last does not necessarily mean that he has not done well.   In the honest judgment of any judge, the speaker he places last may have been only a mental step or two behind the one he awarded first.   In a national contest in which an orator of mine competed (and in which he did not place first), in my judgment any one of five out of six could have been declared the winner and no one could or should have complained. [7]

Unlike the 100-yard dash, in an oratorical contest, there is no photo-finish device to declare the winner in an objective way; each judge must make a subjective judgment upon his past experience as to what he believes constitutes good oratory.   Suppose some personality traits of an orator just somehow rub Judge A the wrong way.   He has every right to take into consideration this total impression as well as specific details as to delivery and composition.   And yet those things which created an unfavorable impression upon Judge A may not have been noticed by Judge B at all!

There will always be controversy over judges' decisions.   Any coach of wide experience could cite many examples of wide disparity in judging.   Judges of course should do everything possible to divest themselves of prejudice, and I am sure most do try.   Yet I am equally sure that human nature being what it is, this ideal situation is more fiction than fact.   Egbert Ray Nichols, a superb oratory coach and a founder of PKD, rightly said:  "The student who chooses a public question must always run the risk of facing prejudiced judges or a hostile audience."[8]   It is humanly impossible for a judge completely to shed his background and prior views on an oration subject.   For example, if one has a strong conviction that our involvement in Vietnam was wrong and immoral from the very beginning, he is likely to lean more to-

ward favoring the orator who espouses that view than one who
favors the Vietnam war.   I do recall, however, instances of
my giving a higher ranking to orators, the "thrust" of whose
orations I did not share, and placing them higher than one
who spoke my own convictions, but spoke them less ably.
Thus the answer at least of this apologist for college oratory
to the charge of some prejudice in judging is not to deny,
but frankly to admit it.   After we have agreed that we should
be as honest and upright in our judgments as we possibly can
be,  there will always remain a residuum of prejudice which
cannot be overcome as long as we are finite human beings.
So to you students, too, I say--be charitable, have compas-
sion--you as a contestant may not think much of a judge, but
please, be charitable and don't tell him so!


## Notes

1.     QJS, January, 1916, p. 26.

2.     "Unfortunately, today in many forensic contests criticism
       is often discouraged and, indeed, in some contests,
       prohibited.  It would seem that if our forensic contests
       are educational opportunities, and if the student has
       spent a great deal of effort preparing for this particu-
       lar event then the least we can offer is sound, construc-
       tive criticism on how he might improve his speaking."
       "Coaching Individual Events," Robert E. Dunham, The
       Ohio State University, former Director of the Ohio
       High School Speech League and the Pennsylvania
       High School Speech League, Directing Forensics:
       Debate and Contest Speaking,  compiled by Don F.
       Faules, Ohio University and Richard D. Rieke, The
       Ohio State University, International Textbook Com-
       pany, Scranton, 1968, p. 228.

3.     Donald W. Klopf and Carroll P. Lahmann, Coaching
       and Directing Forensics, National Textbook Corpora-
       tion, Skokie, Illinois, 1967, p. 253.

4.     "Tournaments, For Better or Worse?" ST, January,
       1957, pp. 65-67.

5.     "The student should not be afraid to deviate from the
       original.  The judges in the better contests do not
       keep a copy of the manuscript before them as they
       listen in order to determine how far one deviates

from the text." Robert E. Dunham, "Coaching Individual Events," ibid., p. 251.

6. "Do You Know How To Listen? Practical Helps in a Modern Age," Ralph G. Nichols, University of Minnesota, The Rhetoric of Our Times, J. Jeffery Auer, ed., Appleton-Century-Crofts, 1969, p. 233.

7. In fact, I do not believe in complaining even if one thinks he has won. I said to my orator while waiting for the announcement of the decision in the national Hearst Tournament of Orators Contest in 1953 (in which our orator, Guy Vander Jagt, won first): "Now if the judges don't vote for you, remember to be a good loser. I think you won, and I know you think so, but we're both prejudiced in your favor, and one can never tell about these things. Remember, you're not being a good loser if you take defeat graciously if you really think you lost; you're that only in cases where you really think you won and still take your defeat in stride, like a man."

8. Egbert Ray Nichols, Writing The College Oration, Nichols Publishing House, Redlands, California, 1950, p. 73.

Chapter XV

AUDIENCE ATTENDANCE

The only excuse for any kind of public
speaking is the presence of an audience, and
college oratory is no exception. [1]
Charles W. Lomas

I. IMPORTANCE OF AUDIENCES

A genuine speech situation requires a speech, a speaker, and an audience. Our young orators have ideas on timely worth-while subjects which deserve very much to be com-
municated and shared. A flyer promoting a new text quotes
the poet John Andrew Holmes as saying: "What could be
more pathetic than an empty speaker pouring himself forth
to a full house?"[2] To me the obvious answer is, a full
speaker pouring himself forth before an empty house! In
this chapter, we concern ourselves with the audience attendance situation, and the need for improving it.

II. TWO KINDS OF AUDIENCES

The usual audience at local oratorical contests is
made up primarily of high school and college faculty and students, and such interested towns-people as can be induced to
attend. Following the local contest, regional, state, interstate, and tournament-convention contests have audiences with
a similar intellectual and academic background. These audiences we shall refer to as campus audiences. All others we
shall designate off-campus audiences. Such would include
luncheon clubs, P.T.A. groups, men's clubs, church groups,
ladies' literary clubs, civic organizations, and others of all
kinds. Most such organizations are eager to secure outside
speakers for their programs. Many coaches have already
made a practice of arranging annual appearances before such
groups. But in this area we have just barely scratched the
surface. A veritable gold mine and veins of rich ore remain

untapped.  The possibilities for publicizing and expanding the
messages of our student orators are immense and rewarding.

III.   INCREASING ATTENDANCE - CAMPUS AUDIENCES
       A.  Local Contests

        Interest in local contest oratory, as measured by at-
tendance, will vary from school to school.  Some coaches
may have unusual or at least above-average success in attracting audiences, while others may find it an annual struggle.  This much is for sure.  An audience is an integral
part of any speech situation.  Therefore, at least an effort
should be made to obtain an audience.  My own efforts and
methods have been briefly mentioned in Chapter XIII.

        Many local contests in high schools and colleges are
held before judges only, and perhaps a few friends of the
competitors.  The sole interest appears to be to decide who
gets the prizes, and who goes on to further competition to
represent the school.  This is not, or ought not to be, suf-
ficient motivation to attract an audience.  It unduly emphasizes the game element.  Being reconciled to having an audience of this type indicates that "who won?" is more important than "what is said?"  Just as this attitude should not be
the proper motivation for the participants, so similarly this
should not be the motivation which prompts the attendance of
the audience.  Concerning the coach, should the lack of audience be his doing, such deprecation on his part of the primary motive of the orator would indicate his failure to recognize the worth of oratory.

        Everyone knows that the average high school and col-
lege campus is a bee-hive of activity.  Students, faculty, and
townspeople must make some hard choices on what events to
attend.  An enterprising publicity campaign is necessary to
attract people in to the honey-comb.  In the effort to get
audiences, there are times we may have to settle for less
than the ideal situation, but to give up trying to get an audience is inexcusable.  Some high school and college contests
are held before compulsory assemblies.  I have held a few
local oratorical contests at the University of North Dakota as
the program of what was at that time a one-hour weekly required convocation.  In Chapter XIII, I made note of my a-
version to "captive" audiences.  Such a practice all too often
results in contests being looked upon as "exhibitions" to be
observed, rather than as situations where an auditor is open

to influence.

    Perhaps I should add here that at Hope College, be-
fore my coming, it was a tradition for the already-chosen
man and woman local contest winners to deliver their orations on successive days at an expanded compulsory chapel
service just prior to their going to the state MISL contest.
Some might think: "My, what a fine ready-made-to-order
audience!" Not so. Neither my orators nor I looked forward to that ordeal. Even one who is now a Representative
in Congress quailed at the prospect. It was so clearly ex-
hibitory that ere long I was able to persuade our faculty to
dispense with that tradition. Even before off-campus audiences, in my capacity as Chairman introducing orators at a
Rotary Club meeting for example, I always make clear that
what they are about to hear is "for real" and not an "exhibition."


                        B. State Contests

    My observation of attendance at state contests is limi-
ted to Michigan. Both the MHSFA and the MISL have done
outstanding work in promoting forensic activity for many decades. Both richly deserve high praise for their past ac-
complishments. But in recent years, both organizations
have fallen short in getting audiences to attend their final
oratory contests. Basically, my regret is not so much that
there are no audiences of any consequential numbers at their
final state oratory contests. Rather, it is that there does
not appear to be a clear recognition that there ought to be,
with the result that no real efforts are under way to improve
the audience attendance situation. And that is deplorable.

    As an example that not enough effort is being made
to attract audiences, and that none is contemplated, I cite
my experience on April 30, 1968. I was invited to judge
three rounds of oratory in the MHSFA contests, climaxed by
judging the finals in Girls' Oratory. These finals were held
in a small classroom seating no more than 25 persons. Present were two other judges, the contestants, and the coaches
of some of the speakers. The orations were far above average, some of them superb! The tight schedule for all the
other events going on simultaneously that day (Serious Interpretive Reading, Humorous Interpretive Reading, Declamation,
Boys' Oratory, Boys' Extemp, Girls' Extemp, Radio News,
and Multiple Reading) no doubt made the recruiting of an audi-

ence difficult. But I hold oratory in too high esteem to combine it with these other events, worthy as they are. Perhaps
sponsorship and prizes could be sought from an individual or
organization as is done in the companion activity of debate.[3]

The University of Michigan at Ann Arbor, under whose
auspices and on whose campus this event was held, is my
alma mater whose enrollment now numbers over 40, 000 students. If student oratory is ever again to attain the status
I covet for it and which I believe it richly deserves, surely
the affair should have been properly publicized, and if it had,
surely out of the thousands of students and townspeople, many
might have been persuaded to find time and inclination to listen to what these young people had to say.

A few words on the attendance situation in state contests in the MISL. For many years, its state contests were
held traditionally and constitutionally on the first Friday in
March, preliminaries in the morning, women's finals in the
afternoon, and men's in the evening. Host schools were rotated alphabetically, and would vie with each other in recruiting audiences. In "the good old days," these state oratorical contests were very well attended. As a 17-year old resident of Kalamazoo, I remember attending the contest hosted
by Kalamazoo College on March 8, 1918. It was held in the
Masonic Temple because most of the student body attended
in those days and Bowen Hall on the campus could not possibly accommodate the audience of townspeople and delegations
from other schools. I have before me a printed program of
the day's events, through the courtesy of Dr. Marion H.
Dunsmore, an alumnus of the college.[4] In those days, host
schools were rotated alphabetically, and this system remain-
ed in effect for at least 15 years beyond the time that I began my work at Hope College in 1939.

Hope College has been host to this final state contest
in 1942 and 1954. In 1942, perhaps with interest enhanced
by reason of our entrance in World War II a few months before, we managed an audience of over 500. In 1954, by
conservative estimate we did even better. To lend prestige
to the event, we secured the services as chairman of a prominent alumnus, Chief Justice John R. Dethmers of the Michigan Supreme Court, one of the 50 distinguished alumni honored at the 50th Anniversary Convention of PKD at Carbondale,
Illinois, in 1963. We wrote letters to local and nearby PKD
alumni soliciting their attendance and support, to clergymen
within a radius of 40 miles, some of whom inserted notices

of the event in their church bulletins.   We secured the cooperation of most local fraternities and sororities who gave
up their traditional Friday evening meeting or met early and
in a few instances attended the contest in a body.

Eleven years later, the state attendance situation
reached its nadir.   In 1964, the MISL dispensed with the
hitherto sacrosanct constitutional provision for Friday afternoon and evening finals.   The next year, both final contests
were held on a Saturday afternoon, the worst possible time
for attracting audiences.   To cap the climax, the two final
contests for men and women were held concurrently!   This
was clearly a devaluation of the worth of oratory.   At the
following fall meeting, the oratory coaches recommended an
attack on the "no audience" problem, and the avoidance of
concurrent contests, and these recommendations were adopted without a dissenting vote.   Fortunately, the following year,
at Eastern Michigan University, Ypsilanti, with the fine cooperation of Professor Thomas J. Murray, President of
MISL, and also the boost of Dr. Harold Sponberg, its president, a former Gustavus Adolphus College orator, there was
considerable improvement in audience attendance.

## C.   Interstate Contests

And what are we to say of the finals in the IOA contests?   The first such contest was well attended on February 27, 1874, "in the City Opera House at Galesburg, Illinois, before the largest crowd ever to assemble."[5]   A good
beginning.   At the some 21 of these contests that I have attended with my orators, the audiences have been disappoint-
ingly small.   This, in spite of the fact that most of them
have been held under the sponsorship of the Speech Departments of three large universities with prestigious reputations
in the forensic field, Northwestern University, Michigan
State University, and currently Wayne State University.

## D.   Tournaments - Conventions

One can hardly expect sizable audiences at tournament or convention contests in oratory.   For both the competitors and the coach-judges are occupied with their own
events.   The officials of the tournaments or convention, however, should publicize the event and make clear that interested townspeople of the community are welcome.

One important suggestion should be made here for the convention orator. Although convention audiences are rather sparse, and not too typical in that the conspicuous presence of the judges accentuates the contest element, you as the speaker should always regard even these small audiences as you would any other. That is to say, your primary intent should be to influence them. You should try to make the few auditors present forget that the occasion is a somewhat artificial one. It is a high accomplishment for you to keep the audience so interested in your message as to make them almost oblivious to their surroundings. Orators, even in contests at conventions, should always be speaking for results.

The campus audience problem at all levels--local, state, interstate--is a long way from being solved. For all contestants and coaches of oratory, it should be a continuing matter of what the Quakers call "concern." Those coaches who are successful in securing sizable audiences could do their colleagues in the profession a great service by writing in the speech journals or speaking at speech conventions to tell of their methods. The late Professor George L. Hinds, for many years a highly successful coach at Wayne State University, Detroit, has already written this kind of article. Citing many years of well-attended contests at his own university, he urges that forensic leaders

> ... utilize sound principles of public relations and promotion to encourage local audiences to attend speech events.
>
> Newspapers can help a great deal. When Mr. Harry Taylor of the Detroit Times held the Hearst national finals in Detroit a year ago, 2200 people attended the contest. If we made our college events good enough, and if we remember that newspapermen are not inaccessible we can secure the help of these powerful media in publicizing outstanding contests. ... Last December, local finals for men in the annual Wayne Oratory Contest saw three state or national champions compete with each other before an audience of 500 people. [6]

IV.  INCREASING ATTENDANCE - OFF CAMPUS AUDIENCES
    A.  Additional Speech Experience

    Think back on what you have read so far in this book a-
bout all the time and effort an orator puts into the preparation
of an oration.  Isn't it on the face of it an inexcusable waste
of brain- power to limit his opportunities for speaking to a
single appearance in a local contest?  Both the contestant
and the coach should be on the look- out to arrange off- campus appearances for all local entries.  Only those, however,
who reach a minimum standard of excellence, and who give
promise of handling the assignment with credit to himself,
his cause, and his school, should be encouraged in making
such appearances.  Many orators report that, with the ten-
sion- producing contest element removed, their concentration
upon the audience and the message is enhanced.


    B.  Audience Adaptation

    Every speech is prepared with a specific audience in
mind, and requires audience adaptation.  Off- campus audiences provide the orator with that invaluable experience.  No
two audiences are exactly alike.  The orator must adjust his
manner and method of presentation to the needs and interests
of the specific audience before him.  This will require the
ability to interpolate extemporaneous material while retaining the basic memorized speech.  To do this successfully
takes skill but with assiduous practice, that ability can be
cultivated.

    In arranging these outside appearances, a coach
should not hesitate to arrange them before any of the three
kinds of audiences:  favorably disposed, indifferent, or hostile.  In the first group, the orator's purpose would be to
strengthen the audience's already- held beliefs, and in the
second to alert an indifferent audience to a problem they had
not previously known or thought about.  But if the intent of
both contestant and coach is to expand the influence of the
message, an audience known to be hostile to the orator's i-
deas should be welcomed as an opportunity.  Perhaps "hostile" is too strong and ominous a word.  There are degrees
in hostility.  In making adaptative changes in the prepared
oration before such groups, the orator should be less concerned with "getting something out of his system" and more
concerned with wooing and winning his audience to his point
of view.  A "come, let us reason together" attitude on the

orator's part is far better for that purpose than an explosive, bellicose attitude of "I'm tellin' you!"

### C.  Promotion "Town-Gown" Relations

An ancillary advantage of appearances of orators before off-campus audiences is the promotion of good "town-gown" relations. This value is not inconsequential for both high schools and colleges. High schools depend upon the public for their financial support. Through the P. T. A., orchestra and band concerts, plays, athletics, and through forensic contests, including oratory, high school administrators covet opportunities to be of service to the community. Likewise, every college president seeks the support, financially and otherwise, of the leaders of the community where the college is located. Bringing together young orators and members of the local community makes for good public relations.

### D.  Recommended by Experts

Off-campus audiences have received official sanction of the body of experts who comprise the AFA. In the opening paragraph of its "Code For Contests in Oratory," one reads: "While competitive speaking events are familiar to the campus, non-academic groups can provide a welcome additional impetus to student development in the skills of advocacy." E. C. Buehler, Professor Emeritus of Speech and Drama at the University of Kansas, co-author of Building the Contest Oration, while serving as President of Delta Sigma Rho, national honorary forensic fraternity, wrote on the "President's Page" of The Gavel, its official organ: "The off-campus forensic activity for many institutions should be an established adjunct of our regular program. It should be explored and developed to a much greater extent."[7]

Following the North Central Association's 1950 Contest Committee report recommending the abolition of interscholastic speech contests, and the Speech Association of America's excellent reply defining the place of speech in the schools, Professor Halbert E. Gulley, currently chairman of the speech department at Northern Illinois University, De Kalb, wrote an article: "The High School Speech Programs and the SAA Report." In it he lists "... some specific changes we should consider which might bring our forensic programs closer to the philosophies expressed by the NCA

and the Speech Association of America.  Among those recommendations is the following:

> We must give more students many more opportuni-
> ties to address audiences.  As many persons have
> pointed out, here is one of the great weaknesses of
> the debate tournament and the individual speaking
> events at our district and state contests.  Speak-
> ing to an empty room and a critic is not necessar-
> ily conducive to the development of good speech.
> School assemblies, programs for community organ-
> izations, etc., are possibilities we all know about.
> We must be more diligent in searching for such
> opportunities. [8]

### E.  Off-Campus Audiences - A Proven Success

In advocating a vast expansion of off-campus audiences, we are not crusading for something new and untried.
Many coaches for many years have carried on this practice.
William Norwood Brigance, a past president of the SAA and
a highly successful coach of orators, took his orators to
many such groups.  Wayne State University has availed itself of these audiences in both oratory and debate for many
years.  George Ziegelmueller, past president of the AFA,
and John Boaz of that school in 1964 wrote of the companion
activity of debate.  They said they were in the seventh year
of the practice of holding debates before various civic organizations in the Detroit metropolitan area.  In the preceding
year, "17,000 Detroiters listened to a total of 64 debates on
the national debate topic."[9]

Both at the University of North Dakota and at Hope
College, we made annual appearances with both debaters and
orators before various civic groups such as the Knights of
Columbus, the American Legion, the Sons and Daughters of
Norway, and at the men's clubs of various church groups.
Following the stock market crash in 1929, North Dakota was
afflicted both by depression and drought.  The Legislature
drastically cut educational appropriations.  One of my orators, Don Holand, who is now himself in the Legislature,
prepared an oration entitled "The Educational Crisis" which
he delivered some dozen times in various cities throughout
the state.

One of the most stimulating articles appearing in recent journals as this is written is entitled: "Participating in Community Affairs," by Dorothy Q. Weirich of Webster Groves Senior High School, Webster Groves, Missouri. One of five contributors to the main article: "Advice For the Beginning Teacher of Speech: A Symposium," even experienced teachers could profit from a thoughtful reading of it. [10] Note this excerpt:

> The schools and the community are inseparable. In no other place is the truth of this statement demonstrated any more effectively than by the use of high school speech students in community life.

The experiences involving the author's speech students with the community in appearances in a wide variety of subjects and occasions, make inspirational reading.


## V.  A BASIC NEED - HIGHER CONCEPTION OF THE WORTH OF ORATORY

Absence of audiences represents one of oratory's present major problems. In her excellent article, Dorothy Q. Weirich says: "As communicators we have failed to communicate the worth of our product." In some circles, this observation is most assuredly true when those in charge hardly make an effort to secure an audience, sometimes upon the wholly mistaken notion that the benefits of oratory can be obtained without one. What prospect would buy from a salesman who held his own product in such low esteem? I believe that high school and college oratory can play a significant role in problem-solving, and in influencing public opinion. The potential is there. But the addition of audiences could make a considerable difference in bringing its potential nearer to reality.

This feeling about the importance of audiences I have held from the beginning of my teaching career. It was rather dramatically confirmed nearer its close. In the summer of 1960, I received a Hope College Summer Study Faculty Grant. The purpose was to visit several German universities, and to confer with leaders in speech education. I reported on that experience in the autumn 1961 issue of the Central States Speech Journal. [11] In the opening paragraph, I stated:

My objectives were to observe the teaching of
classes, particularly in beginning speech, to exchange ideas generally about aims and methods in
speech education, and specifically to discuss the
values--and admitted shortcomings--of extra-curricular activities in the hope that contests in debate,
extemporaneous speaking and oratory might be incorporated into the German speech program in the
foreseeable future.

At that point, I inserted Footnote 3 which reads, "Space
limitations require that a report on this latter phase of my
visit be delayed for a later article." That "later article"
never got written. But I report now the gist of what I would
have said, which is that German colleges and universities
will never have anything comparable to our forensic programs. And the primary reason is the lack of audiences.

I remember well my visits with Dr. Paul Tack of
Bonn University, President of the German Speech Association, and especially my concluding conference at the beautiful Beethoven Halle in Bonn. Dr. Tack had spent a year
here at the University of Wisconsin. As we discussed our
forensic programs with him, and earlier with others, [12] I
could sense that they were being kind, courteous, considerate toward me personally as a guest. Some were rather
reticent. But a few did say orally, in effect, "But what's
the good of it all without audiences, and especially if nothing gets done as a result of the speaking?" In short, the
German visit confirmed my belief that the value of forensics,
including oratory, as a preparation for life in the future
needs to be de-emphasized, and that its value in the here
and now must receive greater emphasis.


VI. SUGGESTIONS FOR INCREASING ATTENDANCE

Oratory coaches who lack a high enough conception of
the worth of oratory, who are content to think of oratory
contests primarily in terms of a game to decide the winner,
who feel the objective of preparation for future adult speaking is met whether the audiences are large or small, may
be few in number. The vast majority would no doubt prefer
to have audiences. But many do not know how to begin.
Some suggestions may be helpful, especially to beginners in
coaching. The situations throughout the country, as to size
and nature of communities and schools are so varied that

one hardly knows how to proceed.   But we shall try.

A high school or college coach should start taking inventory of ideas with himself and with his own campus.   In his own classes, he can radiate enthusiasm for oratory. From there on out, like the concentric circles that form when you plunk a stone into a pond, you should impress your faculty colleagues with your enthusiasm for the task you are engaged in.   Not always directly, but by indirection you should seek their cooperation in helping to boost attendance, for example:   by having your colleagues not only announce up-coming oratory events in their classes but urge attendance; by having them serve as judges if qualified; or by getting them to attend the event themselves.   You should by all means enlist the cooperation and support of the principal or college president.   Keep him informed of what events are going on, invite his support, including that shown by his personal attendance.   If there is a publicity director at your school, be on good terms with him, provide him with such good publicity releases for circulation by him to the news media that he is likely to come himself!   If there is a speaker's bureau on your campus, make known the availability of your orators to go out and speak before community organizations.

The coach is a member of the community as well as a faculty member.   He is no doubt a member of a church, perhaps a luncheon club, and of other civic organizations. In these groups, he should be a booster for oratory at every opportunity.   He should sound out key members of organizations to which he belongs for their willingness to have an oratory program presented at one of their meetings.   Also they should be informed about such events being held on the campus, and their attendance solicited, especially if the subjects that will be discussed are pertinent to their interests. Once the original contact has been established, and the club is pleased with the program, its officers are likely to agree it should be made an annual affair.   We have appeared before the Holland Rotary Club annually for over 12 years.   In Grand Forks, North Dakota, either as debaters or orators, our students appeared annually on an evening program of the Sons and Daughters of Norway.   Both the organization and our speakers looked forward to that event, followed by a social affair afterwards, complete with dancing the polka and the schottische!

Often such appearances snowball; other groups, reading of an event in the local newspaper, will call you for dates. Speaking of the newspaper, get acquainted with the local editor. See that he is supplied with the "Who? What? When? Where? and Why?" of forensic events, complete with biographical information about your contestants. Does your town have a radio or TV station, perhaps a segment of programming devoted to public affairs? Seek to expand the message of your orators by telling the station manager what you have to offer. You may well find that your orators will make a hit. As a result of successful public appearances with their orations, your orators may often be asked to become involved in community affairs and to make other public appearances. Ours, for example, have often been recruited to help out in United Fund Community Chest campaigns, urging people to "Put all your begs in one Ask-it!" At the annual ceremony in Holland on Memorial Day, it is traditional that Lincoln's "Gettysburg Address" is read, and for over 20 years this function has been performed by an orator from the college.

There is nothing startlingly original in these suggestions. One device for increasing attendance, carried out every year of my 12-year stay at the University of North Dakota, was at that time rather novel. One special day in the school year was designated as FORENSIC DAY. On that day, we sought to involve both the campus and community, and to focus attention upon a number of forensic events. FORENSIC DAY usually was held on a Thursday, and began with the midmorning weekly convocation, continued with appearances at luncheon clubs which also met on Thursdays. Afternoon appearances were made at the three area high schools; sometimes another event on the campus in mid-afternoon, climaxed by an outstanding event in the evening on the campus. While these appearances also involved other forensic activity, oratory always played a prominent part in them. We have held an annual Freshman Oratorical contest, a local varsity oratorical contest, a state "old-line" contest, a state IPSA contest, and even on one occasion a western division contest of the IOA.[13] Beginning with three events on the first of such days, we wound up the 12th annual FORENSIC DAY with seven. These events were always well received and attended.

VII.  RECAPITULATION

Concluding this chapter on audience attendance, we draw all the strings together, like a balloon vendor at a circus, and recapitulate these suggestions in tabulated form.

1.  Get a distinguished chairman.

2.  If otherwise qualified, get prominent citizens to serve as judges.

3.  Get a prominent person to present the prizes.

4.  Publicize by posters and placards in halls, and in campus and local newspapers.

5.  Get faculty to cooperate by making announcements in their classes.

6.  Enlist the support of leading campus organizations such as international relations clubs, and fraternities and sororities.

7.  Make known the availability of orators through the speaker's bureau.

8.  If a church school, publicize the event through the churches.

9.  Try to appear on programs such as the A.A.U.W. and others on an annual basis.

10.  Get on "public affairs" programs on radio and TV.

11.  Work in close liaison with the publicity department to publicize events.

12.  Experiment with a FORENSIC DAY.


## Notes

1.  "The College Oration and the Classic Tradition," The Gavel, May, 1949, p. 79, by Mr. Lomas, University of California at Los Angeles.

2.  The book advertised: Speech: Idea and Delivery,

Charles W. Lomas and Ralph Richardson, Houghton
Mifflin Co., Boston, 1963.

3. "In 1970, 33 debaters competed in a 2-day event, including preliminary rounds, in competition for the
John S. Knight Scholarship awards of 1st prize,
$1300; 2nd prize, $900; and 3rd prize, $600. John
S. Knight is editorial chairman of the Detroit Free
. Press, under whose sponsorship the finals in debate
were held since 1947. Since then 100 high school
debaters have shared more than $60,000 in scholar-
ship funds." Detroit Free Press, April 16, 1970.

4. In a letter to me dated November 27, 1970, Dr. Dunsmore writes: "As an indication of the interest in
and attendance at the contests, I'll cite the following. The 1917 contest was held in Holland, and the
Kalamazoo College students chartered a special car
on the interurban. As I remember it, the car was
well filled."

5. According to John W. Low, Nebraska Wesleyan University, "My Paper Doll," 1st in IOA contest, 1947,
WO-1947, p. 29.

6. "Developing University Oratory and Extemporaneous
Speaking Programs," The Gavel, November, 1953,
p. 15.

7. "The Off-Campus Audience as an Adjunct of the Forensic Program," The Gavel, January, 1948, p. 27.

8. CSSJ, Spring, 1954, p. 11.

9. ST, November, 1964, p. 270.

10. ST, November, 1969, pp. 273-76. While the article
makes no specific mention of oratory, the author
assured me at the CSSA Convention in Chicago April
11, 1970 that orators were among those taking part
in these outside appearances.

11. "A Goodwill Visit to Six German Universities," CSSJ,
Autumn, 1961, pp. 35-42.

12. Other professors consulted were: Dr. Christian Wink-
ler, Phillipps University, Marburg; Walter Kuhlman,

Albert Ludwig University, Freiburg; Frau Korwan, Heidelberg University; Dr. Walter Wittsack, Johann Wolfgang Goethe University, Frankfurt; and Dr. Irmgard Weithase, Munich University.

13. The 5th annual FORENSIC DAY, April 7, 1932 was a double feature, the Western Divisional Contest of the IOA, in which Harold LeVander, former Governor of Minnesota, and Raymond Carhart, later the well-known audiologist at Northwestern University, took part, and a debate between the University of North Dakota and Gustavus Adolphus College, which the UND won by a 2-1 decision. It is in University Debaters' Annual, 1931-1932, ed. Edith M. Phelps, H. W. Wilson Co., 1932, pp. 325-375.

Chapter XVI

ORATORY OF THE FUTURE

It is not too much to expect men and
women who are about to become citizens in
this bewildered age, to think about great issues, and to write and speak about them.
Most college students are potentially big e-
nough to rise to the challenge of these times.[1]

Lew Sarett
William Trufant Foster
Alma Johnson Sarett

## I.  CONTINUOUS NEED FOR ORATORY

Oratory deals largely with public problems--peace and
war, racial prejudice, the population explosion, poverty, in-
adequate health care, the pollution of our environment, and a
host of others.  These require research, study, talking about.
If ever they do get solved, other problems will have arisen
to take their place.  Can anyone really be so optimistic as to
believe all perplexing problems will be solved in the foreseeable future?  But we keep on trying.  Thus, there will always be a need for the practice of oratory in society in the
future.  The public platform is only one of many public agencies, such as the pulpit and press, which seek to improve
the lot of man.  This concluding chapter on the oratory of
the future considers the role that educational contest oratory
plays and ought to play in problem-solving.

Oratory, as we all know, can be used for malign as
well as for beneficent purposes.  One may well ask, how do
we know that what student orators say will always be in the
direction of improvement?  Well, we don't, but such at least
is the intent.  Perhaps I should first clarify the term "problem-solving" lest I create the impression that the controversial questions with which most oratory deals, admit of but
one solution.  Recall that I said earlier in Chapter III that

truth on such questions is always in process of discovery.
Orations deal with the kinds of questions upon which honest
men can, will, and do differ. Thus it is not surprising to
find orations where diametrically opposite viewpoints are ad-
vocated. For example, I was present at the IOA finals for
women in 1950 where this happened. First place was awarded to Jeanne Harrell, University of Kentucky, Lexington, for
her oration, "The Quality of Mercy, " a plea for mercy- killing under proper safeguards.[2] In the same contest were two
orations against mercy- killing, "Mercy or Murder?"[3] by
Helen Peterson, of Luther College, Decorah, Iowa, and "A
Call to Arms, "[4] by Helen M. Spano, Duquesne University,
Pittsburgh, Pennsylvania. Similarly, today, it is entirely
possible that one orator may speak for "preventive detention"
and the denial of bail, while another may speak in favor of
the retention of the constitutional guarantees of the Constitution. One orator may speak in favor of our going all- out to
win the war in Vietnam. Another may charge it with being
an immoral war we never should have entered in the first
place, and that we should extricate ourselves from it at the
earliest opportunity. The point is that through oratory, the
communication process is kept open, and auditors are free to
choose in the free market place of ideas. And in that sense,
oratory contributes to problem- solving.


II.   PROBLEM- SOLVING - CONTRIBUTION OF HIGH SCHOOL
      AND COLLEGE ORATORY
      A.   Potential is There and Expandable

      Students in our high schools and colleges are very
much a part of this world. Through oratory participation,
they can and ought and do make some contribution, however
small, toward problem- solving. It has long been my belief,
expressed as early as in Chapter II and more recently in the
preceding chapter, that the student speaker with a message,
speaking in local contests and often before civic groups both
before and after the competitive event, has already exerted
an influence upon the world's life. With less emphasis upon
winning, more upon getting before audiences, that influence
can be vastly expanded in the future.

      To credit high school and college orators with the po-
tential power of making an appreciable impact in curing the
malaise of our society seems on the face of it to be an incredible claim. On the other hand, to consider that the thousands upon thousands of orations delivered annually in ham-

lets, villages, cities, and in colleges and universities dotted
all over the land make absolutely no impact upon the public
opinion which ultimately guides public policy, seems equally
unrealistic. As has been previously indicated, the fact that
pressure groups are all too eager to promote oratorical contests and thus to provide a forum to advance their causes is
a clear recognition that such speaking occasions are thought
to carry some influence.

### B.  Oratory's Influence Not Computable

The real question at issue centers upon the amount
and degree of such influence. And the catch here is that
this is an intangible which is simply not measurable by any
presently known standards of measurement. We have made
incredible advances in the field of scientific achievement and
measurement. Many years ago I read that New York University had developed an amplifier that could measure the sound
of a cat's purr 3, 000 miles away. Yes, in the last decade,
we have even gone to the moon, and measured its distance
from earth. A UPI dispatch dated August 21, 1969, began:
"It's official. The precise distance from earth to the moon,
give or take a silly millimeter, is 232, 271. 3816 miles."
This apparently was computable. But the influence of an
orator upon the life of the world cannot ever be so accurately assessed. For myself, I would rather err in the direction of assuming that high school and college orators exert
much more of an influence, rather than less, than is generally supposed.

### III.  THE CONTRIBUTION OF THE HIGH SCHOOL

No consideration of the future of oratory would be
complete without considering the contributions of high school
oratory. The numbers taking part in high school oratory
are in themselves impressive. E. C. Buehler, Professor
Emeritus of the University of Kansas, and Richard L.
Johannesen, of Indiana University, tell of contests sponsored by the Optimists International since 1928, of high school
contests sponsored by various organizations such as Veterans
of Foreign Wars, Future Farmers of America, the American
Legion, the National Forensic League, the state activities
speech associations of 30 states, and conclude that "the total
number of high school students now participating in contest
oratory well exceeds half a million a year."[5]

There is no inherent reason why a bright high school student cannot write a good oration as well as can his college counterpart. I have heard many excellent ones. I have read of some criticism that coaches sometimes write the orations for their high school students and this I could not, of course, condone.

While I have not taught for so much as a single hour in high school, this hardly disqualifies my testimony. For I have served as judge in a large number of high school oratorical contests sponsored by the state speech associations in North Dakota, Minnesota, Missouri, Illinois, Colorado, and Michigan. Moreover, my some 210 speeches at high school commencements over a period of 35 years have given me some contact with and a deep appreciation for high school students.[6] I admire them for their discontent with the state of the world as they find it. I share their youthful idealism in resolving to do something toward improving it. The subjects high school students discuss in their orations should be adapted to their capabilities. Sometimes they may tackle problems which their elders have never solved and have no prospect of ever solving. And yet, if these youthful Davids do battle with subjects as big as Goliath, I cannot fault them for trying.

## IV. CONTRIBUTION OF THE COLLEGE AND UNIVERSITY

In his address at the Centennial Anniversary of Phi Beta Kappa of Harvard College June 30, 1881, "The Scholar in a Republic," Wendell Phillips, the noted abolitionist orator, said, "I urge on college-bred men, that, as a class, they fail in republican duty when they allow others to lead in the agitation of the great social questions which stir and agitate the age."[7] In my view, this admonition to educated men is hardly necessary for college orators. They are interested and knowledgeable in the controversial questions of the day. I have previously expressed my belief that the contributions of college orators toward problem-solving have been substantial in the past. There is no reason to believe their contributions will be less in the future. Many, if not most, college orators have entered life professions where they exercised their speaking ability for the good of mankind. The idealism engendered within them during college days most likely stays with college orators throughout their more mature years. A few may become cynical, but not many. The vast majority add "the stubborn ounces of their weight" to many a worthy cause in later life.


### A.  Record of Past College Orators

From the vast numbers of people in public life who
took part in college oratory, one hesitates to single out individuals.  But Abraham J. Muste, Mel Ravitz, Harold
LeVander, George S. McGovern, and Abraham Kaplan come
to mind as I write. [8]  Each was a college orator in his day,
and now have outstanding records of achievement in later
life.

There was Abraham J. Muste, a distinguished Hope
College alumnus, second-place winner in the 1903 IOA contest, active in the cause of labor relations and Christian pacifism, for many years Executive Secretary of the Fellowship
of Reconciliation. [9]  Mel Ravitz, a Wayne State University
orator in the MISL in 1944 with his oration "Peace No Less
Renowned Than War," was in a triple tie for first place.
He is now a professor of sociology at his alma mater.   In
the fall Detroit city elections in 1969, he received the largest number of votes for the City Council, and thus became
its president.   Harold LeVander, a Gustavus Adolphus College orator with his oration "Date Kernels" won high honors
in Minnesota as an undergraduate in 1932.   In 1968, he was
a Lutheran Church in America delegate to the World Council
of Churches meeting in Uppsala, Sweden, and at the time of
this writing is serving as Governor of Minnesota.

A South Dakota state winner with his 1946 oration
"From Cave to Cave," from Dakota Wesleyan University,
Mitchell, was Senator George S. McGovern.  His activities
against hunger and poverty, his directorship of the Food for
Peace program, and his opposition to the Vietnam war, are
all well-known.   Finally, there was Abraham Kaplan, from
the College of St. Thomas, St. Paul, Minnesota, a second-
place winner in the national Intercollegiate Peace Association contest in 1936, in competition against 802 orations from
24 states, with his oration "Half Slave, Half Free."  He is
now a professor of philosophy at the University of Michigan
and in the May 6, 1966 issue of _Time_ was featured as one
of ten "Great Teachers" in the country.  All of these persons, and hundreds more, have risen, it will be admitted,
to positions where they can conceivably affect public opinion.
But my mind just cannot make that jump to believe that they
are influential now, but made no appreciable dent and impact

upon their audiences when they were younger.  At just exactly what point did their present maturity and influence begin?


## V.  THE CURRENT REVOLT OF YOUTH

We live today in perilous times.  Our country and our
world,  like a bowlegged girl, are in ba-a-a-d shape.  There
is a mood of revolt on high school and college campuses.  I
intend no learned discourse about it,  nor any effort to sort
out all the component elements of this student rebellion.  I
would like briefly,  however,  to consider it in its relation to
the oratory of the future,  the consideration of this chapter.
I believe we can harness the good elements in it, for there
are such,  and use oratory as the vehicle and outlet for the
many justifiable frustrations of young people today.

For a long period in my teaching career, especially
in the Fifties, students were characterized as "the silent
generation."  It was pathetic to observe in the average student the abysmal lack of interest in, and ignorance of, current affairs happening all around them every day, and their
failure to speak out about them.  A chapel speaker aptly cap-
sulized this attitude by his remark, "The best way to mysti-
fy a college audience is to refer to the morning newspaper."
During this period, debaters and orators were the exception.
They were knowledgeable and interested in the events swirl-
ing about them in the non-academic outside world.

Within the past decade, there has been a dramatic
turn-about in student attitudes toward current affairs.  Truly,
in Bob Dylan's words "The Times They are A-Changin'."  It
is difficult to pin-point the exact time of change.  Its first
faint stirrings probably began in the spring of 1960 with the
sit-ins at Southern lunch counters,  and pickets in Washington
and riots against the House Un-American Activities Committee, in San Francisco.[10]  This awakened interest in the grav-
ity of the problems of the day was accompanied by a demand for action.  "Involvement" became the "in" word.
There was a desire on the part of youth to do something
about the urgent needs surrounding them.


### A.  The Good In It

Anyone must be dull and insensitive who does not see
that today's young people have just reason to complain of the

bad "status quo." They are not "rebels without a cause."
They are seeking meaning and purpose in their lives, and
are questioning our values and priorities as adults. With
environmental disaster and atomic war facing them, and the
draft breathing down their necks in what many believe to be
an unjust and undeclared war, it is wholly understandable
that youth is disillusioned with the failures of the older generation. They became dedicated to humanitarian causes. The
phenomenal and enthusiastic response given by them to President John F. Kennedy's challenge of the Peace Corps was one
evidence of their concern for the poor and the oppressed.
Youth joined in the 1963 March on Washington, and enrolled
in the Southern Summer civil rights projects organized under
the sponsorship of the National Council of Churches. All
over the country appeared evidences of a desire to be helpful. On Hope's campus, the Higher Horizons Program, a
tutorial program for slow learners as also an effort to es-
tablish a Big Brother relationship between college students
and disadvantaged youngsters in the community, was a mi-
crocosm of what was happening throughout the country. The
Reverend Billy Graham, in one of his syndicated daily columns, conceded:

> Society is filled with crime, over-emphasis on ma-
> terial things and the love of pleasure. Some of
> the rebellion of our youngsters is against these
> false values, and, in this, I am on their side.[11]

## B.   The Bad In It

Toward the end of the decade, goaded by the slowness
of "the Establishment" to change its ways, there was a polarization between youth and their elders. A "generation
gap" developed; "don't trust anyone over 30" became the slogan. Campus activists took the path of force and violence.
Destroying draft records, imprisoning deans, burning build-
ings, heckling and denying the opportunity for those of opposing viewpoints to be heard, resulted. But violence is not
the way of the educated man, the one who is committed to
reasoned discourse in human relations for bringing about
change. William Norwood Brigance, former president of
SAA, had the East-West confrontation and international war
in mind when he wrote the following, but what he said is
equally applicable to campus and domestic strife:

> There are two kinds of nations and two kinds of
> people in the world: Those who in disagreements
> and crises want to shoot it out, and those who
> have learned to talk it out. To shoot it out is the
> way of the concentration camp, machine gun, and
> the bomb. To talk it out is the way of mediation,
> parliamentary discussion, and political campaigns
> settled by the ballot. [12]

On both sides of the present polarization between the younger
and the older generation, there is a notable absence of listening to what the other side is saying. Someone has aptly
put it: "When communication ceases, reason dies." Time
rightly wrote: "Violence is, essentially, a confession of ultimate inarticulateness."[13] What John W. Gardner, Chairman of the Urban Coalition, former Secretary of Health, Education and Welfare, predicted on July 15, 1969, has deplor-
ably come true: "Over and over, we have seen that violence
and coercion do not lead forward to constructive change but
backward to repressive countermeasures."[14] A sound train-
in oratory, in its reliance upon talk to produce action, would
be of immense value in countering the violence prevalent today.

It has been said that today action, and not talk as
represented by oratory, is the mood of the hour. But let
us remind ourselves that some of the best orations have e-
merged as a result of prior involvement in action. For example, in Holland, Michigan, each year a community ambassador is selected through cooperation with the Experiment in
International Living for a summer's live-in with a foreign
family. At least six Hope College orations have resulted
from that international experience in action, usually followed
by an appeal for some kind of further action in various specific ways for improved international relations. On the domestic front, orations have been prepared after a summer's work
in a mental hospital, social welfare work with elderly persons, and in the slums of a metropolitan city. Such orations
are personalized ones, the most effective type, based upon
action, and not divorced from it.

### C.   One Student's Lament

The mood of frustration in today's students was well
put in an excerpt written by student Roger Black of the University of Chicago as his contribution to a symposium in

Life Magazine:

> We share a large degree of outrage--outrage at the
> hypocrisies of an older generation that outlaws mar-
> ijuana while drinking and smoking itself to the
> grave; outrage at politicians who try to enforce or-
> der by approving laws that plant the seeds of a po-
> lice state; outrage at an educational structure that
> makes people blind and mindless functionaries in a
> system which they don't understand and which, as
> a result, is out of control; outrage at the race to
> build instruments of destruction when we already
> have enough arms to kill every man, flower and
> bug on earth a hundred times over; outrage at the
> 'fact that we have so befouled our environment that
> even if we aren't blown up we may all be poisoned
> or suffocated to death; outrage most of all at the
> war that goes on and on, killing men for a cause
> that is now an admitted mistake, spending billions
> of dollars on the other side of the globe while mil-
> lions of our people are hungry or cold or so des-
> perate that they have taken to rioting in the streets.
> But because of the outrage we also share a convic-
> tion that people must love each other not only to
> be happy, but to survive. This is so obvious to
> us it is a cliché. But it is not obvious to every-
> one or we would not be in the fix we are in.[15]

### D. Today's Student Mood - A Golden Opportunity For Oratory

What a fine cataloguing and listing of excellent subjects for orations in this indictment! And what a golden opportunity for talking about these subjects, not only in contests but before non-academic audiences, and for influencing
public opinion in the direction of the action you want taken.
While I believe past oratory has done much more good than
is generally supposed, I also believe as a profession we have
failed to capitalize fully on its possibilities of bringing to
public attention and discussion the urgent problems of our
times.

## V. A PHILOSOPHY OF ORATORY

In this handbook we have considered many details of
contest oratory. It is now time for a more comprehensive

look at the future of oratory in modern society.  It is as if
a house-builder, having completed the various rooms of a
house, steps outside and takes a long last look at the completed structure.


### A.  A Talk With Teachers

I believe all who teach speech, and specifically we
who are coaches of oratory, have an obligation to seek,
through our teaching, the moral betterment of mankind.  The
potential for helping to do that presents itself in our work
with orators.  That idea is not original with me.  I am simply appropriating as applicable to oratory the statements of
some leading textbook writers in the profession.  Read what
Robert T. Oliver, for many years chairman of the department at Pennsylvania State University and currently a research
professor of International speech, says:

> In the present unsettled state of the world, there
> is a renewal of the ancient demand that speech be
> used as a moral force for the betterment of man-
> kind. ...  The author has ... emphasized much
> more than has been customary the social responsi-
> bility of the public speaker.[16]

Note, too, these observations from Giles Wilkeson Gray, professor emeritus at Louisiana State University, and Professor
Waldo W. Braden, current chairman of the department at
that institution:

> The authors have felt that it was high time to call
> attention again sharply to the fact, sometimes over-
> looked, that speech is a terrific force in human re-
> lations for either good or ill; that because of its
> potentialities, the acquisition of ability in speaking
> carries with it a deep responsibility for its ethical
> use; that in scarcely any period in our history has
> the need existed as it exists today for a type of
> honest thinking and speaking that is motivated by a
> genuine concern for the well-being of humanity.
> [Emphasis mine].[17]

If we agree with these sentiments, it should be a
source of encouragement to us as we go about our daily and
sometimes humdrum routine tasks.  The oratory of the future is unpredictable.  The direction it will take will largely

depend upon our efforts as coaches. If we can keep students
on the path of reasoned discourse rather than violence, if we
can get more of them to take part in oratory, not only in
contests but in appearances before off-campus audiences, if
we can minimize the importance now accorded to winning,
then the future cannot be other than bright. We can then
look forward to enjoying a banner year in 1974 when this oldest educational forensic activity celebrates its centennial year.

### B. A Chat With Students

How I would like to talk personally at length to everyone of you students who read this! But I must confine myself to a few remarks as related to the future of oratory,
and your part in it. You have in this educational device a
powerful means of making your voice heard. Use it, take
full advantage of it. Perhaps the one single thing I most
want to say is: Do not under-rate yourselves!

So often through the years, and more especially recently, I have had to listen to the wail, "Is there any hope
for the younger generation?" Many times I have said to my
classes, I would like to turn that around and have it read,
"Is there any hope for the older generation?" I find myself
in tune with the noted preacher Phillips Brooks, as recorded
by his biographer A. V. G. Allen:

> The worst thing that I see about getting old, or
> older, is that you get further away from the young
> people who are the best people in the world ...
> Most of the wisdom of old age is humbug.[18]

Keep abreast of what's happening in the world. Read,
study both sides of controversial questions, speak your mind
about your feeling about them, subject always to change when
new light dawns. Do you object to or favor the Vietnam
war? Say so! Do you believe clergymen should speak out
about moral issues, or should they confine themselves to
"preaching the gospel"? Whichever way you feel, say so!

In connection with not under-rating yourself and
your potential, consider this excerpt from the great Albert
Schweitzer's book, Out of My Life and Thought. It has been
a great inspiration to me as I hope it will be to you:

However much concerned I was at the problem of
the misery in the world, I never let myself get
lost in broodings over it; I always held firmly to
the thought that each one of us can do a little to
bring some portion of it to an end. [19]

Consider, too, the statement of Dr. Irwin J. Lubbers,
former president of Hope College, spoken at the Hope College
commencement exercises June 3, 1963: "The Biblical admonition not to think of yourself more highly than you ought
does not preclude thinking of yourself highly." Truly, as the
apostle Paul encouraged Timothy: "Let no man despise thy
youth." It is good advice. Heed it.

But forget that talk about "don't trust anyone over 30."
There are millions of us who still have the qualities of youth,
who believe that poverty can be eliminated, that the disgrace
of involuntary unemployment can be wiped out, that racial
hatred can become a thing of the past, and that peace at home
and abroad is not an impossibility. You have allies in these
causes. Come what may, I shall always believe that what
bright young students have to say as they grope for solutions
that plague our country and our world deserves a hearing by
the minds and hearts of all of us. I shall always cherish
the hope that their orations may create dialogue, provoke
discussion, change minds and contribute if only in some small
measure to cure the many ills of our troubled world.

## VII.  A FEW FINAL PERSONAL WORDS

In 1924, in Hill Auditorium, at the University of
Michigan, I delivered my last oration as a student on the
momentous subject, "Is Human Progress a Delusion?" And
do you know, I've been wondering about that ever since! I
close my eyes and in my imagination hear our teacher,
Thomas C. Trueblood, tell our class of the beginning of a
lecture by T. Dewitt Talmage, the noted chautauqua lecturer,
when he appeared on the University Lyceum series. In deep
bass sonorous tones, mimicked perfectly by Professor Trueblood, Talmage began: "Evolutionists tell us whence we
came; theologians tell us whither we are going. But the fact
is, we're here!" (Professor Trueblood never did say what
came next, or at least I don't remember it.)

I do not want to get into a philosophical discussion of
the doctrine of the perfectability of man. But, being here,

as Talmage said, I am perfectly sure of one thing: neither
I nor anyone is absolved from the responsibility of trying to
make this world over into a better place to live for all of
its inhabitants.

When God created the world, He looked it over and
pronounced it good! Man has despoiled it. I am not so
naive as not to know that authors, columnists, educators,
poets, preachers, statesmen have been at this business of
improving mankind since recorded history. But the fact that
we have not fully succeeded and have met with only intermittent success, does not absolve us from making the effort.
In the symphony raising our paean of praise to our Maker,
our instrument of oratory may not be the most important in
the orchestra. But we ought to make the most of it, even
if it be but like the tinkling of the triangle, or the piping of
the piccolo!

I close this chapter on the oratory of the future with
a nostalgic, wistful look at its glorious past. I quote from
an article, "College Orations Old and New," from the pen of
Edgar E. Willis, a Wayne State University orator, winner of
second place in the IOA contest of 1933, and currently department chairman at the University of Michigan.

> The speeches in both periods vibrate with optimism.
> There is in all of them the same disgust for injus-
> tice and discrimination, the same regard for the
> good and the true. Ideas at the forefront of man's
> thinking are hurled defiantly at the barriers of con-
> vention and conservatism. With the passing of the
> years the emphasis may have changed from inter-
> nationalism to save us from war to world govern-
> ment to save us from extinction, but the basic fla-
> vor remains the same. There is throughout the
> strong implication that although the speaker may
> not have quite all the answers, he is confident of a
> goodly share of them. In short, in all of these
> orations we hear the brash, unrestrained voice of
> youth. May it never be silenced. [20]

Yea, verily, may it never be silenced!


                              Notes

1.    Lew Sarett, William Trufant Foster, Alma Johnson
       Sarett. Basic Principles of Speech, Third Edition,

Houghton Mifflin Company, Boston, 1958, p. 192.

2.  WO-1950, pp. 17-21.

3.  Ibid., pp. 15-17.

4.  Ibid., pp. 39-41.

5.  E. C. Buehler, and Richard Johannesen, Building The
    Contest Oration, The H. W. Wilson Company, New
    York, 1965, p. 31.

6.  The following was written, quoting me in an interview
    for a newspaper feature story concerning my com-
    mencement speaking activities: "Trite as it may
    seem, the future of our world depends upon the
    young people of today. One simply cannot travel to
    these commencements in the spring of the year with-
    out feeling that youth is sound at the core. Too of-
    ten we forget that the exceptions make news. We
    read of the one bank teller who absconds with funds
    but never of the 999 who were faithful to their trust.
    After all, it isn't the young people but the older ones
    who have brought on the tensions of the status quo.
    After a dreary winter, I find these visits to high
    schools refresh my spirit and I come away with new
    faith in the future." Grand Rapids Press, May 31,
    1959.

7.  James Milton O'Neill, Models of Speech Composition,
    The Century Co., New York, 1921, p. 807.

8.  Others who come to mind are winners in the Northern
    Oratorical League contests. Paul Blanshard, author
    and sociologist, represented the University of Michi-
    gan in 1913 with a speech entitled: "Christianity
    and the Social Order." Senator Wayne Morse rep-
    resented the University of Wisconsin in 1923 with a
    speech entitled: "The Supreme Court and the
    People." Harold Stassen represented the University
    of Minnesota in 1927 with a speech entitled: "Nation-
    al Will or International Good Will?" Sander Vanocur,
    NBC newsman, represented Northwestern University,
    and won first place in 1949, with his oration, "A
    State of Mind."

9.  His biography is worth reading: Nat Hentoff, Abraham

J. Muste, Peace Agitator, The Macmillan Company, New York, 1963.

10. Peter Schrag, Christian Century, April 17, 1961, pp. 9-11.

11. Detroit Free Press, April 6, 1970.

12. Speech - Its Techniques and Disciplines in a Free Society, Appleton- Century- Crofts, Inc., 1952, Foreword, p. ix.

13. Time, May 18, 1970, p. 15. Reprinted by permission.

14. "You Can Remake This Society," Look, July 15, 1969, p. 85.

15. "Campus '69: The Quiet Year--So Far," Life, December 12, 1969, p. 43.

16. Training for Effective Speech, The Cordon Company, Inc., New York, 1939, Preface, p. vii.

17. Public Speaking: Principles and Practice, Harper & Brothers, New York, 1951, pp. xi, xii.

18. The Life of Phillips Brooks, E. P. Dutton & Co., Inc., 1907, p. 269. Reprinted by permission.

19. As quoted by Robert J. McCracken, Riverside Church, New York, in National Radio Pulpit, sermon, "An Honest Man's the Noblest Work of God," April 3, 1960, pp. 3-9.

20. CSSJ, Spring, 1956, pp. 18-21.

## Appendix A

## CODE FOR CONTESTS IN ORATORY*

[This Code has been adopted as the official statement of American Forensic Association policy on oratory contests. It was formulated by the A. F. A. Committee on Professional Relations in cooperation with officials of the American Legion, Optimist International, Intercollegiate Peace Speech Association, International Toastmistress Clubs, and the National Forensic League.]

The American Forensic Association regards with approval the strong interest of service and professional organizations in original speaking contests. While competitive speaking events are familiar to the campus, non-academic groups can provide a welcome additional impetus to student development in the skills of advocacy. Our association believes that such events, properly conducted, contribute to student growth in the art of effective speech and broaden student understanding of significant contemporary issues.

The rules for each contest should prescribe one or more of the following methods of delivery: (a) writing out a speech and reading it from manuscript; (b) writing out a speech and delivering it from memory; (c) speaking extemporaneously (which is not to be confused with impromptu speaking, for it requires much preparation preceding delivery: thinking, investigating, planning, incorporating that planning into an outline, adapting content to the listeners, practicing the speech aloud with or without outline or notes--all is prepared save the actual wording, which is spontaneously evolved in preliminary practice and in the contest speech itself); (d) speaking impromptu, which requires no specific preparation.

We recognize the preference of organizations for contests in oratory, and the reasons customarily advanced for utilizing this type of public speaking: (a) the desire for a manuscript for publication; (b) the companion objective of attaining the best speech as well as the best speaker; and (c) the requirement of performance consistency in local, regional, and national progression gained by making the speech text relatively constant.

The American Forensic Association recommends the following guideposts to be followed in planning and conducting contests in original oratory:

A.   Standards for directing and evaluating orators should stem from recognized principles and procedures of effective speech training.

1.   A basic criterion should be the conception of a significant, single idea.   The oration must be an original work of the student with specific limitation on quoted material.   The speech purpose should be to persuade or inspire. Extemporaneous reference to timely events is permissible.

2.   The student should be allowed reasonable latitude in subject development so he can advance his own convictions.   Strong, sincere feeling is implicit in persuasive speech; contest regulations should offer opportunity for creative thought reflecting the speaker's beliefs and experience.

3.   The orator should achieve distinction in composition.   He should begin with responsible ideas and employ incisive analysis, cogent reasoning and supporting materials, orderly arrangement, and unaffected dignity of expression. The goal of the orator should be mature content expressed in clear, arresting oral style.

4.   The orator should strive for straightforward, unaffected communicative presentation.   He should give vitality and meaning to his points with direct, animated delivery.   Bombastic, artificial delivery has no place in modern speechmaking; the orator's basic task is to communicate his ideas impellingly.

5.   The orator should be evaluated or judged by standards which embrace the elements of content, composition, and delivery.   Critics should not be confronted with nebulous ballot items such as "power of truth" or "ability to thrill."   Evaluation criteria should be clear and specific.

6.   There should be opportunity for individual

criticism of speakers following the event. This obviously enhances the learning value of speech contests to the contestants.

B. Contests should be judged only by persons competent in speech evaluation.

1. Normally such competence will derive from speech education or from professional experience in public speaking. Judging short of this standard is educationally indefensible. The contest becomes a sham if the occasion for judging is misconceived as an opening for honoring local dignitaries or exploiting their publicity value, or is simply misunderstood as an incidental aspect of the contest situation. Competent criticism should be a right of the participants.

2. A reasonable honorarium, plus expenses, should be provided for the services of the judge. An institution or agency sponsoring a speech contest should budget this sum in advance as a normal contest expense along with publicity, mailing, and awards.

The success of oratory contests for sponsoring organizations and their educational contribution to participants seem inseparable. The Committee on Professional Relations of the American Forensic Association stands ready to advise groups on recommended conduct of contests in oratory. Individual members of the association throughout the United States also are available for consultation and assistance.

---

*Reprinted by permission of the American Forensic Association.

Appendix B

COLLATERAL READINGS

Chapter II:
Edgar E. Willis, "College Orations Old and New,"
CSSJ, Spring, 1956, pp. 18-21.

Thorrel B. Fest, "The Vanishing College Orator?"
QJS, February, 1943, pp. 45-48.

Chapter VI:
Marilyn Myers and Lionel Crocker, "One Hundred
Questions for Public Discussion," ST, November,
1953, pp. 266-72.

Chapter VII:
Russell Wieder Gilbert, "Speech Titles," Today's
Speech, November, 1960, pp. 8-11.

Lew Sarett and William Trufant Foster, Chapter 14 -
"Finding, Choosing and Recording Ideas," Basic Prin-
ciples of Speech, rev. ed., Houghton, Mifflin Company,
Boston, 1946, pp. 331-48.

Arleigh B. Williamson, Charles A. Fritz, Harold
Raymond Ross, Chapter V - "Choice of Subject and
Material," Speaking in Public, Prentice-Hall, Inc.,
New York, 1948, pp. 63-84.

Chapter VIII and IX:
Sarett and Foster, Chapter 16: "The Introduction,"
ibid., pp. 384-421.

William Norwood Brigance, Chapter 12: "Beginning
and Ending the Speech," Speech - Its Techniques and
Disciplines in a Free Society, Appleton-Century-Crofts,
Inc., New York, 1952, pp. 228-244.

E. Christian Buehler, and Wil A. Linkugel, "Dimen-

sion Five--Organization," Speech Communication, Harper & Row, New York, 1962, pp. 138-146.

James C. McCroskey, Chapter 11: "Introducing and
Concluding Messages in Rhetorical Communication,"
An Introduction to Rhetorical Communication, Prentice-
Hall, Inc., Englewood Cliffs, New Jersey, 1968, pp.
188-206.

Chapter X:
J. Jeffery Auer, Chapter 23: "The Persuasive Speaker and his Audience," The Rhetoric of Our Times,
Appleton-Century-Crofts, New York, 1969, pp. 255-
277.

Joseph H. Baccus, "Building a Stock of Illustrations,"
QJS, June, 1935, pp. 373-75.

Chapter XI:
Horace G. Rahskopf, Chapter 12: "The Speaker's
Memory," Basic Speech Improvement, Harper & Row,
New York, 1965, pp. 201-09.

Charles J. Stewart, and H. Bruce Kendall, "Speaking
From Manuscript," by Harold P. Zelko and Frank E.
X. Dance, in On Speech and Speakers, Holt, Rinehart
and Winston, Inc., New York, 1968, pp. 83-98.

Chapter XII:
Jane Blankenship and Robert Wilhoit, "Reducing Tensions," by Otis M. Walter, and Robert L. Scott, in
Selected Readings in Public Speaking, Dickenson Publishing Company, Inc., Belmont, California, 1966,
pp. 192-95.

Lew Sarett, William Trufant Foster, and Alma
Johnson Sarett, Chapter 6, "Growing in Confidence
and Poise," pp. 184-208, and Chapter 10: "Commu-
nicating Meaning Through Action," pp. 310-334, Basic
Principles of Speech, Third Edition, Houghton Mifflin
Company, Boston, 1958.

Chapter XIII:
Fred B. Goodwin, "Oratory By the Seat of Your
Pants," Forensic, October, 1961, pp. 12-14.

Phillip K. Tompkins, and Eldon E. Baker, "Coaching

the Contest Oration," Forensic, January, 1961, pp. 12-15.

C. Horton Talley, "Manuscripts Win Oratory Contests," AFA Register, Spring Issue, 1963, pp. 14-18.

George Ziegelmueller, Chapter 3: "The Role of the Coach," in Don F. Faules, and Richard D. Rieke, Directing Forensics: Debate and Contest Speaking, International Textbook Company, Scranton, Pennsylvania, 1968, pp. 79-94.

Chapter XIV:
Glenn R. Capp, Chapter 2: "How To Judge What Constitutes a Good Speech," How To Communicate Orally, Prentice-Hall, Inc., Englewood Cliffs, N.J., 1961, pp. 17-30.

Donald Klopf, Diane Evans, and Sister Mary Linus DeLozier, "The Controversy Over Judges' Qualifications," Forensic, March, 1966, pp. 7-10.

C. William Colburn, "Let's Develop The Proper Attitude," Forensic, January, 1964, pp. 5-6.

Chapter XV:
Lester Thonssen, and Ross Scanlan, Chapter 4: "Analyzing the Audience," Speech Preparation and Delivery, J. B. Lippincott Company, New York, 1942, pp. 36-48.

Chapter XVI:
John D. Rockefeller 3rd, "In Praise of Young Revolutionaries," Saturday Review, December 14, 1968, pp. 18 ff.

Angelo M. Pelligrini, "Public Speaking and Social Obligations," QJS, June, 1934, pp. 345-51.

# INDEX

262

CSSJ, 14, 19, 157, 181, 231-232, 234, 238, 252, 258
Curiosity-arousing titles, 98
Current events, 18, 50-55
Current youth revolt, 245-249
Curry, Herbert L., 46-47, 124, 195
Curry, S. S., 57
Curtis, George William, 162

Daily Bulletin, 185, 186
Dakota Wesleyan University, 244
Darrow, Clarence, 27
Da Vinci, Leonardo, 174
Davidson, Peggy A., 33
De Pauw University, 210
De Vries, Calvin, 93
"Decalogue For an Ideal Citizen," 15, 168, 193
Dedmon, Donald N., 67
Defining oration, 40-42
Delivery of oration, 169-181
Delivery rehearsals, 195-202
DeLozier, Sister Mary Linus, 260
Demmink, Gerrit, 142, 143
Demosthenes, 162
Dennis, Ralph, 209-210
Dethmers, John R., 227
Detroit Free Press, 82, 238, 246
Detroit Times, 229
Developing oration, 88-100
Dickens, Milton, 129
Dickenson, Jeanne-Mann, 85
Diem, W. Roy, 44, 67, 154
Diem Report, 42, 44, 152
Dimnet, Ernest, 49
Direct Discourse (Colloquy),

134-135
Directness in delivery, 172-174
Dress rehearsal, 202
Drummond, Alexander M., 36
Drew Theological Seminary, 155
Dubois, W. C., 50
Dunham, Robert E., 222
Dunsmore, Marion H., 238
Duquesne University, 241
Dylan, Bob, 245

Earlham College, 79
Earnestness, 177-179
Eastern Michigan University, 228
Eastman, Max, 14, 162, 176
Educational oratory, 10-13
Edwards, Jonathan, 104, 160
Eisenhower, Dwight D., 53
Elmhurst College, 14, 157
Emerson, Ralph Waldo, 50, 54
Emotional appeals, 114
Enunciation, 171-172
Epigrams (paradox), 135-136
Erickson, Kenneth, 132
Ervin, Sam J., 82
Eulogies, 40, 64
Euphony, 136
Evans, Diane, 260
Ewbank, Henry L., 15, 37, 161
Eye directness, 173, 180
Experiment in International Living Program, 25, 95, 118, 247
Extemporaneity vs. memorization, 158-159
Extemporaneous oratory, 154-156

"Face the Nation" scripts (CBS), 91
Faules, Don F., 222, 260

263

264

176, 260
Scanlan, Ross, 260
"Scent-a-chase" organization, 94
Schrag, Peter, 254
Schrier, William, 51, 154, 168, 184, 185, 191, 193, 195, 206, 234, 235, 251
Schroeder, Clifton P., 103
Schweitzer, Albert, 64, 251
Schwinn, Doris, 61, 85
Scott, Robert L., 60
Sears, Lorenzo, 37
Shelley, Percy Bysshe, 104
Short, Robert L., 52
Shylock, 145
Sillars, Malcolm, 123
"Sinners in the Hands of an Angry God," 104
Sioux Falls College, 86
Sizoe, Joseph R., 96
Skeirik, Habeeb J., 61
Slang, 137
Smith, Howard Van, 174
Sobrepena, Enrique C., 61
Sockman, Ralph W., 104, 135
Sons and Daughters of Norway, 232, 235
Sources for oration, 89-91
South Dakota State College, 132
Southern Illinois University, 60, 61, 85, 148
Spano, Helen M., 241
"Speaking From Manuscript," 259
Specific, see Concrete
Specific Purpose Sentence (SPS), 92-95
Spectra, 18
Speech, 129
Speech 11 contest, 183
Speech rally, 182
Spencer, Herbert, 129
Sponberg, Harold, 228

ST, 45, 46, 215, 232, 233, 258
Stassen, Harold E., 253
Steele, Harland, 131, 200
Steensma, John, 85
Steere, Douglas, 138
Steffens, Gretchen, 110-111
Steininger, George, 107
Stewart, Charles C., 259
Stidger, William L., 50
Storrs, Richard, 170
Student interest and recruitment, 59-60, 76-77, 182-187, 250-251
Subjects for orations, 59-87
Swanlund, Judi, 135
Swift, Jonathan, 49

Tact (in coaching), 190
Talk with teachers, 249-250
Talley, C. Horton, 60, 260
Talmage, T. Dewitt, 251
Tardiff, Vivian, 108-109
Taylor, Harry, 229
Television programs, 143
Temple Time broadcast, 131
Temple University, 139
Tennyson, Lord Alfred, vii
Texas Christian University, 102, 167
Thomas, James W., 86
Thonssen, Lester, 260
Thoreau, Henry David, 55, 64
Thurston, 171
Time, 22, 83, 98, 132, 244, 247
Titles (orations), 97-99
Today's Speech, 258
Tompkins, Phillip K., 181, 259
Trent, Jimmie, 26, 220
Trueblood, Thomas C., vi, 10, 251
Turner, Patricia Ann, 85
Twain, Mark, 162
Twenty-third Psalm, 147